WITHDRAWN
FROM STOCK
UL LIBRARY

QMW Library

23 1101321 X

KU-573-993

0162531
16.1.90

Language Change

Trends in Linguistics
Studies and Monographs 43

Editor

Werner Winter

Mouton de Gruyter
Berlin · New York

Language Change

Contributions to the Study of Its Causes

Edited by

Leiv Egil Breivik and Ernst Håkon Jahr

Mouton de Gruyter
Berlin · New York 1989

QUEEN MARY & WESTFIELD UNIV. LONDON COLLEGE

Mouton de Gruyter (formerly Mouton, The Hague)
is a Division of Walter de Gruyter & Co., Berlin.

Library of Congress Cataloging in Publication Data

Language change : contributions to the study of its causes /
edited by Leiv Egil Breivik, Ernst Håkon Jahr.
    p.   cm. — (Trends in linguistics. Studies and mono-
graphs : 43)
    Bibliography: p. Includes index
    ISBN 0-89925-564-7 (alk. paper)
    1. Linguistic change. I. Breivik, Leiv Egil. II. Jahr, Ernst
Håkon, 1948 —   . III. Series.
P142.L26   1989
417′.7 -- dc20
                                                89-13147
                                                CIP

Deutsche Bibliothek Cataloging in Publication Data

Language change: contributions to the study of its causes / ed.
by Leiv Egil Breivik; Ernst Håkon Jahr. — Berlin ; New York :
Mouton de Gruyter, 1989
    (Trends in linguistics : Studies and monographs ; 43)
    ISBN 3-11-011995-1
NE: Breivik, Leiv Egil [Hrsg.]; Trends in linguistics / Studies
    and monographs

⊗ Printed on acid free paper

© Copyright 1989 by Walter de Gruyter & Co., Berlin, Federal Republic of Germany.
All rights reserved, including those of translation into foreign languages. No part of
this book may be reproduced in any form — by photoprint, microfilm, or any other
means — or transmitted or translated into a machine language without written
permission from Mouton de Gruyter, A Division of Walter de Gruyter & Co., Berlin.
Typesetting: Arthur Collignon GmbH, Berlin — Printing: Gerike GmbH, Berlin. —
Binding: Lüderitz & Bauer, Berlin: — Printed in Germany.

Preface

Most of the papers in this volume were presented at the symposium "The causes of language change: Do we know them yet?" held at the School of Languages and Literature, University of Tromsø, October 15–17, 1987. The symposium was made possible by generous financial support from the University of Tromsø and the Norwegian Research Council for Science and the Humanities.

Tromsø, December 1988   Leiv Egil Breivik
                                                                Ernst Håkon Jahr

Contents

Introduction

The past two decades have witnessed an upsurge of interest in historical linguistics, with attention to all areas of language. There has been a flourishing of new journals and scholarly work — dissertations, monographs, articles, and introductory texts. A great number of contributions have been prompted by the International Conferences on Historical Linguistics (ICHL), the first of which was held in Edinburgh in 1973 and the eighth and latest in Lille in 1987; by the international conferences on historical phonology (1976), historical morphology (1978), historical syntax (1981), historical semantics/word formation (1984), historical dialectology (1986), and historical linguistics and philology (1988), all of which were organized by the Institute of English, Adam Mickiewicz University, Poznań; by special sessions of recurring meetings and congresses, e. g. those of the Chicago Linguistic Society in 1976 and the 14th International Congress of Linguists in 1987; and by special symposia, such as those held at Santa Barbara in 1974 and 1976.

The present volume also reflects the current activity in the field. It is the outgrowth of a symposium, entitled "The causes of language change: Do we know them yet?", held at the University of Tromsø, October 15—17, 1987. The title of the symposium was intended to provide an association to a much-cited statement by Leonard Bloomfield; in 1933, in his book Language (ch. 21.9), Bloomfield claimed that "the causes of sound change are unknown". Undoubtedly, there is still much that is unknown in diachronic linguistics, much that still has to be investigated. However, recent research has delved more deeply into the complex causes of not only phonological change but of language change in general; there now seems to exist a better understanding of the motivations for, and mechanisms of, language change through time. This improved understanding has been made possible by the development and expansion of disciplines such as sociolinguistics, language contact research, communication theory, child language and creole studies — together with innovations in the study of language-internal developments as well as in the study of language universals and linguistic typology. We feel it is safe to claim that historical linguistics has now left the stage where all the causes of language change are unknown.

This volume contains eleven papers which were prepared for the Tromsø symposium (Breivik's paper was not presented, and Romaine read a different one from that included here). The collection of papers covers a wide range of approaches; they draw their data from a variety of languages and language types, but all focus on the main topic of the symposium: the causes of language change.

In the first paper, Henning Andersen emphasizes the importance of understanding the circumstances which motivate speakers to change their language. He argues that the social dimension should be integrated into the description of language, thus eliminating the distinction between linguistic and extralinguistic factors. The functions that innovations have for speakers of a language are also discussed. The author views innovations as a metadialogue through which members of a community propose and reject or adopt new norms.

Leiv Egil Breivik's paper is concerned with the relationship between typological shifts and specific linguistic changes in English; it examines the ways in which sentences with existential *there* have changed and developed over the centuries, and tries to provide an explanation for the diachrony by appealing to various parameters. His data show that syntactic and semantic changes in these constructions are closely correlated with pragmatic factors; indeed, in a number of cases, pragmatics seems to be the primary causal factor.

A similar conclusion is arrived at by Jan Terje Faarlund, who examines the various properties pertaining to the Old Norse nominative NP and the Modern Norwegian subject. He argues that the grammatical changes that have taken place since the Old Norse period have been induced by thematic and contextual factors. Faarlund's general hypothesis is that, in a diachronic perspective, syntax is motivated by the pragmatics of previous stages. It is claimed that this hypothesis is supported by the cross-linguistic data.

Ernst Håkon Jahr considers the relationship between language planning and linguistic change. Particular attention is given to cases where a deliberate and successful effort has been made by political authorities or prescriptive linguists to change a spoken language or a spoken variety of a language in a desired direction. Examples of this are provided from Norwegian and Icelandic.

Charles N. Li's paper addresses two related issues: the diachronic development of switch reference in Green Hmong and the function of switch reference. The fact that switch reference can emerge in a prototypal isolating language which is verb-medial is intriguing from a typological as well as from a diachronic point of view. The Green Hmong data also pose a challenge to the standard interpretation of switch reference, under which it is restricted to tracking the reference of subjects. Finally, the data are discussed within the context of the causes of syntactic change.

Helmut Lüdtke focuses on a set of phenomena which are not planned or intended but nevertheless a result of man's activity. He argues that such 'invisible-hand processes' are important causes of language change; they happen continually and inevitably. For example, the development from Latin to Romance provides evidence for the existence of the quantitative process whereby meaningful elements grow shorter and shorter as regards their phonological realization (shrinking). Invisible-hand processes are discussed in relation to a number of parameters.

Peter Mühlhäusler is concerned with the causes of the dramatic linguistic changes that are taking place in many parts of the Pacific area. He argues against the widely held assumption that language change should be explained in terms of changes in linguistic systems. In his view, most causes of change are person-made causes in linguistic ecology. Accelerated linguistic change in the Pacific is a consequence of modernization; the way man has caused language change is similar to the way he has brought about cultural change.

In his paper, John J. Ohala brings the study of linguistic change into the laboratory, arguing that modern instrumental phonetics allows us to identify some of the causes of sound change or at least locate the domain in which they lie. He discusses three mechanisms in detail (confusion of similar sounds, hypo-correction and hyper-correction), and gives recipes for eliciting in the laboratory sound changes caused by these mechanisms. Ohala's account is entirely non-teleological; for example, sounds are not claimed to change in order to be easier to pronounce.

The main topic of Suzanne Romaine's paper is the role of children in the overall communicative structure of the speech community: does variation in children's language use lead to long-term restructuring of the language system? Her data suggest that there is often a parallelism between first language acquisition and historical change, but she points out that much more research needs to be done on the ontogenetic/ diachronic parallels and dependencies; we do not know as yet why the normal acquisition of language by children effects long-term changes only in certain cases.

Peter Trudgill examines the relationship between linguistic development and social context, with reference to the role of *contact* in linguistic change. The paper considers the extent to which changes that occur in situations of low contact are significantly different from those which take place in high-contact contexts. Trudgill stresses the importance of studying low-contact varieties; his thesis is that insights into the causes and mechanisms of linguistic change are most likely to be found in investigations of data from isolated languages.

Language contact is also the topic of P. Sture Ureland's paper, the first part of which is devoted to a selective overview of recent works dealing with linguistic change. The author points out that the ethnic and language-contact hypothesis as formulated by medieval language philosophers has often been neglected by linguists working in this area. In his view, this is unfortunate since the impact of foreign influence is an extremely important causal factor. Contact-induced structures from several language areas are cited in support of this claim. Particular attention is given to Scandinavia, Holland, and the Engadine in the Swiss Canton Grison.

Understanding linguistic innovations

Henning Andersen

0. Introduction

The title of the symposium posed a question about the causes of linguistic change — do we know them yet? I suppose most linguists would hesitate to answer this question with a categorical yes or no, but would be inclined in one direction or the other. For my own part, I think an affirmative answer is in order, but for this answer to be unqualified, I feel the question would have to be phrased slightly differently. It should concern linguistic innovations and ask whether we can understand them yet.

I have formulated the title of this paper accordingly. In the remarks that follow, I will clarify the sense of the three words I chose for my title (sections 1 – 3) and will then try to substantiate my affirmative answer (section 4). As it happens, my title allows of an interpretation that is quite different from the one that probably comes to mind first, but which seems to be no less relevant. I will explicate this alternative reading of the title in my conclusion (section 5).

1. Understanding

The question the organizers of our symposium raised is straightforward, and it has been given straightforward answers in the past. And so it might be useful to take as point of departure a confrontation of two of the best known statements on the causes of linguistic change.

On one hand we have Bloomfield's position (cf. (1)), which sums up his evaluation of the theories that would explain sound-change by reference to economy of effort:

(1)   Although many sound-changes shorten linguistic forms, simplify
         the phonetic system, or in some other way lessen the labor of
         utterance, yet no student has succeeded in establishing a corre-
         lation between sound-change and any antecedent phenomenon:
         the causes of sound-change are unknown. (1935: 385)

On the other, there is Coseriu's position:

(2)   In one sense, the most general one, the so-called 'causes' are
         actually not unknown, but perfectly well known and observable
         every day, for they coincide with the very conditions of speaking
         and are part and parcel of every speaker's experience. In another
         sense — as cultural and functional determinants — the 'causes'
         of change derive from the general conditions of language and
         are, whenever a given language is adequately documented, by
         and large open to investigation. (1952: 83, 1967: 123 f.; my
         translation, HA)

The two quotations might seem to express diametrically opposite
opinions of one and the same matter. But it would be a mistake to
interpret them in this way — and not only because the question of the
causes of linguistic change is not a matter of opinion. What the apparently
opposite judgements of Bloomfield and Coseriu reflect is first and foremost a difference in metatheoretical premises, a difference in scientific
ideology, which it is instructive to make explicit.

Note that Bloomfield's statement is couched in orthodox positivist
terms: it speaks of efficient causality, carefully referring to causality in
its observable aspect, as correlations between antecedent phenomena and
their consequents. Given this physicalist understanding of the notion of
'cause', few linguists would probably disagree with Bloomfield's conclusion that such causes of linguistic change are unknown. But at the same
time, if the notion of 'cause' is restricted in this fashion few linguists
today, probably, would find the question of the causality of change very
interesting. To my knowledge, at least, no modern advocates of theories
of economy of effort subscribe to the crude, efficient-causality view of
the relation between explanantia and explananda which Bloomfield rejected.

Coseriu, by contrast, explicitly distances himself from such an understanding of the sources of sound-change, and of linguistic change generally, by using the word 'causes' in quotation marks. Instead he speaks

of the conditions of speaking and the conditions of language, and reveals in his choice of the term 'conditions' a more cautious view of the relation between the circumstances that surround language use and grammar and the changes that occur as time goes by.

To Coseriu, none of these circumstances acts as a cause of change. Change in language, as well as the absence of change, is produced by its speakers as part of that excercise of their free will which speaking is. In speaking, they may be motivated by the diverse circumstances under which they speak to deviate from the usage that is traditional in their community. But such a motivation is not a cause in the sense in which Bloomfield and his predecessors understood the word, for the individual speaker is free to let himself be moved, or not moved, by the given circumstance or circumstances. In Coseriu's view, the only true 'causes' of change are the speakers, who use their language — and, in doing so, observe or neglect their linguistic traditions as they see fit.

This is undoubtedly a fairly realistic way of looking at language change, not only because it assumes that any change may be conditioned by a number of coexisting circumstances, but also because it acknowledges the intentional character of speaking, whether it follows or breaks with tradition, and hence, by implication, an element of intention in both stability and change. In accordance with this latter aspect of Coseriu's theory, the language historian's task is one not of causal explanation, but of rational explication.

But a full account of the diverse kinds of change that occur in the history of languages must consider not only the aspects of change which are governed by the intentions of the speakers. It must include as well a number of different kinds of change which cannot by any stretch of the imagination be viewed as intentional in the usual sense of the word. Among these are changes of the kind Bloomfield was considering in the passage quoted above. We will look at such changes below, and I will try to show how such non-intentional changes, too, are compatible with the notion of rational explication (section 4.2.4).

1.1 Description, classification, explication

In discussions of linguistic change (as of any other phenomena), it is necessary to distinguish three different levels of inquiry — the particular, the general, and the universal (cf. Coseriu 1974: 23 ff.).

In diachronic linguistics, inquiry on the particular level (which Coseriu calls the historical one, and which might also be termed the idiographic) is concerned with individual historical changes and seeks to establish all the circumstances relevant to any such change, that is, to describe as fully as possible what actually occurred in the given instance.

Besides investigations of this kind there is a general level of inquiry, where similar changes in different languages are compared and contrasted, subsumed as tokens of types, and categorized from diverse points of view. Here different changes are examined with the aim of forming generalizations about that usually happens under such and such circumstances and, ultimately, of establishing what kinds of change are possible.

On this level of inquiry, where our experience with concrete linguistic changes is systematized, it is apparent that although all changes in some sense must be products of man's free will, they still give evidence of a fair degree of determinism. This is not surprising, considering that all languages conform to definite universal principles of use and of structure, which are not subject to human will. Coseriu, in my opinion, has tended to underemphasize this aspect of language change, and Itkonen denies its existence (1986). But to others it seems obvious that even on the particular level of inquiry, where we seek to describe and interpret individual changes as fully as possible, our success in identifying the relevant motivating circumstances and determinants and in clarifying their relative weight depends on our understanding of the universal principles which govern language use and grammar formation, and which thereby define the limits within which speakers are free to exercise their will.

These principles are central to the universal level of inquiry (which Coseriu has called the rational or philosophic one), where such problems are considered as what language change is, what the reasons for language change are, that is, why change is an invariable concomitant of any living language tradition — the problem of the mutability of language. Here it is essential to recognize that any language is a joint product of nurture and nature. On one hand, it is a cultural institution, assimilated by the individual and freely manipulated by him according to his needs and skill, and in relation to the limits set by social convention. On the other hand, it is acquired, maintained, and elaborated entirely by the grace of the natural language faculty that all members of our species share. It is against this background that the different types of rational explication must be applied which we will look at below.

Among the three different levels of inquiry sketched here — the particular, the general, and the universal — the question posed by the organizers of this symposium clearly refers to the last. No one would claim that we understand all the particular changes that have ever taken place in the languages of the world or even all the changes that are known to have taken place. It might even be hazardous to claim that all the possible types of change are known. But one can reasonably hold that we have an adequate understanding of the universal mechanisms of change and of the reasons why languages change.

It is in this sense that I interpret — and answer — the question posed in the title of our symposium, and I will consequently offer a survey of the major categories of change below (section 4) and a characterization of the different reasons for each of them.

2. Linguistic

There would be no need to explicate the second word in my title, *linguistic*, were it not for the fact that historical linguists, at least since the nineteenth century, have been concerned to make a distinction between the linguistic and the extra-linguistic (or non-linguistic), but have disagreed both on where the boundary between these two domains should be drawn and on the very relevance to their inquiry of allegedly extralinguistic facts.

Here I will mention only the relation between linguistic and other social values, which has been particularly troublesome and remains of current interest. I will contrast two different points of view and suggest a synthesis.

In their seminal essay on the theory of language change, Weinreich et al. illustrate the remarkable backwardness of some of their predecessors in the field with the following quotation from Kuryłowicz, a consistent advocate of a formal, algebraic structuralism and of immanent explanations in diachronic linguistics (1968: 177):

(3)   One must explain linguistic facts by other linguistic facts, not by heterogeneous facts. ... Explanations by means of [heterogeneous] social facts is a methodological derailment. (The bracketed word is missing in the quotation, but occurs in the original; cf. Kuryłowicz 1948: 84, 1960: 246).

The omission by Weinreich et al. of the bracketed occurrence of 'heterogeneous' makes Kuryłowicz appear not to have considered language a social phenomenon, which is unjust. But the reinstatement of the word does not change the fact that Kuryłowicz (and some other structuralists) for one reason or another demanded a strict separation of what was properly linguistic from what was not and assigned exclusive relevance in historical explanations to the former.

The major contribution of Weinreich et al. — which has been universally acclaimed — was in arguing for social realism in the theory of linguistic change, in demonstrating how "sociological factors ... explain distributions and shifts in linguistic phenomena which, from a structural point of view, would have been seen as random" (177), and in clarifying how "the changing linguistic structure ... is embedded in the larger context of the speech community", and how "social factors bear on the system as a whole" or, perhaps more often, unequally on different parts of it, inasmuch as "linguistic structures [are] embedded unevenly in the social structure" (185).

Throughout the subsequent flowering of sociolinguistic studies it has proven practically impossible to escape the conceptual difficulties these few, randomly chosen quotations exemplify, first, the false dichotomy between the linguistic and the social, and, secondly, the notion that language is embedded in society.

This being so, it seems well worth emphasizing that the supposed dichotomy between language and society is non-existent in two respects. For one thing, language is an entirely social phenomenon and can in no way be separated from its social functions. For another, when linguistic rules make reference to social categories such as age, sex, or class, these categories are eo ipso linguistic categories. These categories can be, and should be, strictly distinguished from such notions as chronological age, biological sex, or socioeconomic status, which can be defined prior to, and without regard to, the investigation of any language. Of course, such language independent notions can be used as preliminary, auxiliary means to establish the social value of linguistic expressions. But what linguistic expressions index are culture specific categories such as 'youthfulness', 'femininity', or 'upper class', not as defined in universal, naturalistic terms, but as conventionally encoded and understood by speakers of the language in question at the given time. Far from being "sociological factors" or "social factors bear[ing] upon linguistic features" (186), these are simply linguistic features. They are language particular categories of content, indexed by linguistic elements of expression, and they are selected for expression in discourse by speakers in accordance with their communicative intentions and with the same degree of freedom (and responsibility) as other categories of linguistic content.

Secondly, while it is a commonplace that language is totally embedded in society (linguistic facts are social facts, cf. (3)), what is important to understand is that through the sociolinguistic categories of content indexed by linguistic expressions, the categories of a society are ("unevenly", that is, selectively) embedded in its language.

What should distinguish our generation of linguists from that of Kuryłowicz is the understanding that social categories which are thus integrated into a language are not heterogeneous to it. If we look back at Kuryłowicz's methodological admonition with this, it seems, superior understanding and grasp the difference between "sociological factors" and sociolinguistic features of content, we can in fact give Kuryłowicz's statement our unqualified endorsement.

In speaking of "linguistic" innovations in my title I want to imply as broad an understanding of the word 'linguistic' as is necessary to accommodate the fact that the realms of content encoded by linguistic expressions extend far beyond what is given individual morphemic expression. No elements of meaning symbolized or indexed by linguistic expressions can be considered non-linguistic or extra-linguistic (cf. Hjelmslev 1961: 125 ff.).

3. Innovations

The third word in my title was chosen in an effort to pinpoint the phenomena that have to be explicated and understood in linguistic diachrony and to avoid the confusion and the misunderstandings that the word 'change' has traditionally given rise to.

To some extent speakers of a language can have the impression that their language is changing or has changed in their time. There is no reason why the word 'change' should not be used to describe this naive, subjective impression.

But in linguistics the word 'change' has come to be more of a liability than an asset. Several attempts have been made to define it as a technical term (Coseriu 1958: 45 f., 1974: 63 f., cf. Andersen 1975: 19, 22, 54;

Lüdtke 1985: 187), but perhaps it is best avoided altogether. It has been noted time and again — but is often not sufficiently appreciated — that in the literal sense of the word 'change', "linguistic change does not exist" (thus Coseriu 1985). What happens diachronically — in discourse as in grammar — is that innovations are made which for a time may occur or exist side by side with the corresponding traditional forms, and eventually may become established as traditional themselves. In such a diachronic development, which informally can be called 'a change', nothing strictly speaking changes into anything else. The key concept here is that of innovation, which we return to below.

Often, in the scholarly literature, the word 'change' is used indifferently about diachronic developments as just described and about an entirely different, purely metalingual notion, equally distinct from anything properly called change and therefore better denoted by a more precise, descriptive label. I use the term 'diachronic correspondence' for this, the relation between an entity belonging to one stage of a language and an equivalent entity of a later stage. Diachronic correspondences are, so to speak, the raw material on the basis of which the linguist determines whether there have been innovations or not during a given segment of time.

The simple fact that a diachronic correspondence may be the result of a series of diachronic developments ('changes') would in itself argue for a consistent, explicit distinction between the two notions. In fact, however, linguists have tended to take little interest in the actual diachronic developments in which a language tradition is preserved and renewed as it is passed on from speaker to speaker — which should be the historical linguist's primary object of inquiry. Instead they have focused their attention on diachronic correspondences, calling these metalingual relations 'changes', and speaking of them as of objects changing into other objects, bizarre as it may seem. Consider, among recent works, Bynon (1977), who speaks variously of grammars turning into subsequent grammars (e. g., pp. 46, 57, 67) and of surface representations changing into later, different surface representations (e. g., pp. 53, 64); these are the "pseudo-connections" highlighted by Andersen (1973: 767); or see Itkonen (1983: 208 ff.), who defines several schematic types of diachronic correspondence, calls these abstractions changes, and theorizes that some of them are more rational than others. In other words, the word 'change' has commonly been employed not to describe anything going on in the object of inquiry — language in diachrony — but rather to sum up a reified version of the linguist's observations (cf. Coseriu 1985).

In order to describe effectively the reality of diachronic developments, I use the term 'innovation' to refer to any element of usage (or grammar) which differs from previous usage (or grammars). The notion of innovation makes it possible to break down any diachronic development ('change') into its smallest appreciable constituent steps. The notion has sufficient flexibility to allow ad hoc qualification — we can recognize passive innovations, in decoding competence, along with active ones, speak of collective as well as of individual innovations, or consider a train of cumulative innovations as a single innovation — without losing sight of the term's ideal, minimal extension. In this regard, the term 'innovation' differs very favourably from the word 'change', which has traditionally tended to subsume arbitrarily large segments of development.

Most importantly, as the notion of innovation allows us to analyse any diachronic development into its constituent steps, it also lets us recognize that these are of necessity quite differently conditioned and leads us to inquire whether any given innovation in usage or in grammar is intentional, to what extent it is determined by universal or language specific features of discourse or grammar, and whether it affects or is codetermined by one or another of the different levels of grammatical organization of the language — its received norms, its functional system, and its type (thus Coseriu 1971) or groundplan (as Sapir sometimes called it).

4. Finality, determinacy, fortuity

In section 3, I sketched the usual course of events in diachronic developments: an innovation arises, the new entity (of usage or of grammar) cooccurs or coexists for some time with the corresponding traditional one and is then eventually established as traditional itself — if it does not go out of use, yielding to the traditional one or to a new innovation. To understand any such particular development it is necessary to understand the reason for the initial innovation, why it was accepted, adopted or acquired, or duplicated by others, and finally, why it was generalized or given up in competition with alternative linguistic entities.

To speak meaningfully about such developments in general, one needs to recognize that each and every step in such a development is an innovation, not only the initial act, through which a new linguistic entity comes into being. It is through innumerable individual acts of innovation — of acceptance, adoption, and acquisition — that any new entity gains currency and enters into competition with traditional entities in the usage of a linguistic community. Among all the different kinds of innovation, however, the initial innovations show the greatest variety and involve the most varied kinds of motivation.

A consistent analysis of diachronic developments into the steps of which they are composed leads to the identification of three major categories of innovation, which differ by the distinct kinds of motivation they involve. They are, first, the pragmatically motivated innovations, which involve finality (section 4.1), secondly, the innovations that arise in the transmission of a language from generation to generation, which involve different degrees of determinism (section 4.2), and finally, the innovations that arise, as it were, fortuitously out of nowhere (section 4.3).

4.1 Adaptive innovations

An adaptive innovation is a purposeful elaboration of an innovator's competence (a covert innovation), typically motivated by immediate communicative needs and immediately realized in discourse (in an overt innovation). An adaptive innovation enables the innovator to overcome a perceived shortfall of his competence vis-à-vis his communicative needs, and in thus extending his competence it can be said to adapt his grammar to — that is, bring it into greater conformity with — the demands of discourse. The simplest illustrations are new words coined to express new notions; Andersen 1975 and 1980a offer systematic overviews with lexical, morphological, morphophonemic, and phonological examples.

Adaptive innovations may be premeditated (as, for instance, terminological neologisms typically are), but most are not. Some are unquestionably intentional or may be rationalized ex post facto as intentional. But many appear to be made without conscious intent and may be produced in the here-and-now of discourse even without the innovator's being aware of their novelty. Maybe most kinds of adaptive innovations conform to Coseriu's conception of innovations as products of the speaker's free will, but some must be recognized as involuntary. The unifying feature of all adaptive innovations is their purposefulness (or goal-directedness — finality, as the philosophers would say), the fact that they are modifications of a speaker's grammar aimed at achieving specific communicative ends.

This makes it natural to categorize adaptive innovations according to the diverse functions discourse serves, as suggested in Andersen (1975: 19 f., 1980 a: 7 ff.). Minimally one can distinguish six categories, corresponding to Jakobson's six functions of discourse, innovations facilitating (1) reference precision, (2) emotive expressiveness, (3) aesthetic aptness, (4) conative effectiveness, (5) channel efficiency, and (6) code conformity (cf. Jakobson 1960: 353 ff.). All of these can evidently be divided into subcategories, with differences in detail from culture to culture.

4.1.1 Contact innovations

Contact innovations, which include the last-mentioned category above, are noteworthy in several regards, first of all by being necessarily involved in every diachronic development: it is through contact innovations that any overt innovation spreads and is generalized in a speech community, by being (passively) accepted, (intentionally) adopted, or (voluntarily or involuntarily) acquired by other speakers. More importantly, it is through contact innovations (especially adoption and acquisition) that members of a language community manifest their linguistic solidarity, and that any community language is maintained as such. Furthermore it is through contact innovations that speakers of any language bridge communication gaps between themselves and speakers of other languages.

It stands to reason that very different conditions for contact innovations obtain under these different circumstances. Active participation in the linguistic tradition of one's own speech community is one thing. Adoption of the norms of another sociolect or dialect is quite another. Adoption of a different grammatical system, yet another, not least where the languages in contact are typologically distant. The consequences of contact innovations undoubtedly depend on whether the adaptation is unilateral or occurs in a context of mutual code adjustment, and whether it is based on adoption alone or includes acquisition (cf. Andersen 1988). Again, much probably depends on the relative stability of the contact situation and on how long it obtains: the development of a shared ecology of speaking may be a prerequisite for such relatively orderly amalgamations of grammars as Zamboangueño (Frake 1971) or Michif (Rhodes 1977), as well as for the development of linguistic alliances (Sprachbünde), whereas the confrontation of widely different ecologies may inevitably produce the sort of cataclysmic results described by Mühlhäusler elsewhere in this volume.

But while a great deal remains to be learned about the conditioning of contact innovations, there is no doubt about the reason for them. Speakers of all languages naturally look to the fitness of their linguistic competence and will adopt or acquire novel expressions they encounter by reason of their apparent utility — be it with respect to referential precision, emotive expressiveness, aesthetic aptness, conative effectiveness, channel efficiency, or code conformity. Thus the reasons for contact innovations include all the reasons why adaptive innovations are made. And all the reasons for adaptive innovations may result in code conformity, not just the common desire to speak like one's fellows.

4.1.2 Finality and indeterminacy

If one considers the logical structure of innovations and views any innovation as a conclusion derived from a set of premises, then the purposive character of all adaptive innovations can be seen to consist in the fact that their "final cause" — the goal of the innovation — is the chief of these premises, the single sufficient condition, the reason for the innovation.

In addition, two sets of conditions are invariably involved in adaptive innovations, elements of the innovator's pragmatic competence — which, for instance, determine the fact and the extent of the innovation — and elements of his grammatical competence. The latter may determine the character of the innovation positively — for instance, where a productive pattern of word formation is used to coin a neologism, or negatively — such as when an adaptive innovation goes beyond the customary means of the innovator's competence, as typically innovations in word order or contact innovations.

There is a notable difference between contact innovations and the other five types mentioned above, which I call accommodative innovations. In contact innovations, the covert innovation is a hypothetical (abduced) account of elements of a model usage, defined on the basis of the innovator's prior competence, in terms of which these elements have been observed. In accommodative innovations, by contrast, the goal of the individual covert innovation is not part of the innovator's prior experience and is largely determined by his grammatical competence. As a consequence, accommodative innovations are less determinate than contact innovations. Note that contact innovations typically contribute to linguistic convergence, whereas accommodative innovations often result in divergence, as one and the same communicative problem is solved differently by different members (in different parts) of a community.

4.2 Evolutive innovations

I have suggested the term 'evolutive innovations' for the unintentional and purposeless innovations in grammar and in usage that occur as a language is transmitted from generation to generation — or, perhaps more accurately, is acquired by generation after generation — in a language community (cf. Andersen 1973: 778).

4.2.1 Continuity

The continuity of a linguistic tradition rests entirely on the interplay of two activities, in which all members of a language community are engaged from cradle to grave. These two activities, which it is useful to view in logical terms, are discourse — the (logically deductive) derivation of observable usage by means of internal grammars — and language acquisition — the (abductive) construction of internal grammars on the basis of observed usage.

Leaving aside performance errors and adaptive innovations, the usage of discourse is logically entirely determined by the internal grammars with which it is produced; such is the nature of deduction. If internal grammars were similarly determined by the usage from which they are inferred — as many linguists have believed — no innovations would arise in the transmission of language, or at most one would expect to record random, individual fluctuations due to acquisition errors, or imperfect learning, as it is usually called.

In fact, of course, diachronic shifts do occur in all linguistic traditions, and they may affect any part of grammar and range from almost imperceptible shifts in the shape, value, or distribution of single entities to wholesale systemic shifts, and even typological shifts. What is more, when such shifts occur, they are typically actuated in discourse in a gradual and generally orderly fashion. These are the two major explananda for a theory of evolutive innovations.

4.2.2 Bifurcations

Historical dialectology sheds considerable light on the reason for such diachronic shifts. The analysis of dialect boundaries provides massive evidence suggesting that in general, to any diachronic shift which occurs in some language area at some time, there is a logical alternative, often attested in a complementary area (on the other side of an isogloss) or known from the history of some other language (cf. the notion of 'bifurcation' in Andersen 1975).

What this means is two things. First, whereas the construction of a grammar by and large may be sufficiently determined by evidence available to the learner, this is probably never the case in all particulars, the observable usage being susceptible to more than one interpretation in some, perhaps in numerous, respects. Secondly, the lack of determinacy involved can more often than not be ascribed to ambiguities — with respect to distinct parameters — which must be resolved in the course of the acquisition process by cognitive operations such as segmentation, valuation, or ranking, which are equally relevant to the expression side, the content side, and the syntactic specifications of any linguistic entity; cf. Andersen 1975, 1980a. It is the fact that many of these operations involve binary decisions which explains why the attested diachronic shifts typically imply logical alternatives. Any ambiguity in the observed discourse data which different learners may resolve differently is sufficient reason for an (abductive) innovation.

4.2.3 Norms and system

Since usage is logically entirely determined by the internal grammars with which it is produced, all abductive innovations might be expected to have immediate observable consequences. However, a grammatical competence develops, throughout a speaker's life, as a dual structure composed of a (hypothesized) system of the productive rules of the language and a (similarly hypothesized) account of its norms, the principles of usage which guide the speaker in his efforts to speak as he should. Consequently speakers are able to produce usage conforming relatively closely to the same norms despite differences in their internal grammatical systems. Or, to put this into a diachronic perspective, even relatively significant systemic shifts may be shielded from immediate manifestation by the speakers' adherence to received norms of usage. In ontogenetic terms, an abductive interpretation of some part of a grammatical system which turns out to be untenable may — instead of being revised — be covered up, or patched up, with adaptive rules formulated in subsequent contact innovations; this is the scenario exemplified in Andersen 1972. Or, elements of the received usage may be acquired 'by rote' as part of the norms before any generalizations are made regarding the productive system, in which case observable usage might not offer any evidence at all of the innovative or non-innovative character of the speaker's system.

This, in outline, is the theory adumbrated with regard to diachronic morphophonemics in Andersen 1969 (821 ff.) and elaborated with reference to phonology in Andersen 1972. An essential element in this theory is the asymmetrical relationship between norms and system which follows from the generality and simplicity of the system and the fact that the norms, which prevent the system from full, immediate manifestation, in many regards have to be acquired piecemeal. First, in every respect in which a speaker is not familiar with the norms, he will be guided in his usage by the productive system he has constructed for himself. As a consequence, deductive innovations will arise in community usage side by side with entities conforming to the received, unproductive patterns. Secondly, since the novel entities bear a simpler relation to the productive system than the received ones, they may be evaluated by the speakers as simpler and more natural than the received ones and hence not be subject to censure, at least in some styles. Thirdly, the actual occurrence of the novel entities in the usage of the community will tend to increase the frequency with which the innovative, productive patterns will be constructed by subsequent learners. As a consequence, the unproductive patterns defined by the norms will gradually be curtailed and superseded by the productive patterns of the system, and observable usage will gradually approach complete comformity with the rules of the system.

The theory that has been summarized here departs from what can be observed in order to explain it. What can be observed when a shift is actuated is that minor alterations of usage gradually lead to a new systematic regularity. The theory, by contrast, assumes that the shift precedes the actuation. It views the actuation of a systemic shift as a series of innovations in usage, conditioned by the novel interpretation of the system and allowed to increase in frequency, number, and variety as the norms are gradually brought into conformity with the novel interpretation of the system.

The dynamic relation between norms and system implied in this conception is in essence a theory of double standards. It provides an account of the tension between received community norms and individual interpretations of the system, which is presumably relevant to other value systems than language. Be this as it may, the functional advantage of the differentiation of grammar into norms and system is evident. Since grammar construction is based on abduction, there are no safeguards against divergent interpretations of the data of usage. The norms protect against the undesirable consequences a diversity of interpretations would have for communication. They secure a relative homogeneity (or ordered heterogeneity) and continuity of usage whether or not there are differences among the grammars constructed by different speakers.

4.2.4 Determinacy and ambiguity

Unlike adaptive innovations, evolutive innovations are not purposeful. To be sure, the efforts through which each speaker acquires his competence are evidently purposeful. But the purposeful character of the acquisition process as a whole merely means that the acquisition of any part of a grammar is purposeful, and not that innovation would be either more or less purposeful than the absence of innovation. There is no need for the concept of finality in discussions of evolutive innovations.

As mentioned above, observable usage is in principle (leaving aside performance errors and adaptive innovations) entirely determined by the internal grammar from which it is (deductively) derived, whereas the system of an internal grammar is not fully determined by the usage data from which it is (abductively) inferred.

The reduced determinacy of the abductive process, however, is far from being a play of chance. In the first place, it is mainly around certain threshold values that the observable usage corresponding to given parameters is ambiguous. This is clear from the geographic consequences of bifurcations when a language area is differentiated into dialects; these are typically neat bisections of an area and not random distributions of the two logical alternatives. Secondly, there is evidence to suggest that abductive innovations are conditioned not just by ambiguous usage data, but also by prior analytic decisions the learner has made (cf. Andersen

1973: 767 f.). In fact, such prior decisions may determine innovations even in cases where there are apparently no ambiguities in the data (cf. Andersen 1980 a: 37 f.). Thirdly, central among the premisses that condition the results of the acquisition process are universal principles of grammar formation, which determine which aspects of the usage data will be cognized, the strategies of analysis used, and the form the results of abduction will have. To give just one example, there is probably a universal, possibly holding by default, to the effect that of two alternants, the longer will be derived from the shorter (cf. Andersen 1980 b: 299). This universal would be an essential part of the explanation for the remarkable fact mentioned by Bloomfield in (1) (section 1) that linguistic forms tend to shorten. On the whole, it seems that there is copious evidence in documented language histories for an extensive codetermination of abductive innovations by other facts of grammar with which given innovations seem to cohere, and hence, by implication, evidence for the character of this coherence. Perhaps due to the absence of a generally accepted theory of evolutive innovations, this evidence has not attracted quite the attention it deserves.

While many questions regarding the conditioning of evolutive innovations remain to be answered, the reason why they occur is clear: it is in the intrinsic fallibility of the abductive mode of inference. In other areas of cognition, the fallibility of abduction is offset by the possibility of inductive observation. But in the inference of mental objects, such as the grammatical patterns that underlie language behavior, this corrective procedure is not, for obvious reasons, available.

4.3 Spontaneous innovations

The last of the three major types of innovation has long seemed the most enigmatic. What I call spontaneous innovations are like some adaptive innovations in that they extend the innovator's competence relative to that of his models. But unlike adaptive innovations, they serve no discourse purpose. In Andersen 1972 (785 f., 790), I described them as a kind of evolutive innovations. But they differ from what I have discussed as evolutive innovations above (section 4.2 – 4.2.4) by having no basis whatever in tradition. In fact, they are the innovations from which traditions spring.

Spontaneous innovations are the innovations by which speakers interpret as regular variation what is objectively mere fluctuation. I will mention only two areas in which the effects of spontaneous innovations are most notable.

One is the ascription of social value to all novel linguistic entities. When innovations — any innovations — are first introduced in usage, they may convey whatever linguistic and pragmatic content they are intended to convey, but they have no social value. Social value is ascribed to them by individual speakers as they receive them, depending on the social group membership of the speakers from whom they hear them and on the context in which the innovations are heard. These individual (abductive) ascriptions of sociolinguistic and stylistic indexical content, which are tantamount to conditions of use, determine each individual's own use of the innovation if he adopts or acquires it. Only as an innovation gains currency in the speech of the community does a collective understanding of its social value develop on the basis of the use patterns of those who have adopted it (cf. section 5).

Such use patterns may remain stable, but more often they will drift. Whenever a condition of use is defined by a markedness relation, the given entity's use will be less clearly defined at one end of the given dimension than at the other, and the resulting skewed fluctuation will give rise to subsequent revaluations of the categories that are indexed.

The other area I will mention, in which spontaneous innovations play an important role, is low level phonetics. It is through spontaneous innovations that the naturally occurring mutual adjustments of contiguous phonic elements (intrinsic allophones) are elevated to conventional, that is, rule governed indexes (extrinsic allophones). By such innovations, phonetic fluctuation — that is, to put it in Saussurean terms, the amorphous sound material just beyond what is linguistically formed — is given linguistic form as rules of allophonic variation and, in this way, semioticized (cf. Andersen 1979: 380 f., Dressler 1982: 116 f.). That the resulting variation, which originates as a result of individual spontaneous innovations, is idiosyncratic at first and may gain currency only if it is ascribed social value, perhaps goes without saying.

4.3.1 Fortuity and contingency

Spontaneous innovations appear to arise fortuitously, with the flimsiest conceivable basis in reality, or even without any at all. As innovations, they serve no apparent purpose. On the basis of these characteristics one would expect there to be very cogent reasons for their occurring, and for the results of spontaneous innovations to be readily adopted and acquired by members of language communities. These expectations seem to be fulfilled.

The likely reason why spontaneous innovations arise is that man's ability to acquire language is so superior to the task that even the merest cues may suffice for the identification of some existing regularities, and even fluctuations may be interpreted as rule governed variation. If this is so, learners must bring to many of their analytic decisions definite expectations regarding the kinds of values to assign to alternative expressions and the kinds of phonetic dimensions to pick out for allophonic variation — to remain with the two areas of spontaneous innovation mentioned above. For example, alternative expressions become indexes of social group membership, but never of hair colour, body height, or other physical characteristics. Similarly allophonic alternations are created which highlight existing phonemic distinctions, not in any conceivable, random way, but in apparent accordance with universal regularities (cf. the notions of 'linking' in Chomsky and Halle 1968: 419 ff. and of 'secondary diphthongization' in Andersen 1972: 19 ff.).

If spontaneous innovations are readily adopted and acquired by members of a community even though they serve no immediate communicative purposes in discourse, the reason may well be that they serve essential functions in their grammar.

In several earlier writings I have suggested that allophonic rules (or, more generally, implementation rules), by virtue of their phonological indexing function, encode important information about the system of distinctive oppositions to which they refer. If this is so, one may guess that only such innovative patterns of variation will be acceptable to members of a community which are compatible with their interpretation of the phonological system (cf. Andersen 1973: 786, 1979: 381). Similarly the patterns of sociolinguistic indexing distributed across the grammar of a language evidently encode significant information about the system of social categories which is thus embedded in the language (cf. section 2). And one may guess that the spontaneous innovations by which social value is ascribed to any novel entities are viable or not depending on their compatibility with the system of social categories tacitly recognized by the community. This interpretation of the function of spontaneous innovations is directly related to the discussion in section 5.

5. Understanding linguistic innovations

It was my intention with the title of this paper simply to refer to one of the chief concerns of historical linguists. But the verbal noun in the title — understanding — can be construed with different subjects and almost invites us to expand our perspective, at least for a brief moment, and ask the question as to how members of a speech community understand linguistic innovations. This is not an idle question. Indeed, if the historical linguist's primary object of inquiry is really the actual diachronic developments in which a language tradition is preserved and renewed as it is passed on from speaker to speaker (as I claimed in section 3), then the question of how speakers understand innovations in their language cannot be neglected.

In a stimulating paper published some years ago, "Linguistic change as a form of communication", Labov concluded that innovations may be used to signal a variety of messages, such as 'stronger meaning', 'group solidarity', 'greater intimacy', or their opposites (1980: 253 ff.). Labov's study is a very nice clarification of some of the reasons why innovations are adopted, but it is interesting by its key assumption alone. It assumes, in fact, that any novel expression, apart from the content invested in it by grammar and pragmatics, has a specific value by virtue of being different from a traditional expression with the same grammatical and pragmatic content (cf. the notion of connotative content, defined in Hjelmslev 1960: 114 ff.).

In Labov's study, the specific values carried by the novel expressions he examined are all immediately referable to such established categories of connotative content as those mentioned above. This is what one would expect, for they all exemplify innovations which have already been widely adopted as parts of community languages, and for which one can consequently identify a definite, collectively understood connotative content.

But does not Labov's idea of language change as a form of communication apply just as well to the period in the life of an innovation before this stage of consolidation of its value has been reached?

I would suggest that it does, and that it is reasonable to recognize two kinds of metadialogue which take place concurrently with the use of language for its regular, communicative purposes.

One of these metadialogues concerns the constitution of the linguistic system. It consists of learners' experimentation with their language and was briefly sketched at the end of section 4.3.1. Its messages are the substantive innovations a learner produces and the perceived feedback regarding the successfulness and acceptability of these innovations, which serves to confirm or disconfirm the learner's hypotheses about the productive system and the norms of the language.

The other metadialogue concerns the norms of usage more narrowly, for it is focused on the social value of novel expressions. This is a dialogue in which all members of a speech community participate throughout their lives. In this metadialogue, the use of an innovation in a specific context is tantamount to a motion that it be accepted for general use in such contexts, a motion which the interlocutors may second, reject or, for the moment, leave undecided. As they select novel and traditional expressions in accordance with their individual hypotheses about their appropriateness — relative to the genres of discourse, styles of diction, categories of role and status and social class recognized in the culture — the speakers in effect negotiate the norms that they look upon as their community norms.

Nothing prevents a speech community from verbalizing this metadialogue about the norms, and in some cultures explicit discussions of proper usage are standard. But the verbalized metadialogue can never be more than fragmentary. The full metadialogue, by contrast, is part and parcel of the life of any language tradition. For no community values can be established except through the dialectic of usage, and no values can be maintained except through renewal. Thus it is by the temporary consensus mediated by this unspoken dialogue that the tacit conventions of a language are shaped and constantly reshaped as long as the language is spoken.

References

Andersen, Henning
   1969   "A study in diachronic morphophonemics: the Ukrainian prefixes", *Language*
            45: 807—830.
   1972   "Diphthongization", *Language* 48: 11—50.
   1973   "Abductive and deductive change", *Language* 49: 765—793.
   1975   "Towards a typology of change: bifurcating changes and binary relations",
            in: *Historical linguistics* II, ed. by John M. Anderson & Charles Jones, 17—60.
            (Amsterdam: North-Holland).
   1978   "Vocalic and consonantal languages", in: *Studia Linguistica A. V. Issatschenko
            a Collegis et Amicis oblata*, ed. by L. Durovic et al., 1—12. (Lisse: De Ridder
            Press).

1979   "Phonology as semiotic", in: *A semiotic landscape. Proceedings of the First Congress of the International Association for Semiotic Studies*, ed. by Seymour Chatman, 377–381. (The Hague: Mouton).
1980 a   "Morphological change: towards a typology", in: *Historical morphology*, ed. by Jacek Fisiak, 1–50. (The Hague: Mouton).
1980 b   "Russian conjugation: acquisition and evolutive change", in: *Papers from the 4th International Conference on Historical Linguistics*, ed. by Elizabeth C. Traugott et al., 285–302. (Amsterdam: John Benjamins).
1988   "Center and periphery: adoption, diffusion and spread", in: *Historical dialectology*, 39–85, ed. by Jacek Fisiak. (Berlin: Mouton de Gruyter).
Bloomfield, Leonard
1935   *Language.* (London: George Allen & Unwin).
Bynon, Theodora
1977   *Historical linguistics.* (Cambridge: Cambridge University Press).
Chomsky, Noam – Morris Halle
1968   *The sound pattern of English.* (New York: Harper & Row).
Coseriu, Eugenio
1958   *Sincronía, diacronía e historia.* (Montevideo: Universidad de la Republica).
1971   "Synchronie, Diachronie und Typologie", in his: *Sprache. Strukturen und Funktionen. XII Aufsätze zur allgemeinen und romanischen Sprachwissenschaft*, 91–108, hrsg.: Uwe Petersen. (Tübingen: Narr).
1974   *Synchronie, Diachronie und Geschichte. Das Problem des Sprachwandels*, trsl. by Helga Sohre. (München: Fink).
1985   "Linguistic change does not exist", *Linguistica nuova ed antica* 1: 51–63.
Dressler, Wolfgang U.
1982   "A semiotic model of diachronic process phonology", in: *Perspectives on historical linguistics*, ed. by Winfred P. Lehmann and Yakov Malkiel, 93–132. (Amsterdam: John Benjamins).
Frake, Charles O.
1971   "Lexical origin and semantic structure in a Philippine Creole Spanish", in: *Pidginization and creolization*, ed. by Dell Hymes, 223–242. (Cambridge: Cambridge University Press).
Hjelmslev, Louis
1960   *Prolegomena to a theory of language*, trsl. by Francis J. Whitfield. (Madison, Milwaukee & London: University of Wisconsin Press).
Itkonen, Esa
1985   *Causality in linguistic theory: a critical investigation into the philosophical and methodological foundations of non-autonomous linguistics.* (Bloomington: Indiana UP). [American edition of 1983 publication.]
1986   "Form-meaning isomorphism, or iconicity in diachronic linguistics (and elsewhere)", in: *Symposium on formalization in historical linguistics*, ed. by Mart Remmel, 38–46. (Tallinn, ESSR: Academy of Sciences of the ESSR).
Jakobson, Roman
1960   "Linguistics and poetics", in: *Style in language*, ed. by Thomas A. Sebeok, 350–377. (Cambridge, Mass.: M. I. T. Press).
Kuryłowicz, Jerzy
1947   "Le sens des mutations consonantiques", *Lingua* 1: 77–85. [Reprinted in his *Esquisses linguistiques* (= *Prace językoznawcze*, 19), 240–247. (Wrocław & Kraków: Ossolineum, 1960).]
Labov, William
1986   "Linguistic change as a form of communication", in: *Human communication*, 221–256, ed. by A. Silverstein. (Hillsdale, NJ: L. Erlbaum).

Lüdtke, Helmut
    1980   "Auf dem Wege zu einer Theorie des Sprachwandels", in: *Kommunikations-theoretische Grundlagen des Sprachwandels*, ed. by Helmut Lüdtke, 182—252. (Berlin: de Gruyter).
Rhodes, Richard
    1977   "French Cree — a case of borrowing", in: *Proceedings of the 8th Algonquian Conference*, ed. by W. Cowan, 6—25. (Ottawa: National Museums of Canada).
Sapir, Edward
    1921   *Language. An introduction to the study of speech.* (New York: Harcourt, Brace & World).
Weinreich, Uriel — William Labov — Marvin I. Herzog
    1968   "Empirical foundations for a theory of language change", in: *Directions for historical linguistics*, ed. by Winfred P. Lehmann and Yakov Malkiel, 95—188. (Austin & London: University of Texas Press).

On the causes of syntactic change in English

Leiv Egil Breivik

0. Introduction

In the past fifteen years or so, there has been a remarkable upsurge of interest in typological universal grammar — the framework generally taken to begin with Greenberg 1963, and which continues in such works as Lehmann 1974, Vennemann 1974, Harris 1978, Comrie 1981, Mallinson and Blake 1981, Andersen 1983, Hawkins 1983, Givón 1984, and Stassen 1985. Recent approaches to morphosyntactic typology utilize the same sort of broad, cross-linguistic data base which has always served as the foundation for phonological theorizing.

A number of linguists have extended the study of typological parameters to the empirically less verifiable field of language change, seeking to determine the motivations for, and mechanisms of, changes in word order systems. Work done by diachronic syntacticians working within this paradigm has yielded valuable insights into the way in which languages change. There can be no doubt, however, that a great deal of fine-grained analysis remains to be done before we can hope to formulate a theory of change within the typological framework (cf. Ashby 1983, Breivik 1984, Lightfoot 1979). The present paper is meant as a small contribution towards this end. It is concerned with the relationship between typological shifts and specific linguistic changes in one area of English grammar; the following sections chart the development of sentences with EXISTENTIAL *THERE*, and try to provide an explanation for the diachrony by appealing to syntactic, semantic and pragmatic parameters.[1] Existential *there* (*there₁*) is the kind of *there* which is constrained to occur in subject position and should be distinguished from LOCATIVE *THERE* (*there₂*):

(1)   There₁ are linguists in Tromsø.

(2)   The linguist is over there₂, just behind the table.

In discussing the historical paths of actuation, I shall frequently adduce data from other Germanic languages in support of my hypotheses. Where details of the history of English *there*₁-sentences are poorly understood, the possibility exists of gaining fresh insight into them in the light of changes that have taken place more recently, or are indeed still taking place, in languages which are genetically and typologically closely related to English. In this connection, I shall assess the plausibility of two theories concerning the development of word order in Germanic, those of Haiman (1974) and Stockwell (1977).

The exposition is organized as follows. Section 1 outlines the most important characteristics of *there*₁-sentences in present-day English. This section forms a necessary background for the detailed treatment of the historical data in section 2, which traces the various types of *there*₁-sentence from the earliest texts up to Modern English. Section 2 also offers a principled explanation for the changes taking place in the period examined. Section 3 summarizes Haiman's (1974) findings concerning the development of verb-second order in the Germanic languages, and section 4 briefly reconsiders the development of English word order in the light of his theory of syntactic change. It is argued that a modified version of his analysis can account for some residual cases from my Old English material. Section 5 presents the basic tenets of Stockwell's (1977) theory of the transitional sequence between Proto-Germanic SOV order and Modern English SVO order. Stockwell himself does not discuss the development of dummy subjects, but it is shown that his theory of word order change is compatible with Haiman's general hypothesis as well as with my historical data. Section 6 advances a tentative hypothesis about the origin of *there*₁. It is suggested that *there*₁ separates from *there*₂ as a result of semantic/syntactic reanalysis. The main results of my investigation are summed up in section 7.

Before turning to the use and non-use of dummy subjects in English, it is necessary to define two terms which will play a prominent role in the subsequent discussion. The term EXISTENTIAL SENTENCE, which was coined by Jespersen (1924: 155), is often applied with a certain vagueness in the literature both in import and extension. Here the term will be reserved to designate all and only sentences (and clauses) containing existential/locative *be* or an intransitive verb which has included in it the meaning 'be in existence' or 'come into existence'. Note that the presence of the morpheme *there*₁ is not taken to be a defining characteristic of existential sentences. Examples of existential sentences by this definition are the following:

(3a)   An account book is on the table.

  b)   There₁ is an account book on the table.

  c)   On the table is an account book.

  d)   On the table there₁ is an account book.

(4a)   An account book lay on the table.

  b)   On the table (there₁) lay an account book.

(5a)   In our department a serious crisis is developing.

  b)   In our department there₁ is developing a serious crisis.

Since the *there₁*-sentence in (6) contains a transitive verb in the passive voice, it does not qualify as an existential sentence. Such cases will be referred to as PASSIVE *THERE₁*-SENTENCES.

(6)   In 1985, there₁ was written a whole series of articles on existential sentences by a number of eminent linguists.

1. *There₁* in present-day English

In both spoken and written English, the vast majority of *there₁*-sentences contain a form of lexical *be* (cf. Bolinger 1977: 96; Breivik 1983: 174). I shall therefore devote most of my attention to this category.

Consider again the examples in (3). These sentences are fully synonymous in that they express the same cognitive content, but they differ in the way this content is presented. In (3a) the message is coded in a marked way. This sentence violates what is sometimes called the TOPICALIZATION PRINCIPLE. According to this principle, there is a tendency for elements containing given information (i. e. the topic) to come first in the sentence, and for elements containing new information (i. e. the comment) to come near the end. Sentences like (3a) are extremely rare in both spoken and written English. By contrast, (3b) represents the unmarked version. Compare (3a) with (7), which is consistent with the topicalization principle:

(7)   The account book is on the table.

It is a common observation that that *there*$_1$ behaves like a subject-NP with respect to a number of transformations (e. g. Subject Raising). Syntactically, it functions as a DUMMY SUBJECT in (3b); that is, when the logical subject is moved to post-verbal position for communicative reasons, *there*$_1$ is inserted in the vacated subject slot. In present-day English, which is a verb-medial (SVO) language, a finite verb cannot normally occur in initial position in declarative sentences:

(8)   *Are two books on the table.

We turn now to (3c—d). The only difference between these two sentences is that *there*$_1$ is absent in (3c), while it is present in (3d). Such sentences are not freely commutable in contemporary English. As we shall see below, the non-use of *there*$_1$ is subject to constraints. If my hypothesis about the syntactic status of *there*$_1$ is correct, it accounts for the fact that restrictions DO apply to (3c): one would expect (3d), which under my analysis has the order subject-verb, to be the unmarked version in a verb-medial language like English. (3c) has inversion of subject and finite verb, the finite verb being preceded by a locative adverbial. Note that both these sentences are in agreement with the topicalization principle. This explains why (3c) sounds better than (3a) when presented out of context.

The above discussion does not imply that all *be*-existential sentences permit the pattern of (3a) and (3c). Note the following:

(9a)   *No sign of life was in the house.
  b)   There$_1$ was no sign of life in the house.
  c)   *In the house was no sign of life.
  d)   In the house there$_1$ was no sign of life.

My hypothesis is that *there*$_1$ is obligatory in *be*-sentences which fail to convey visual impact. In some of my publications (e. g. Breivik 1981, 1983), I have referred to this (pragmatic) constraint as the VISUAL IMPACT CONSTRAINT.

Let us return for a moment to example (3a). When (3a) is presented out of context in informant-reaction tests, native speakers tend to characterize it as dubious, marginal or even unnatural. However, the same speakers find (3a) perfectly natural in the following context:

(10)   We are looking at an extraordinary picture painted by X. A
        middle-aged man and three boys are seated on chairs or stools
        at a spindly square table. *An account book is on the table.*

In order for sentences like (3a) to be acceptable, they must bring something — literally or figuratively — before our eyes.

    The visual impact constraint also applies to *be*-sentences with a pre-
posed locative. The fact that the sentences in (9) cannot make us visualize
a concrete scene in the way described above explains why *there*$_1$ is
necessary here. In this connection, one important point needs to be
emphasized: the visual impact constraint stipulates that *there*$_1$-insertion
is obligatory in examples like those in (9), regardless of style; it does not
stipulate that *there*$_1$-insertion is blocked in cases like (10). In *be*-sentences
satisfying the requirement for visual impact, the use or non-use of *there*$_1$
seems to some extent governed by stylistic factors: *there*$_1$ is more common
in informal than in formal English. The non-use of this particle is
particularly common at the formal end of the register in written English.

    In the preceding paragraphs, I have argued that *there*$_1$ can be dispensed
with if the subject and the locative convey visual impact. So far, I have
not commented explicitly on the pragmatics of *there*$_1$ itself. It is generally
agreed that this morpheme is a non-referring expression in present-day
English; that is, it does not carry semantic information. However, it
would appear that it carries a kind of information which we may call
SIGNAL INFORMATION: *there*$_1$ functions as a signal to the addressee
that he must be prepared to direct his attention towards an item of new
information. If the introduction of new information consists in bringing
concrete objects into the presence of the addressee, there is no need to
prepare him in this way.

    Sometimes it would appear that *there*$_1$ and *be* have become fused into
a single presentative formula *there*$_1$*'s*. Sentences like (11) occur quite
frequently in spoken English:

(11)   There$_1$'s two men here.

From such sentences, it is only a short step to sentences containing a
post-verbal NP with definite reference:

(12)   There$_1$'s always George. (We might ask him.)

In (12), *there*$_1$*'s* is more or less synonymous with 'I could mention',
'Dont't let's forget' etc. In such cases, the formula *there*$_1$*'s* seems to recall

the referent of the post-verbal NP into the focus of attention. Although the subject in (12) is definite, it is contextually independent. *There*$_1$ would have been inappropriate if *George* had represented given information. The hypothesis that *there*$_1$ + *be* functions as a presentative formula, or signal, receives further support from such examples as (13):

(13)   A: Who's attending the meeting?
        B: Well, there$_1$'s (*are) John, Michael and Janet.

Note that in this example the plural form of *be* is disallowed.

We come now to existential sentences containing a verb other than *be*. This type is not subject to the same constraints as *be*-sentences, as shown by (14) and (15):

(14)   An unpleasant smell remains in the house.

(15)   Unicorns exist.

Neither of these sentences conveys visual impact, and they both violate the topicalization principle. However, if the whole of the subject-NP is shifted to post-verbal position in such sentences, *there*$_1$ becomes obligatory:

(16)   There$_1$ exist unicorns that are white in the winter, green in the spring, grey in the summer and black in the autumn.

In (15), the subject is not weighty enough to outbalance the verb, but in (16) the word order (logical) subject-verb would be unacceptable because of the discrepancy in length between these two constituents. In other words, (16) is consistent with the HEAVIER-ELEMENT PRINCIPLE, which states that heavier elements tend to come towards the end of the sentence. It is important to note that the logical subject in (16) represents new information. Thus, when *there*$_1$ occurs in sentences containing a verb other than *be*, it can be regarded as a presentative signal in these sentences too. However, it has not acquired the same pragmatic status here as in *be*-sentences.

There seems to be a unifying principle determining the multitude of verbs that can appear in *there*$_1$-sentences. In his discussion of non-thematic subjects in contemporary English, Firbas operates with a category of verbs which he calls verbs of 'appearance or existence on the scene': "These verbs or verbal phrases undoubtedly imply or even explicitly express 'appearance — a kind of coming into existence — on the scene' (i. e. the scene created by the narrow, *ad hoc* context at the moment of utterance) or simply 'existence' on this scene" (1966: 243). It appears that the verbs which can co-occur with *there₁* are precisely verbs of 'appearance or existence on the scene', i. e. verbs like *appear, be, emerge, exist* and *remain*. If I am correct in claiming that *there₁* is a presentative signal, then this also provides a natural explanation for its co-occurrence restrictions with respect to the verb. Example (17) contains a verb of appearance on the scene; hence *there₁* can be used. This is not the case with (18):

(17)   There₁ appeared a man in front of us.

(18)   *There₁ disappeared a man in front of us.

In (18), the person is not presented on the scene; he disappears from the scene. Consider also (19), which contains a transitive verb in the active voice:

(19)   *There₁ broke a girl a vase.

Break is not a verb of 'appearance or existence on the scene'. Thus my analysis predicts that (19) is deviant.[2]

It must be emphasized that the analysis presented above is not entirely conclusive. It does not account for the non-use of *there₁* in (20) and (21):

(20)   A burglar has been in the room.

(21)   Nobody is in the garden.

These two *be*-sentences do not convey visual impact. Such sentences are of course not counter-examples to that part of my hypothesis which claims that *there₁* is a formal subject. If the subject-NP is moved to post-verbal position, as in (22) and (23), *there₁*-insertion becomes obligatory:

(22)   There₁ has been a burglar in the room.

(23)   There₁ is nobody in the garden.

A further problem for my analysis is presented by the sentence in (24):

(24)   There₁ lacked only the moon. (Hartley, *Eustace and Hilda*, quoted from Erdmann 1976: 138.)

Lack cannot be subsumed under the category established above. However, sentences of this type have a very low frequency in present-day English. Thus they are non-existent in the material of the Survey of English Usage at University College London.

2. *There*$_1$ in earlier English

In the course of the preceding discussion, it has become apparent that the use or non-use of *there*$_1$ in present-day English is conditioned by a complex interplay of syntactic, semantic, and pragmatic factors. Let us now see how the historical data can account for the complicated situation which exists today.

This section traces the development of *there*$_1$-sentences from Early Old English up to Early Modern English. We shall distinguish between four main periods:

I.	-1070
II.	$1070-1225$
III.	$1225-1425$
IV.	$1425-1550$

The reason why we do not go beyond the middle of the 16th century will become clear from the subsequent discussion. The texts examined are listed in the Appendix. In all, the source texts comprise 4,031 pages (Period I: 1,357 pages; Period II: 627 pages; Period III: 571 pages; Period IV: 1,476 pages). In view of the fact that Periods I and IV represent the terminal points of my investigation, it was natural to examine a larger body of material from these two periods than from the intervening periods.

2.1 On the semantics of *there*$_1$

I have argued elsewhere that *there*$_1$ and *there*$_2$ are already differentiated in Old English, and that this differentiation in some important respects resembles that of contemporary English (cf. Breivik 1977, 1983: chapter

4). For example, the hypothesis that *there₁* functions as a non-referring expression in earlier English receives support from the fact that it is interchangeable with the classic dummy form *it*. As is well known, *it* is widely used as an empty 'slot-filler' in certain types of non-existential sentence in Old and Middle English (e. g. in weather statements). Consider the following examples of existential *it* (*it₁*):

(25) forþon *hit* wæs an geleafa & an hiht on þa halgan þrynesse ær
       Cristes tocyme
       'because there was one belief and one hope in the Holy Trinity
       before Christ's advent' (Blickling 81: 26−27).

(26) þa wearð *hit* swa mycel æge fram þam here . þet man ne mihte
       geþeoncean ne asmægian hu man of earde hi gebringon sceolde
       'Then there was so great terror inspired by the host that every-
       body was incapable of devising or drawing up a plan to get them
       out of the country' (Chronicles, Laud 1006: 32−34).

(27) Bot *hit* ar ladyes innoʒe
       'But there are ladies enough' (Sir Gawain 1251).

    A collation of the Lauderdale MS and the Cotton MS of *Orosius* also brings to light evidence for my hypothesis. Consider the following examples from the Lauderdale MS:

(28) þæt *þær* nane oðre near næran
       'that there₁ were no others near' (Orosius 12−13).

(29) ymb þone tieman wæren swa micel snawgebland
       'At that time there₁ were so strong snowstorms' (Orosius 186:
       33−34).

Corresponding to the existential sentences in (28) and (29), the Cotton MS has (30) and (31) respectively:[3]

(30) þæt nane oðre near næran.

(31) *hit* ymbe þone timan wæron swa micel snaw-gebland.

It will be seen that (28) contains *þær* (= *there₁*), while (29) has the zero form of the existential particle. In (30), *þær* is left out, while *hit* (= *it₁*) is inserted in (31).

The alternation of *there*$_1$, *it*$_1$ and zero is also illustrated by other Old and Middle English texts, e. g. by the various MSS of *Cursor Mundi*. Thus, in line 2210, all three possibilities are represented:

(32a) Þat tim *it* was bot a langage
'At that time there was only one language' (Cotton).
b) Þat time was bot an langage (Fairfax).
c) Þat time *it* was bot a langage (Göttingen).
d) þat tyme was *þer* but o langage (Trinity).

We have seen that *it* can be inserted in existential sentences in earlier English. In (33), *there*$_1$ has encroached upon the territory of *it* in a sentence with an extraposed clausal subject:

(33)   and some deme þat *þer* shall be condyssendyd þat iff E.P. come to London þat hys costys shall be payed fore (Paston 302: 26 – 27).

2.2 Word order types in Old English

Before embarking on a detailed discussion of *there*$_1$-sentences, it is necessary to outline some of the major tendencies of Old English word order. Three basic types of serial order can be distinguished:[4]

A. S(v)V(O)(...)
(S = subject; v = auxiliary verb; V = lexical (main) verb; O = object/verb complements. Parentheses indicate that the element is optional.)
B. S(O)(...)V(v)
C. i. (X)(v)VS(...)
ii. (X)vSV(...)
(X is a cover term for various elements, some of which will be specified below.)

It must be emphasized that the above classification does not claim to be exhaustive: only such patterns are listed as are relevant to our discussion of *there*$_1$-sentences. Among patterns which are omitted, I may mention the common construction in which a pronominal object is placed between the auxiliary and the main verb, whether or not a main clause is involved (cf. Traugott 1972: 109). The discussion of word order patterns in Old English will be resumed at various places below.

Type A word order is of course the same as the usual Modern English order. It is used in most non-dependent clauses containing an affirmative proposition:

(34)   Ic eom soðlice cristen
         'I am truly a Christian' (Ælfric 1 XXII: 208).

Type B is the dominant order in subordinate clauses:

(35)   Gif ic godes man eom . forbærne eow godes fyr
         if I God's man am   consume you God's fire
         'If I am a man of God, let God's fire consume you' (Ælfric I XVII: 248).

Type C is employed by *yes/no*-questions, in which case the X position is empty:

(36)   willaþ ge astigan on eorðan & min þær onbidan
         'Will you go ashore and wait for me there₂?' (Blickling 233: 30).

The X position may be empty in declarative main clauses too:

(37)   Hæfde he bisceopseðl   in þære stowe, þe   geceged is
         Had   he episcopal seat at the place   which called is
         Liccedfeld
         Lichfield
         'He had an episcopal seat at the place which is called Lichfield' (Bede 262: 11).

If the X position is filled, the elements that occur are, most typically, the negative particle *ne* and adverbials of place and time:

(38)   *Ne* synd ge na wyrðe . þæt wundor to geseonne
         'You are not worthy to see that wonder' (Ælfric 1 VII: 196).

(39)   *Ðær* wærð East Engla folces seo yld ofslagen
         'There₂ were slain the chief men of East Anglia' (Chronicles, Laud 1004: 16−17).

(40)   *Nu* mæg soð hit sylf gecyþan
        'Now the truth itself may be told' (Blickling 187: 15–16).

Finally, let us briefly look at Old English from the point of view of the function of word order as a typological parameter. Stockwell (1977, 1984) claims that Old English prose is characterized by a word order norm that is best described by the verb-second constraint, i. e. the constraint whereby the finite verb must be the second constituent in a declarative main clause. Or, as Stockwell himself puts it: "In declarative main clauses of late OE prose, represented e. g. by the Homilies and Saints' Lives of Ælfric, the V-2 rule characterizes a word-order norm that is not fully grammaticized. By that, I mean that it is very common but not obligatory or fully categorical" (1984: 576). Examples of verb-second patterns are given in (34), (39) – (40).

Stockwell's hypothesis is confirmed by Bean's (1983) study of the development of word order patterns in the *Anglo-Saxon Chronicle*. Her data show that the verb-second rule characterizes 70% to 80% of all main clauses after the earliest period. According to Bean, XSVO (which is the Modern English order) is never higher than 10% in prose after the earliest period. It may also be mentioned that Vennemann (1974) presents evidence to show that Old English is a verb-second language similar to Modern German and not a subject-verb language similar to Modern English.

As will emerge from the subsequent sections, my own data also provide support for the view that Old English is predominantly a verb-second language.

2.3 Criteria for the classification of sentences in which *there₁/it₁* can be inserted

In the following, we shall be concerned only with sentences which contain an indefinite subject. We shall distinguish between existential sentences in which *there₁/it₁* is absent (Types A/B and C) and existential sentences in which *there₁/it₁* is present (Type D). Types A and B have been collapsed into one category (A/B) on the grounds that there are no unambiguous instances of Type B in the material. All the relevant sentences exhibit one of the following patterns: SvV..., SV..., or SV; that is, they are either unambiguously Type A (SvV..., SV...) or indeterminate between A and B (SV).

We saw above (section 1) that *there*$_1$ can co-occur with a passive VP in present-day English. This is the case in earlier English too. *There*$_1$/*It*$_1$-sentences with a passive VP will be referred to as E sentences. The example in (71) is the only passive *it*$_1$-construction in the corpus. In Period III, a new type of *there*$_1$-construction crops up, that containing a transitive verb in an active VP (cf. example (19) above). This construction will be referred to as Type F. No instances of *it*$_1$ co-occurring with a transitive verb in the active voice are attested.

It must be stressed that serial order is not used as a criterion to establish Classes D, E, and F. However, the dummy subject occurs in pre-verbal position in the vast majority of cases throughout Periods I − IV.

2.4 Presentation of data

Sections 2.4.1 − 2.4.5 present data from Periods I − IV. Then follows a discussion of the use and non-use of *there*$_1$/*it*$_1$ in my historical material (section 2.5). It must be emphasized that figures given for Classes D, E, and F are based only on sentences which (as I interpret them) contain unambiguous instances of *there*$_1$. Similarly, only unambiguous instances of *there*$_2$ have been included in Class C. (Recall that the X element in sentences of Class C can be filled by *there*$_2$.) The frequencies of Classes A/B, C, D, E, and F will be cross-tabulated against two clausal categories: main clauses (MC) and subordinate clauses (SC).

2.4.1 Frequency counts

Table 1. Distribution of existential sentences between Types A/B, C, and D in the material from Period I.

	MC	SC	Total
Type A/B	57 = 12.1%	24 = 30.4%	81 = 14.7%
Type C	354 = 75.0%	33 = 41.8%	387 = 70.2%
Type D	61 = 12.9%	22 = 27.8%	83 = 15.1%
Total	472 = 100%	79 = 100%	551 = 100%

Table 2. Distribution of existential sentences between types A/B, C, and D in the material from Period II.

	MC	SC	Total
Type A/B	34 = 14.3%	3 = 12.5%	37 = 14.2%
Type C	137 = 57.8%	9 = 37.5%	146 = 55.9%
Type D	66 = 27.9%	12 = 50.0%	78 = 29.9%
Total	237 = 100%	24 = 100%	261 = 100%

Table 3. Distribution of existential sentences between types A/B, C, and D in the material from Period III.

	MC	SC	Total
Type A/B	1 = 0.5%	7 = 9.5%	8 = 3.0%
Type C	39 = 20.2%	2 = 2.7%	41 = 15.4%
Type D	153 = 79.3%	65 = 87.8%	218 = 81.6%
Total	193 = 100%	74 = 100%	267 = 100%

Table 4. Distribution of existential sentences between types A/B, C, and D in the material from Period IV.

	MC	SC	Total
Type A/B	19 = 6.5%	3 = 2.3%	22 = 5.2%
Type C	27 = 9.2%	1 = 0.8%	28 = 6.7%
Type D	247 = 84.3%	124 = 96.9%	371 = 88.1%
Total	293 = 100%	128 = 100%	421 = 100%

Table 5. Frequency of sentences of Type E in the material from Periods I—IV

	MC	SC	Total
Period I	10	1	11
Period II	2	0	2
Period III	18	9	27
Period IV	38	46	84
Total	68	56	124

Table 6. Frequency of sentences of Type F in the material from Periods III—IV

	MC	SC	Total
Period III	7	6	13
Period IV	13	3	16
Total	20	9	29

My data show that *there₁* vastly outnumbers *it₁* in all of the four periods. The ratios are: 81/2 (Period I), 68/10 (Period II), 213/5 (Period III), 367/4 (Period IV). It may be mentioned that *it₁* lingers on after 1550 in archaic ballad style, as in *It₁ is an ancient mariner, And he stoppeth one of three* (Coleridge).

2.4.2 Textual examples from Period I

Type A/B

(41) Micel yfelnyss wæs on iudeiscum mannum
'There was great evilness in Jewish men' (Ælfric 1 XI: 317).

(42) 7 gyt ma wæs þe þæt don ne wolde
'but there were yet more who would not do so' (Bede 48: 21).

(43) Manige men beoð þe beforan oþrum mannum hwæt hugu god begangaþ, & raþe hie hit anforlætaþ
'There are many men who, before other men, begin to do a little good and quickly abandon it' (Blickling 57: 1—3).

Type C

(44) On ðam ylcan dæge com sum bisceop helenus gehaten
'On that same day came a bishop who was called Helenus' (Ælfric 1 II: 57—58).

(45) Nis nan leahter swa healic þæt man ne mæg gebetan
'There is no sin so great that a man may not atone for it' (Ælfric 1 XII: 157—158).

(46) Nu synd ðreo heah-mægnu. ðe menn sceolan habban
'Now there are three chief virtues which men must have' (Ælfric 1 XVI: 246).

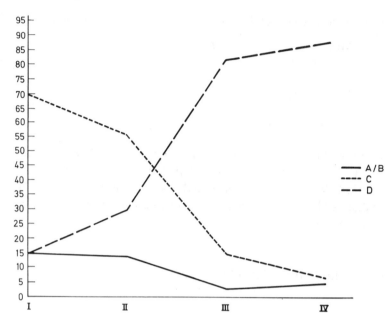

Figure 1. Percentage changes in the various types of existential sentence in Periods I—IV.

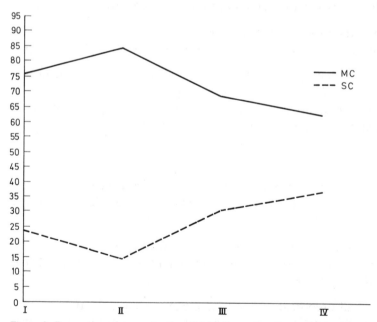

Figure 2. Percentage changes in the distribution of main and subordinate *there₁*-clauses (Types D—F) in Periods I—IV.

(47)   Wæs sum Godes þeow of þæm broðrum þære cirican æt Agos-
         taldes ea, þæs noma wæs Bothelm
         'There was a servant of God among the brethren of the church
         at Hexham, whose name was Bothelm' (Bede 156: 15–16).

(48)   Þa wæron ·ii· ciningas on Cent. Wihtred. 7 Wæbheard
         'There were then two kings in Kent, Wihtred and Wæbheard'
         (Chronicles, Laud 692: 3–4).

Type D

(49)   Gif ðær beoð fiftig wera wunigende on þam earde
         'If there are fifty men living in the place' (Ælfric 1 XIII: 196).

(50)   þær wæs an cyrce of scinendum golde . and of gymstanum
         standende on þam felda
         'there was a church of shining gold and of precious stones
         standing in the field' (Ælfric 1 XXI: 352–353).

(51)   þa onget he þæt ðær næs fyrod genoh ongen heora fynd
         'he then perceived that there was not a sufficient army to meet
         their enemies' (Ælfric 2 XXX: 295–296).

(52)   Þær wæron bisceopas of gehwilcum burgum to þære ge-coren-
         nysse
         'There were bishops from every city at the election' (Ælfric 2
         XXXI: 267–268).

(53)   Forþon þrym gearum ær his cyme in þa mægðe þæt þær nænig
         regn in þæm stowum cwom
         'For three years before his coming to that province, no rain had
         fallen in those localities' (Bede 302: 25–27).

(54)   Ðonne is þær on neaweste sum swiþe mære burh
         'Then there is a very famous city in the neighbourhood' (Blickling
         196: 18).

(55)   nis þær on þam londe lað-geniðla
         'there is no enemy in the country' (Exeter IV: 50).

(56)   Þær bið swyðe mycel gewinn betweonan him
         'There is very much strife among them' (Orosius 20: 17–18).

Type E

(57)   Þær wurdon gehælede at ðære halgan byrgene eahta untrume
        menn ... wundorlice þurh god
        'At the holy tomb there were healed eight sick men, miraculously,
        by the power of God' (Ælfric 1 XXI: 132−134).

(58)   ne bið ðær nænig ealo gebrowen mid Estum, ac þær bið medo
        genoh
        'no ale is brewed among Estonians, but there is enough mead'
        (Orosius 20: 18−19).

2.4.3 Textual examples from Period II

Type A/B

(59)   An preost wes on leoden: Laȝamon wes ihoten
        'There was a priest in the nation who was called Laȝamon'
        (Laȝamon 1).

(60)   Ðreo tide beoð on þissere worlde
        'There are three periods in this world' (OEH 1 89: 9−10).

(61)   Two kinne festing beð
        'There are two kinds of fasting' (OEH 2 63: 21).

(62)   Fuwerkinne mannisshe liuen on þis woreld
        'Four kinds of men live in this world' (OEH 2 85: 5−6).

Type C

(63)   Stod an hali mon of feor, biheold al þis ilke
        'A holy man stood at a distance and watched the whole affair'
        (Ancrene 13: 11−12).

(64)   Þa wes i Kent an eorl. Aldolf i-haten
        'Then there was in Kent an earl who was called Aldolf' (Laȝamon
        5662).

(65)   on þis niht beð fowuer niht wecches
        'In this night there are four night-watches' (OEH 2 39: 32).

(66)   Nu bien sume oðre ðat healden hem seluen wise and ȝeape
        'Now there are some others who consider themselves wise and
        crafty' (Vices 79: 10−11).

Type D

(67) *þer* is remunge iþe brune. ant toðes hechelunge iþi snawi weattres
'There is shrieking in the flame, and chattering of teeth in the snowy waters' (OEH 1 251: 19—20).

(68) for nis *þer* na steuene bituhhe þe fordemde bute wumme
'for there is no voice between the damned but woe me' (OEH 1 253: 20—21).

(69) ȝif *ðar* cumþ ani þoht oðer ani word a godes half, hie bieð hire swiðe welcume
'If there comes any thought or any word on the part of God, they are very welcome to it' (Vices 99: 28—29).

(70) Ac *hit* bieð sume ðe to michel þar of þenceð
'But there are some who think too much of them' (Vices 137: 20—21).

Type E

(71) and þarfore *hit* is iset lage bi ure drihtenes wissunge. þat me sal children fuluhtnie
'and therefore there is a law ordained according to our Saviour's direction that children shall be baptized' (OEH 2 17: 16—17).

(72) *Þer* is iboren an luttel child: inne þere leoden
'A little child is born in the nation' (Laȝamon 4551).

2.4.4 Textual examples from Period III

Type A/B

(73) A knyȝt wes/þet zuor/be godes eȝen (Ayenbite 45: 31).

(74) Also yif ony persone be, that wil auenture toward þe forsayd Costes of Normandy wyn, ale, beer, fissh, flessh (BLE, War with France X: 11—13).

Type C

(75) Betuene ham and paradys ne is bote a lyte woȝ (Ayenbite 72: 14—15).

(76)   Item atte ende of Tryggeslane is a Steyre greuously broken (BLE,
        From Pleas and Memoranda III: 245 – 246).

(77)   Thanne is here necessite in the toon and in the tothir (Chaucer/
        Boece, Book V, Prosa 3: 60 – 61).

Type D

(78)   I wene *ther* wer a-boute a xxx craftes (BLE, Appeal of Thomas
        Usk 192 – 193).

(79)   Item *þer* is a donghill in þe watergatestrete (BLE, From Pleas
        and Memoranda III: 264).

(80)   Whilom *ther* was a man that hadde assaied with stryvynge wordes
        another man (Chaucer/Boece, Book II, Metrum 6: 123 – 124).

(81)   Estward *ther* stood a gate of marbul whit (Chaucer/Knight
        1893 – 1894).

Type E

(82)   Also is ordeined þat vche ȝer *þer* schul four wardeines be chosen
        to reule þe fraternite þat ȝer (BLE, London Guilds I: 83 – 84).

(83)   for *ther* nys no thing doon for cause of yfel (Chaucer/Boece,
        Book IV, Prosa 6: 170 – 171).

Type F

(84)   Also þat *þer* schal non of þe wardeyns make none newe statutes
        ne newe ordinances withoute assent of alle þe bretherhede (BLE,
        London Guilds III: 87 – 88).

(85)   *Ther* may no man clepen it cowardye (Chaucer/Knight 2730).

2.4.5 Textual examples from Period IV

Type A/B

(86)   A Man was whiche of his craft was a Rope maker (Caxton 87:
        32).

(87)   And somme ben that can neuer kepe theyr tongue (Caxton 184:
        7).

Type C

(88)   And in alle the world is no gretter treson/ than for to deceyue gentyll wymmen (Caxton 12: 15−16).

(89)   I remembred that I had redde in many a boke/ That in this place of plesure were many a stormy blast (Nevill 220−221).

(90)   In that castell was also a garnisson of Frenshemen (Paston 412: 24−25).

Type D

(91)   *There* was a knyght/ that hadde two doughters (Caxton 17: 36).

(92)   Now on a nyght *there* cam to her a Vysyon/ that she drewe and took oute of a donghylle a vessell/ lyke to a plater of syluer (Caxton 21: 5−7).

(93)   And anone *there* began a grete stowre and much people were slayne (Malory 32: 21−22).

(94)   For as for chaunteryes, though *ther* be many, no one man can haue any greate lyuynge therby (More 81: 27−28).

(95)   And God sayd: let *there* be a fyrmament betwene the waters, and let it devyde the waters a sonder (Tyndale, Genesis I: 6−7).

(96)   But I will seperate the same daye the londe of Gosan where my people are, so that *there* shall no flyes be there (Tyndale, Exodus VIII: 22).

(97)   *Ther* ys nothing that lackys in me/ But that I haue not (Wyatt XXI: 3−4).

Type E

(98)   And *ther* was sene at her deth a grete clerenes and lyght alle full of lytel children (Caxton 38: 27−28).

(99)   So than *there* was made grete ordynaunce in thys ire (Malory 17: 11).

(100)   And *there* was ordeyned an hors-bere (Malory 90: 20).

(101)   As for bevere, *þer* is promysid me somme (Paston 148: 10−11).

(102)   Iffe *ther* be any suche thynge begune ther by suche a fryere or prest, as it is seyde, I mervayle þat ye sente me no worde theroff (Paston 312: 24−25).

Type F

(103)   But without any such thyng proued before/ *ther* wyll no reason nor good conscyence bere it (More 106: 5−7).

(104)   And *þer* knoweth no man how soon God woll clepe hym, and þer-for it is good for euery creature to be redy (Paston 30: 11−13).

2.5 Discussion

Let us now attempt an explanation for the trends evident in the corpus. My hypothesis is that in Old English constructions like (50), *there*$_1$ is inserted as an empty topic to move the verb into second position. Sentences like (41) and (44) satisfy this constraint without *there*$_1$. As appears from Table 1, C is the dominant pattern in Old English. The proportion of this type is especially high in non-embedded contexts. Although verb-initial sentences like (47) occur, the vast majority have verb-second order.

As already stated, English is now a verb-medial language. I would claim that *there*$_1$ is syntactically reanalysed as a subject-NP when English develops from a verb-second into a verb-medial language. Reanalysis is not an uncommon phenomenon in the history of the English language. This is demonstrated by cases like *Hem nedede no help* → *They needed no help*: here the old dative *hem* is reinterpreted as the subject, and the old subject *no help* becomes the object under the pressure of the SVO syntax. The quantitative data show that existential sentences of Type C are increasingly being ousted by sentences with a pre-verbal *there*$_1$ under the pressure of the SVO syntax (cf. Tables 1−4 and Figure 1). *There*$_1$-sentences represent a compromise in the conflict between pragmatic and syntactic structure: the initial subject slot is filled by a dummy subject, while the logical subject, the communicative core, is shifted to post-verbal position. As the presentative construction with *there*$_1$ becomes established, there is also a decrease in the proportion of A/B-sentences. In other words, it would seem that the increasing use of *there*$_1$ in earlier English is part of a series of parallel syntactic changes, acting in a coordinated manner and pushing the language from one typological category to another. In view of the gradual nature of syntactic change, it is not surprising that we should find survivals of the verb-second stage in present-day English. Thus examples like (3c) and (4b) illustrate the specialization of a once general rule.

It is sometimes claimed that changes in word order affect main clauses before subordinate clauses (cf. Mallinson and Blake 1981: 402). My data offer support for this view. As appears from Figure 2, *there*$_1$ is much more common in non-embedded than in embedded contexts in the material. After Period II, however, we witness a marked increase in the proportion of subordinate clauses.

My account of the use and non-use of *there*$_1$ in present-day English made crucial reference to pragmatics. The development in my historical corpus suggests that the pragmatic and syntactic functions of present-day English *there*$_1$ do not have an arbitrary relationship to each other. It is arguable that the signal function of *there*$_1$ is a concomitant to, and a development from, its function as a non-referential subject-NP. Since this morpheme has come to be associated with the introduction of new information, it has itself acquired the status of a presentative signal. A scrutiny of my material reveals that by the beginning of Period IV, the use or non-use of *there*$_1$ is governed by virtually the same syntactic factors as those operative today. This is the reason why it was not found necessary to extend the investigation beyond 1550. To judge from the historical data, however, Early Modern English *there*$_1$ has not acquired quite the same pragmatic status as it has in contemporary English. Thus it can be omitted freely in *be*-existential sentences which do not convey visual impact, as shown by the examples in (86)—(90). It is also worth pointing out that *there*$_1$-sentences like those in (12) and (13) crop up in the language long after full-fledged existential sentences like (1) have become established; the former type is non-existent in my material from pre-1550 English.

As we saw in section 1, passive *there*$_1$-sentences (Type E) still occur in English. However, it should be pointed out that constructions like (6), where the whole of the VP occurs before the subject-NP, are exceedingly rare in the present-day language. Thus they are non-existent in the spoken material of the Survey of English Usage. Sentences like (105) are not subject to the same restrictions:

(105)   There$_1$ had been a secret meeting held.

Here the VP *had been held* is split up, with *had been* coming before the subject-NP. Consider also the following specimens from the spoken Survey material:

(106)   There$_1$ has been some paint spent on the department.

(107)   There$_1$ was nothing taken.

(108)   There$_1$ should be an additional Yale lock fitted on the door.

The low frequency of passive sentences like (6) in present-day English is perhaps not surprising in view of the pragmatic role of the archetypal *there*$_1$-sentence, namely that containing *there*$_1$ plus a form of existential/ locative *be*. Sentences like (1) and (3b) may be regarded as devices for presenting new information: *there*$_1$ functions as a point of departure from which the utterance may be developed, by way of the communicatively weak item *are/is*, to the communicative core — the real subject. The data also suggest that *there*$_1$ + *be* is often regarded as a single presentative formula for a foregrounded NP (cf. the examples in (11)−(13)). In sentences like (6), the sequence 'presentative signal + *be* + foregrounded NP' is interrupted by a prominent element (*written*). In (105)−(108), on the other hand, the passive subject is brought into distinct relief by the preceding elements. Note that the subject-NP's in (105)−(108) are relatively light. Most native speakers of English find (109) unacceptable:

(109)   *There$_1$ had been held a secret meeting.

By increasing the communicative prominence of the subject, we can facilitate the use of the pattern in (109). In (6) the subject-NP is so heavy that it overshadows the preceding VP. The constraint discussed above is purely pragmatic, and does not seem to be operating in earlier English. (109) should be compared with the passive sentences in (99)−(101).

If we are correct in claiming that the pragmatic function of *there*$_1$ has become more and more prominent over the centuries, we also have an explanation for the decay of sentences of Type F. In section 1, it was argued that the presentative particle is disallowed in sentences containing a transitive verb like *break* or *hit* for pragmatic rather than syntactic reasons (cf. *There$_1$ *hit a man the boy*). Cases like (84), (85), (103), and (104) resemble the E sentences attested in my material in that *there*$_1$ has apparently not acquired the status of a presentative signal but functions primarily as a syntactic device. This is of course different from claiming that F sentences do not have a contextually independent subject. According to Visser (1970: 52), the sentence type under discussion falls into disuse in the course of the 16th century. In this connection, it is interesting to note that in present-day German the dummy subject *es* functions as a purely syntactic device, also in F sentences, to keep the verb in second position:

(110a)   *Es* ist noch etwas Wein in der Flasche.
        'There is still some wine (left) in the bottle.'
    b)   In der Flasche ist (*es*) noch etwas Wein.

(111a)   *Es* hat jemand gestern deine Schwester geküsst.
        'Somebody kissed your sister yesterday.'
    b)   Gestern hat (*es*) jemand deine Schwester geküsst.

On the basis of the historical data, then, it appears that the conglomeration of factors underlying the use and non-use of *there*₁ in present-day English reflects an ongoing change. If this assumption is correct, it is not surprising that *there*₁-insertion should be less common in written than in spoken *be*-existential sentences (cf. above, section 1). Nor is it surprising that non-*be*-sentences like (24) should be restricted to formal written English. Here the verb cannot be characterized as a verb of 'appearance or existence on the scene'. In contrast to sentences of Type F, non-existentials like (24) have not yet been eliminated from the language. As is to be expected if we are dealing with a linguistic change in progress, different native speakers often express different acceptability judgments with regard to the use and non-use of *there*₁ (cf. Breivik 1983: chapter 3).

Not explained by the analysis developed above is the fact Old English *there*₁ occurs post-verbally in such cases as (54), (55), and (58). The existential dummy subject also appears in other contexts where the verb-second constraint does not obtain. Thus it can show up in embedded structures, as in (49) and (51). Sometimes it even occurs in subordinate clauses where the finite verb stands at the end of the clause. (53) is a case in point. In an attempt to solve the problems presented by *there*₁, we shall take a look at its counterparts in other languages.

3. Haiman's theory of syntactic change

In his seminal book on syntactic change, Haiman (1974) discusses the use of dummy subjects in various languages. This section outlines the basic tenets of Haiman's theory.

Following Perlmutter (1971), Haiman makes a typological distinction between Type A and Type B languages. According to Haiman (91), a Type A language must have all the the following features:

(i)   Allow no deletion of unstressed personal pronoun subjects.
(ii)   Must have subjects for impersonal verbs.
(iii)   Have special indefinite pronoun subjects like *on* and *man*.
(iv)   Have dummy subjects to replace extraposed sentences.
(v)   Have a dummy pronoun *there* (or some equivalent) to stand in the place of logical subjects that have been displaced from sentence-initial position.

Type B language may dispense with superficial subjects. The class of Type A languages is co-extensive with the Germanic languages, plus French and Romansh. Haiman writes (90):

> Among those type A languages mentioned in Perlmutter's study were English, French, and German. To these we may add the remaining Germanic languages and Romansh. The type B languages which he enumerated included Latin, Spanish, and Italian, Arabic, Walbiri, Hebrew, Hausa, and Basque. To these we may add the remaining Romance languages, all the Slavic languages, and all the other Indo-European languages attested at any time, as well as the Uralic languages, the Altaic languages, and, apparently, most of the other languages of the world.

Haiman hypothesizes that while the Germanic languages are Type A languages by heredity, French and Romansh are Type A languages by borrowing from Germanic dialects.

We thus see that languages which are genetically closely related to English have a dummy element which is inserted in subject position in existential sentences. Equally important, Type B languages do not have a rule corresponding to *there*$_1$-insertion in English or *es*-insertion in

German. Note also that some Type A languages (e. g. French, German, and Norwegian) employ the same morpheme both in existential sentences and in other constructions which require a dummy element in subject position. Consider the following Norwegian examples:

(112)   *Det* er mange folk her.
        'There₁ are many people here.'

(113)   *Det* snør.
        'It is snowing.'

(114)   Det vart sunge.
        it   was sung
        'There₁ was singing.'

(115)   Det er usannsynleg at han vil gjere det.
        'It is unlikely that he will do it.'

In many varieties of Norwegian, *der* can replace *det* in sentences like (112) and (113).

Haiman contends that dummy subjects are properties of languages which either are or have been subject to the verb-second constraint. His hypothesis is that we begin with a language having the underlying order VSO. In order to satisfy the verb-second constraint, various constituents of the sentence can be fronted. If nothing can be fronted, as in impersonal passives, a dummy pronoun is inserted to move the verb into second position (cf. example (114)). From this stage, the language eventually develops obligatory subject pronouns and SVO order. Haiman posits (127 ff.) four stages in the historical development of dummy pronouns.

(116)   Stage 0: VSO base order
        a) fronting
        b) # V → # pronoun, V

Note that pronoun insertion is ordered after fronting. This means that either the first or the second rule may apply, but not both: "fronting applies to VSO structures and creates derived structures to which the rule of *es*-insertion, by virtue of its structural index, can no longer apply" (Haiman, 141). This stage is exemplified by Modern Icelandic, where all cases of *það*-insertion follows the application of the fronting rule:

(117a) Það voru blöð, blek og pennar á borðinnu.
      'There₁ were papers, ink and pens on the table.'

  b) Á borðinnu voru (*það) blöð, blek og pennar.
      'On the table there₁ were papers, ink and pens.'

  c) Voru (*það) blöð, blek og pennar á borðinnu?
      'Were there₁ papers, ink and pens on the table?'

A similar situation obtains in Faroese, where only weather statements can have the dummy subject in post-verbal position. In Modern German, fronting always precedes *es*-insertion in existential sentences and impersonal passives.

(118) Stage 1: SVO base order
     a) # V → # pronoun, V
     b) fronting
     c) subject-verb inversion
     d) V pronoun → V Ø (obligatory)

The underlying order VSO of Stage 0 has been reinterpreted as SVO. Furthermore, pronoun insertion now precedes the fronting rule. This means that both (a) and (b) may apply in the same derivation. Observe, however, that the pronoun is obligatorily deleted by rule (d). Attestation of Stage 1 is provided by Romansh.

(119) Stage 2: SVO base order
     a) # V → # pronoun, V
     b) fronting
     c) subject-verb inversion
     d) V pronoun → V Ø (optional)

At this stage, rule (d) is optional: dummy subjects begin to appear optionally in positions where they are not motivated by the verb-second constraint. According to Haiman, the rule which deletes post-verbal dummy subjects becomes more and more restricted and finally ceases to operate at all:

(120) Stage 3: SVO base order
     a) # V → # pronoun, V
     b) fronting
     c) subject-verb inversion

d) ------------------------

(the rule is dropped)

We have now reached the stage in the historical development where the presence of a dummy subject is completely independent of the surface verb-second constraint: when rule (d) is dropped from the grammar, dummy subjects begin to appear OBLIGATORILY in positions where the verb-second constraint does not require them. Both Stage 2 and Stage 3 are well attested in Type A languages. Consider the following data from Dutch:

(121a) *Er* is hier veel sneeuw.
'There is much snow here.'
b) Is (*er*) hier veel sneeuw?
'Is there much snow here?'
c) Hier is (*er*) veel sneeuw.
'Here there is much snow.'
d) ... dat (*er*) hier veel sneeuw is.
'... that there is much snow here.'

(122a) *Er* wordt gezongen.
'There is singing.'
b) Hier wordt (*er*) gezongen.
'Here there is singing.'
c) Wordt (*er*) hier gezongen?
'Is there singing here?'
d) ... dat (*er*) hier gezongen wordt.
'... that there is singing here.'

In Modern Danish, Norwegian, and Swedish, hardly any traces remain of an original interdependence between the verb-second constraint and the presence of dummy subjects in sentences. Thus *det* cannot be left out in the following examples from Norwegian:

(123a) *Det* er løver i Afrika.
'There$_1$ are lions in Africa.'
b) I Afrika er *det* løver.
'In Africa there$_1$ are lions.'
c) Er *det* løver i Afrika?
'Are there$_1$ lions in Africa?'

d) ... at *det* er løver i Afrika.
'... that there₁ are lions in Africa.'

(124a) *Det* regnar i Bergen i dag.
'It is raining in Bergen today.'
b) I Bergen regnar *det* i dag.
'In Bergen it is raining today.'
c) Regnar *det* i Bergen i dag?
'Is it raining in Bergen today?'
d) ... at *det* regnar i Bergen i dag.
'... that it is raining in Bergen today.'

For English and French, both of which have lost the verb-second constraint, Haiman postulates the following stages with respect to the phenomenon of word order:

(125) Stage 2: SVO base order
a) fronting
b) subject-verb inversion (optional)

(126) Stage 3: SVO base order
a) fronting
b) -----------------------
(the rule is dropped)

Stage 2 is claimed to describe Middle English and Middle French, while Stage 3 is claimed to describe the modern languages. According to Haiman, the loss of rule (b) (subject-verb inversion) is the only factor which prevents English and French from being verb-second languages.

Throughout Stages 0−3, the verb-second constraint is a TARGET; that is, it is an outcome of a number of rules that conspire to keep the verb in second position. Haiman points out (50) that targets must be distinguished from surface structure constraints: targets motivate rules, while surface structure constraints screen the output of rules, filtering out ill-formed sentences. The changes outlined above are hypothesized to be the result of satisfying the verb-second target at earlier and earlier stages in the derivation.

4. English dummy subjects revisited

We shall now reconsider the English data in the light of Haiman's theory. Haiman's own examination of the diachrony of English dummy subjects is very cursory. As far as *there*$_1$ is concerned, he contents himself with the following statement (125 – 126):

> ... modern English requires a more or less obligatory (and relatively early – i.e. cyclical) rule of *there*-insertion in existential sentences where the subject noun has been moved from the head of the sentence. Again, in Old English, this rule does not seem to have existed, or at least, not to have been obligatory, provided always that no violation of the V/2 constraint should arise through the failure of its application.

This statement is not accurate with respect to the situation that obtains in Old English. First, the evidence is overwhelming that the rule of *there*$_1$-insertion exists in this period. Secondly, the non-use of *there*$_1$ can violate the verb-second constraint in both Old and Middle English, as shown by the examples in (47) and (63).

Nor is Haiman's claim about the dummy subject *hit* 'it' correct. According to him (127), *hit*-insertion follows the application of the fronting rule in Old English; that is, *hit*-insertion is claimed to be sensitive to word order in the same way as *það*-insertion in Modern Icelandic (cf. the examples in (117)). We have already seen that *it*$_1$ can appear post-verbally in Old English existential sentences like (26). In non-existential sentences, too, the dummy subject *hit* can show up in post-verbal position, where fronting has occurred. Sentences like (127) and (128), which both contain an extraposed clausal subject, are by no means rare in my Old English material:

(127)   ða gelamp *hit* amang þam þæt sume hlosniende menn ðær be- tweonan eodon . and þisra seofona georne heddon
        'Then it befell them that some spying men went amidst them and carefully observed these seven' (Ælfric 1 XXIII: 136 – 137).

(128)   Ða gelamp *hit* þet se cyng Æðelred forðferde ær ða scipu comon
        'Then it happened that king Æthelred passed away before the ships arrived' (Chronicles, Laud 1016: 35 – 36).

Compare the above examples with (129):

(129)   *Hit* gelamp þa sona . swa hi ofslagene wæron . þæt mycel liget
com . ofer þa manfullan hæðenan
'It happened then, as soon as they were slain, that a great flash
of lightning fell upon the wicked heathens' (Ælfric 1 IV: 422 –
423).

Although there are difficulties with Haiman's analysis in the form
presented, it has certain appealing aspects. As we have seen, he contends
that Stage 2, at which dummy subjects appear optionally in positions
where the verb-second constraint does not require them, describes the
situation in Middle English (cf. (119) and (125)). However, if we assume
that Old English has reached Stage 2, then we can account not only for
sentences in which *there*$_1$ occurs pre-verbally but also for such residual
cases as those mentioned in section 2.5. Observe that all the Old English
there$_1$-sentences we failed to come to grips with in section 2.5 have
parallels in other Type A languages. Compare the examples in (49), (51),
(54), (55), and (58) with those in (121)–(124). As appears from (122d),
even the serial order of (53) is attested. Needless to say, the hypothesis
proposed above also accounts for the distribution of the dummy subject
it in Old English.

At first sight, verb-initial variants like (47) do not mesh with my
modified version of Haiman's theory: while such sentences represent Stage
0, Old English *there*$_1$-sentences represent the advanced Stage 2. The study
of language drift and syntactic change is still very much in its embryonic
stage. Yet we do know that the actualization of word order change is a
gradual process which spans centuries or even millennia (cf. Kohonen
1978, Li 1977). It is not inconceivable, therefore, that constructions like
(47) are relics from the VSO stage.

In this connection, one important point needs to be emphasized. The
existence of verb-initial sentences like (47) is not the only reason why
Old English is not a consistent verb-second language. As shown by Bean
(1983), XSV (verb-third) order is an important pattern in main clauses,
especially in the earliest period (cf. above, section 2.2). In XSV constructions, the subject is preceded by an adverbial element, as in the following
examples (from Bean, 62):[5]

(130)   Her Cyneheard ofslog Cynewulf cyning
'In this year Cyneheard slew King Cynewulf.'

(131)   & on Pasches he weas on Northamtune
         'and at Easter he was at Northampton.'

The fact that subject-verb inversion is not obligatory in declaratives which have undergone fronting is yet another argument in favour of my hypothesis that Old English has reached Stage 2.

Apart from the crucial facts noted above, my data are consonant with Haiman's hypothesis about English. Thus, from what was said in section 2.5, it will be clear that there is no reason to disagree with his claim that the following changes take place subsequent to Stage 2: (i) the rule of subject-verb inversion is dropped from the grammar; (ii) the rule of dummy subject insertion begins to operate within the cycle. Equally important, my data show that English becomes verb-medial (verb-third) long before dummy subjects begin to appear obligatorily in positions where they are not required by the verb-second constraint.

5. Stockwell's theory of syntactic change

In this section, we shall briefly look at Stockwell's (1977) theory of the transitional stages between Proto-Germanic and Modern English. Stockwell does not explicitly discuss the development of dummy subjects, but we shall see that his theory of word order change is compatible with my data as well as with the changes hypothesized by Haiman.

It is generally assumed that Proto-Germanic is verb-final (SOV) in main clauses (cf. Hopper 1975). Stockwell posits a sequence of five transitional stages between Proto-Germanic and Modern English. In the first stage, verb-initial variants arise by a rule of COMMENT FOCUSING. Using Stockwell's notation, we can state the rule as follows:

(132)   SO(V)v → vSO(V)

Stockwell writes: "The rule may have been inherited from IE, since VSO variants must have existed (they are the early norm in Celtic and, to a lesser extent, in Slavic); or in Gmc. it may have been extended from a narrower function such as the imperative or presentative. This rule would code some semantic content such as 'vividness' of action: i.e., the action, not the participants, would be primary in the expression" (291–292). We may also note that Heusler (1931: 168) speaks of VSO order in Old Icelandic as the 'moving' order. McKnight (1897: 138) refers to it as 'dramatic' or 'pathetic'. Givón (1977) assumes VSO as intermediate between SOV and SVO for Hebrew, Spanish, and several Bantu languages.

In the second stage, the vividness of vSO(V) constructions is contextualized by explicit linking words like *then* and *there*:

(133)   vSO(V) → xvSO(V)
        (x = *then, there* etc.)

Stockwell puts forward the hypothesis that the linking construction xvSO(V) is the origin of verb-second clauses in Old English. He also assumes a rule of topicalization which moves NP's as well as adverbials into the initial slot x. This rule produces Haiman's (1974) verb-second structure and Vennemann's (1973, 1974, 1975) TVX structure (where T stands for a topical element and X for whatever remains to the right of the verb).

The remaining stages can be summarized in the following way:

(134)   Stage 3
        TvX(V) → SvX(V) by subject = topic

(135)   Stage 4
        SvX(V) → SvVX by exbraciation

(136)   Stage 5
        Subordinate order → main order by generalization
        (or elimination of whatever differences exist)

6. On the genesis of *there$_1$*

Kimball (1973: 262) writes: "The difficulties with the rule of *There* Insertion are, as with most known rules, insurmountable. It fails to explain why *there* is inserted and not, say, *chop suey*; or, whether the *there* that is inserted is the same as the deictic *there*, or what relation the two bear to each other".[6] We are now in a position to look into this problem.

Danish, Norwegian, and Swedish are, genetically, closely related to English. The fact that these languages, just like English, have an existential dummy subject that is formally identical with a locative adverb strongly argues that English *there$_1$/there$_2$*, Danish and Norwegian *der$_1$/der$_2$*, and (Southern) Swedish *där$_1$/där$_2$* ultimately derive from a common source.

A possible explanation for how *there$_1$* splits off from *there$_2$* is to be found in Western 1921. In his discussion of what he calls the *skinnsubjekt* 'sham subject' in Norwegian, Western claims (61) that *der$_1$* (= *there$_1$*) ultimately derives from the fully stressed locative adverb *der$_2$*, as in (137):

(137)   *Der$_2$* bor en gammel mann.
        'There$_2$ lives an old man.'

In order to make the referent of *der$_2$* explicit, a co-referential locative adverbial is often added:

(138)   *Der$_2$* bor en gammel mann, i det huset.
        'There$_2$ lives an old man, in that house.'

According to Western, the addition of a second locative leads to a semantic reanalysis of *der$_2$* in cases like (138): *der* becomes redundant as an indication of place; it loses its stress as well as its locative meaning. In Western's view, it is only a short step from the use of *der* in (138) to its use as a dummy subject in (139):

(139)   *Der$_1$* bor en gammel mann i det huset.
        'There$_1$ lives an old man in that house.'

Western does not deal with the equivalents of *der$_1$* and *der$_2$* in other languages. However, *mutatis mutandis*, his hypothesis about Norwegian *der$_1$* offers a plausible explanation for how *there$_1$* comes to be employed as an empty topic/subject in English. It fits in very well with sequence of events hypothesized by Haiman (1974) and Stockwell (1977). In section 2, we saw that the development of *there$_1$* is parallel to the gradual stabilization of the SVO syntax. This development lends support to the hypothesis that *there$_1$* has functioned as a subject-NP ever since Late Old English. I now postulate the following stages in the development of *there$_1$*:

(140)   Stage 1
There$_2$ is semantically reanalysed in certain contexts and becomes a non-referring expression, i. e. *there$_1$*.

(141)   Stage 2
There$_1$ is inserted in pre-verbal position by linkage or topicalization (vSO(V) → *there$_1$* vSO(V)); that is, *there$_1$* is inserted as an empty topic in Stockwell's TvX(V) structure.

(142)   Stage 3
This empty topic is syntactically reanalysed by topic = subject (TvX(V) → SvX(V)).

7. Summary and concluding remarks

In the present paper, we have examined the ways in which English *there$_1$*-sentences have changed and developed over the centuries. One fact emerges very clearly from the preceding sections: sentence-internal accounts of the synchrony and diachrony of *there$_1$*-constructions can have only a provisional and incomplete validity. The historical data show that syntactic and semantic changes in these constructions are closely correlated with pragmatic factors (cf. section 2). Extensive text counts revealed that *there$_1$* becomes more and more common from Old English onwards. While Old English is predominantly a verb-second language, Modern English is verb-medial (verb-third). The increasing use of the existential dummy subject in earlier English reflects the typological shift from verb-second to verb-medial. Sentences with a pre-verbal *there$_1$* represent a compromise in the conflict between the topicalization principle and the SVO syntax: the insertion of a dummy subject in pre-verbal position allows the logical subject, the new information, to be postponed.

In view of the fact that the actualization of word order change is a slow process, it is not surprising that the various synchronic stages of English exhibit inconsistencies with regard to the use and non-use of *there$_1$*. Thus it appears that the conglomeration of factors underlying the use and non-use of *there$_1$* in contemporary English reflects an ongoing change, the causes of which can be unravelled only by a detailed examination of the historical data.

As implied above, pragmatics proved to be an enlightening context in which to seek motivations for the establishment of the *there₁*-construction in earlier English. Equally important, the data suggest that the syntactic and pragmatic functions of present-day English *there₁* do not have an arbitrary relationship to each other. It is not unreasonable to assume that the signal function of *there₁* is a concomitant to, and a development from, its function as a non-referential subject. Such an explanation receives support from the cross-linguistic data. As pointed out by Hopper and Thompson (1980: 281), numerous languages have syntactic and morphological devices which reflect foregrounding and backgrounding.

The hypothesis that *there₁* has increasingly come to function as a marker of a foregrounded subject also provides a natural explanation for the decay of F sentences like **There₁ hit a man a boy*: in contrast to verbs like *be* and *appear*, the transitive verb *hit* does not allow the logical subject to receive a foregrounded interpretation in the way defined in section 1. In other words, it would appear that the decay of this sentence type is primarily induced by pragmatic factors. Pragmatics also seems to be a causal factor in the decrease of passive sentences like *Since 1970, there₁ have been published a number of articles on this topic*.

My data are consonant with Haiman's (1974) theory of dummy subjects (cf. sections 3−4). Or, to be more precise, they are consistent with the sequence of changes he hypothesizes for verb-second languages: they do not necessarily bear out his central hypothesis that this sequence should be explained in terms of one basic principle − a target-moving process which seeks to eliminate disparities between surface forms and underlying forms. Whether or not this is a diachronic principle which has explanatory force with regard to verb-second languages is a question we cannot go into here. Haiman's book draws its data from a tiny minority of the world's languages, and we cannot be sure that the generalizations based on them are principled and not coincidental (cf. Lenerz 1979, Steele 1977). Targets are of course an artefact of the theoretical framework in which Haiman works. The notion of target presupposes that surface structures and underlying structures differ substantially, and it would be unnecessary in syntactic theories like the Extended Standard Theory or the Revised Extended Standard Theory. It should be noted that a purely syntactic principle would be incapable of giving a fully coherent account of the development of *there₂*-sentences after English lost the verb-second constraint.

In section 5, we saw that Stockwell's (1977) theory of the transitional stages between Proto-Germanic SOV order and Modern English SVO order is consistent with the sequence of events posited by Haiman as well as with the development in my historical material. Having shown that the verb-second constraint plays a crucial role in the diachrony of dummy subjects, I was in a position to return to a residual problem from my English data considered in isolation, the origin of *there*₁. In section 6, it was suggested that *there*₁ separates from *there*₂ as a result of semantic/syntactic reanalysis. After the separation, which must have occurred before the Old English period, *there*₁ embarks on its long and eventful journey towards present-day English.

Appendix

Primary texts

Period I

Ælfric 1 = *Ælfric's lives of saints* I.i, edited by Walter W. Skeat (London: EETS, 1881); I.ii, edited by Walter W. Skeat (London: EETS, 1885). Reprinted as one volume 1966.
Ælfric 2 = *Ælfric's lives of saints* II.i, edited by Walter W. Skeat (London: EETS, 1890); II.ii, edited by Walter W. Skeat (London: EETS, 1900). Reprinted as one volume 1966.
Bede = *The Old English version of Bede's ecclesiastical history of the English people* I.i, edited by Thomas Miller (London: EETS, 1890); I.ii, edited by Thomas Miller (London: EETS, 1891).
Blickling = *The Blickling homilies* I, edited by Richard Morris (London: EETS, 1874); II, edited by Richard Morris (London: EETS, 1876); III, edited by Richard Morris (London: EETS, 1880). Reprinted as one volume 1967.
Chronicles = *Two of the Saxon chronicles parallel* I, edited by Charles Plummer — John Earle (Oxford: Oxford University Press, 1892).
Exeter = *The Exeter book* I, edited by Israel Gollancz (London: EETS, 1895).
Orosius = *King Alfred's Orosius* I, edited by Henry Sweet (London: EETS, 1883).

Period II

Ancrene = *Ancrene wisse* VI — VII, edited by Geoffrey Shepherd (Manchester: Manchester University Press, 1972).
Laȝamon = *Laȝamon: Brut* (Caligula MS), edited by G. L. Brook — R. F. Leslie (London: EETS, 1963).
OEH 1 = *Old English homilies and homiletic treatises of the twelfth and thirteenth centuries* I.ii, edited by Richard Morris (London: EETS, 1868).
OEH 2 = *Old English homilies of the twelfth century* II, edited by Richard Morris (London: EETS, 1873).
Vices = *Vices and virtues* I, edited by Ferd. Holthausen (London: EETS, 1888).

Period III

Ayenbite = *Dan Michael's Ayenbite of Inwyt*, edited by Richard Morris (London: EETS, 1866).
BLE = *A book of London English 1384 — 1425*, edited by R. W. Chambers — Marjorie Daunt (London: Oxford University Press, 1931).

Chaucer/Boece = *Boece* (by Geoffrey Chaucer), *The works of Geoffrey Chaucer* (2nd ed.), edited by F. N. Robinson (London: Oxford University Press, 1974), 320–380.

Chaucer/Knight = *The knight's tale* (by Geoffrey Chaucer), *The works of Geoffrey Chaucer* (2nd ed.), edited by F. N. Robinson (London: Oxford University Press, 1974), 25–47.

Cursor Mundi = *Cursor Mundi* I (Cotton MS), edited by Richard Morris (London: EETS, 1874).

Sir Gawain = *Sir Gawain and the green knight*, edited by W. R. J. Barron (Manchester: Manchester University Press, 1974).

Period IV

Caxton = *The book of the knight of the tower* (translated by William Caxton), edited by M. Y. Offord (London: EETS, 1971).

Malory = *The tale of the death of King Arthur* (by Sir Thomas Malory), edited by Eugène Vinaver (London: Oxford University Press, 1955).

More = *The apologye of Syr Thomas More, knyght*, edited by Arthur Irving Taft (London: EETS, 1930).

Nevill = *The castell of pleasure* (by William Nevill), edited by Roberta D. Cornelius (London: EETS, 1930).

Paston = *Paston letters and papers of the fifteenth century* I, edited by Norman Davis (London: Oxford University Press, 1971).

Tyndale = *William Tyndale's five books of Moses called the Pentateuch*, edited by J. I. Mombert – F. F. Bruce (Fontwell: Centaur Press, 1967).

Wyatt = *Sir Thomas Wyatt and his circle, unpublished poems*, edited by Kenneth Muir (Liverpool: Liverpool University Press, 1961).

Notes

1. The paper is a substantial revision of Breivik 1983: chapters 4–6.
2. In this connection, we may note the following statement by Bolinger (1977: 102): "There is a notably low percentage of active transitive expressions in presentative constructions. If the verb is part of a phrase that is a kind of semantically analytic intransitive, that is, one that amounts to a single verb, its appearance here is normal enough so long as the sense is appropriate... . But elsewhere the transitives seem to involve too many entities, and to violate the loose constraint against saying more than one thing at a time." In the following example, the verb is part of a phrase that is equivalent to a semantically analytic intransitive: *There$_1$ was slowly making its way toward* (= *was approaching*) *us a figure in black*. Passive *there$_1$*-sentences will be briefly discussed in section 2.5 below.
3. (30) and (31) are taken from Bosworth's (1859) edition, which is based on the Cotton MS.
4. For two excellent surveys of research into Old English syntax, see Bean 1983: chapter 6 and Kohonen 1978: 10 ff.
5. For main clauses, Bean (chapter 4) distinguishes five major and five minor word order types. The five major types are VSX, XVS, SVX, XSV, and SXV. The five minor orders are OSV, OVS, SXVX, SV$_1$XV$_2$, and Miscellaneous.
6. In a recent article in *Linguistic Inquiry*, Williams (1984) discusses *there$_1$*-insertion in present-day English. He starts out by stating categorically that *there$_1$* is an NP: this "assertion is unarguable — at least, no one has argued against it yet" (131). Williams here shows an incredible lack of familiarity with the relevant literature. His statement is perhaps true of linguists working within the framework to which he himself subscribes

(GB), but otherwise the view that *there₁* derives (synchronically) from a locative constituent has enjoyed considerable popularity in recent years, among generativists as well as non-generativists. Thus Anderson 1971, Bolinger 1977, Fillmore 1968, Sampson 1972, Walters 1974, 1975 all claim that *there₁* is a syntactic remnant of a locative adverb. The chief exponent of this theory is Lyons, who has discussed the relationship between the two *there*'s in a number of publications (e. g. 1967, 1968a, 1968b: 389—390, 1975, 1977: 722—723). In a paper published in *Language* (Breivik 1981), I examined Lyons' hypothesis about the source and function of *there₁*, and I concluded that the synchronic data fail to confirm his claim that this morpheme is a locative adverb in present-day English. The arguments brought against Lyons' position can also be construed as arguments against other synchronic analyses which derive *there₁* from a locative constituent. It will be evident to anyone who is familiar with the literature that Williams' analysis is incomplete and renders important generalizations inexplicable. Consider, for example, the following claim which he makes (147) about the co-occurrence restrictions of *there₁* (for a fuller discussion of Williams' analysis, see Hannay 1985: 81 ff.):

First, it follows from the fact that *there* is an NP that it can occupy only NP positions — but why only the subject position, and WHY ONLY THE SUBJECT POSITION OF *BE*? [My emphasis] If *there* is a scope marker, as I have suggested above and will explore more thoroughly below, then it cannot occupy positions to which theta roles are assigned. Consequently, *there* must be the subject of a verb that does not assign a theta role to its subject. The copular *be* is one of the few such verbs; as we have seen, even MV *be*, if it does not assign a theta role to its subject, at least ascribes intentionality to it.

References

Andersen, Paul Kent
  1983   *Word order typology and comparative constructions* (Amsterdam: John Benjamins).
Anderson, John M.
  1971   *The grammar of case: towards a localistic theory* (Cambridge: Cambridge University Press).
Ashby, William J.
  1983   Review of Harris 1978, *Language* 59: 414—420.
Bean, Marian C.
  1983   *The development of word order patterns in Old English* (London—Canberra: Croom Helm).
Bolinger, Dwight
  1977   *Meaning and form* (London—New York: Longman).
Bosworth, Joseph
  1859   *King Alfred's Anglo-Saxon version of the compendious history of the world by Orosius* (London: Longman, Brown, Green, and Longmans).
Breivik, Leiv Egil
  1977   "A note on the genesis of existential *there*", *English Studies* 58: 334—348.
  1981   "On the interpretation of existential *there*", *Language* 57: 1—25.
  1983   *Existential THERE: a synchronic and diachronic study* (Bergen: Department of English, University of Bergen).
  1984   "On the typological distinction between subject-prominence and topic-prominence", *Folia Linguistica Historica* 5: 3—23.

Comrie, Bernard
1981   *Language universals and linguistic typology: syntax and morphology* (Oxford: Basil Blackwell).
Erdmann, Peter
1976   *THERE sentences in English: a relational study based on a corpus of written texts* (München: Tuduv).
Fillmore, Charles J.
1968   "The case for case", in: *Universals in linguistic theory*, edited by Emmon Bach—Robert T. Harms, 1—88 (New York: Holt, Rinehart and Winston).
Firbas, Jan
1966   "Non-thematic subjects in contemporary English", *Travaux Linguistiques de Prague* 2: 239—256.
Givón, Talmy
1977   "The drift from VSO to SVO in Biblical Hebrew: the pragmatics of tense-aspect", in: Li 1977: 181—254.
1984   *Syntax: a functional-typological introduction* I (Amsterdam—Philadelphia: John Benjamins).
Greenberg, Joseph H.
1963   "Some universals of grammar with particular reference to the order of meaningful elements", in: *Universals of language*, 2nd ed., edited by Joseph H. Greenberg, 73—113 (Cambridge, MA: MIT Press).
Haiman, John
1974   *Targets and syntactic change* (The Hague: Mouton).
Hannay, Michael
1985   *English existentials in Functional Grammar* (Dordrecht: Foris).
Harris, Martin
1978   *The evolution of French syntax: a comparative approach* (London: Longman).
Hawkins, John A.
1983   *Word order universals* (New York—London: Academic Press).
Heusler, Andreas
1931   *Altisländisch* (Heidelberg: Carl Winter).
Hopper, Paul J.
1975   *The syntax of the simple sentence in Proto-Germanic* (The Hague: Mouton).
Hopper, Paul J.—Sandra A. Thompson
1980   "Transitivity in grammar and discourse", *Language* 56: 251—299.
Jespersen, Otto
1924   *The philosophy of grammar* (London: George Allen & Unwin).
Kimball, John P.
1973   "The grammar of existence", in: *Papers from the 9th Regional Meeting, Chicago Linguistic Society*, 262—270.
Kohonen, Viljo
1978   *On the development of English word order in religious prose around 1000 and 1200 A.D.: a quantitative study of word order in context* (Åbo: Research Institute of the Åbo Akademi Foundation).
Lehmann, Winfred P.
1974   *Proto-Indo-European syntax* (Austin: University of Texas Press).
Lenerz, Jürgen
1979   Review of Haiman 1974, *Beiträge zur Geschichte der deutschen Sprache und Literatur* 101: 277—282.
Li, Charles N., ed.
1977   *Mechanisms of syntactic change* (Austin—London: University of Texas Press).
Lightfoot, David
1979   Review article on Li 1977, *Language* 55: 381—395.

Lyons, John
1967   "A note on possessive, existential and locative sentences", *Foundations of Language* 3: 390—396.
1968 a   "Existence, location, possession and transitivity", in: *Logic, methodology and philosophy of science* III, edited by B. van Rootselaar—J. F. Staal, 495—504 (Amsterdam: North-Holland).
1968 b   *Introduction to theoretical linguistics* (Cambridge: Cambridge University Press).
1975   "Deixis as the source of reference", in: *Formal semantics of natural language*, edited by Edward L. Keenan, 61—83 (Cambridge: Cambridge University Press).
1977   *Semantics*, 2 vols. (Cambridge: Cambridge University Press).
McKnight, George
1897   "The primitive Teutonic order of words", *Journal of English and Germanic Philology* 1: 136—219.
Mallinson, Graham—Barry J. Blake
1981   *Language typology* (Amsterdam—New York—Oxford: North Holland).
Perlmutter, David M.
1971   *Deep and surface structure constraints in syntax* (New York: Holt, Rinehart and Winston).
Sampson, Geoffrey
1972   "*There₁, there₂*", *Journal of Linguistics* 8: 111—117.
Stassen, Leon
1985   *Comparison and universal grammar* (Oxford: Basil Blackwell).
Steele, Susan M.
1977   Review of Haiman 1974, *Language* 53: 209—212.
Stockwell, Robert P.
1977   "Motivations for exbraciation in Old English", in: Li 1977: 291—314.
1984   "On the history of the verb-second rule in English", in: *Historical syntax*, edited by Jacek Fisiak, 575—592 (Berlin—New York—Amsterdam: Mouton).
Traugott, Elizabeth Closs
1972   *A history of English syntax: a transformational approach to the history of English sentence structure* (New York: Holt, Rinehart and Winston).
Vennemann, Theo
1973   "Explanation in syntax", in: *Syntax and semantics* 2, edited by John P. Kimball, 1—50 (New York—London: Seminar Press).
1974   "Topics, subjects, and word order: from SXV to SVX via TVX", in: *Historical linguistics. Proceedings of the First International Conference on Historical Linguistics* I, edited by John M. Anderson—Charles Jones, 339—376 (Amsterdam—Oxford: North-Holland).
1975   "An explanation of drift", in: *Word order and word order change*, edited by Charles N. Li, 269—305 (Austin—London: University of Texas Press).
Visser, F. Th.
1970   *An historical syntax of the English language* I (Leiden: E. J. Brill).
Walters, Ingeborg O.
1974   "The *there be* construction, I", *Norwegian Journal of Linguistics* 28: 131—206.
1975   "The *there be* construction, II", *Norwegian Journal of Linguistics* 29: 35—100.
Western, August
1921   *Norsk riksmåls-grammatikk* (Kristiania [Oslo]: Aschehoug).
Williams, Edwin
1984   "*There*-insertion", *Linguistic Inquiry* 15: 131—153.

Pragmatics and syntactic change

Jan Terje Faarlund

1. Introduction

The syntax of a given synchronic stage of a language may be seen as conditioned by two types of factors: Universal constraints on 'possible grammars', and the 'choices' made by a particular language through its history. It is the task of diachronic syntax to describe and explain those choices.

In the following, certain changes in the history of Norwegian syntax will be described and tentatively explained according to such a perspective. A comparison will be made between two stages of Norwegian, Medieval and Modern. Medieval Norwegian or Old Norwegian, is a dialect of Old Norse. There are only minor, if any, syntactic differences between Old Norwegian and other dialects of Old Norse, such as Old Icelandic. Most of the Medieval data used here is from 13th century Old Norse. The Modern Norwegian data is from *nynorsk*, a standard language based on the spoken dialects which descend directly from Old Norse.

Since Proto-Germanic was verb-final (Hopper 1975: 58 f.), the typical verb-object order of Modern Norwegian as well as Modern English must be the result of a choice made between OV and VO at some stage in the history of these languages. For such a choice to have been possible, there must have been a time where the two forms, OV and VO, coexisted. However, at the stage where the two forms do coexist, the choice is not primarily historical, but rather pragmatic; i.e. the choice of one form over the other is conditioned by information structure and other contextual features.[1] In a synchronic perspective, syntax is unmotivated, whereas pragmatics is motivated by discourse structure and contextual factors. In a diachronic perspective, syntax is motivated by the pragmatics of previous stages. Thus today's syntax may be the product of yesterday's discourse pragmatics.

A comparison of Medieval and Modern Norwegian reveals several important differences between what is traditionally referred to as the subject in Old Norse, i. e. the nominative NP, and the Modern Norwegian subject. The term 'subject' is used here with regard to the syntax (of historical stages) of specific languages. I will not attempt — and I do not even consider it feasible — to provide a definition of 'subject' as part of universal grammar. The term is defined for each language treated, and it is a matter of descriptive adequacy whether the apparatus needed to describe a given language should include the category 'subject'.

In section 2 I will describe the different sets of subject properties in Old Norse and Modern Norwegian, and also examine the relationship between the morphological category 'nominative' and the syntactic category 'subject' in Old Norse. The outcome of this investigation is that in Old Norse, there is no basis for defining the subject by any other criteria than its morphological case. Whenever the term 'subject' is used in the following with reference to Old Norse, it means 'the referring NP in the nominative case'. Section 3 will be a description of the changes that have taken place in the grammar. Section 4 is an attempt to explain these changes by describing their discourse pragmatic cause. In section 5 some present trends in the development of the subject in Nordic are discussed.

2. Subject properties

In Old Norse, NPs are marked for one of four cases. In traditional grammatical descriptions of the language, the subject is identified with the nominative case, and no other subject criteria are given (e. g. Nygaard 1906: 81).

In Modern Norwegian, the case system has been abolished, except that there is a nominative-accusative opposition in personal pronouns of the first and second person, and in the feminine singular of the third person.

(1a)   Derfor   likte   eg   henne
        therefore liked I-N her-A
        'Therefore I liked her.'

b) Derfor likte ho meg
    therefore liked she-N me-A
    'Therefore she liked me.'

In Modern Norwegian, the subject may, on the other hand, be defined positionally in the following way: the NP furthest to the right among those which precede the (position of a) non-finite verb. In subordinate sentences the auxiliary and the main verb are always adjacent, which means that the subject always precedes both verbs, as in (2a). In main sentences the subject comes immediately after the finitive verb,[2] but before any non-finite verb, (cf. 2b); or − as is most frequently the case − it is fronted to topic position,[3] as in (2c).

(2a) viss ho har gjort det
    if she has done that
  b) Det har ho gjort
    that has she done
  c) Ho har gjort det
    she has done that

Whenever a case distinction is made, the subject is always in the nominative case.

The following survey of subject properties in Old Norse and Modern Norwegian is therefore aimed at answering two questions: First, what are the syntactic differences between the Modern Norwegian subject and the Old Norse nominative NP? And second, can the subject be defined independently of morphological case in Old Norse? For a more detailed discussion of subject properties in Old Norse, see Faarlund 1980 b.

2.1 Syntax

The following syntactic properties are relevant to the comparison of the two stages of Norwegian: *position, dispensability, verb agreement, reflexivization, subject deletion* in imperative sentences, *conjunction deletion,* and *subject control* in infinitival clauses. Most of these subject properties also occur on Keenan's (1976) list of universal subject properties.

2.1.1 Position

In Modern Norwegian, position has already been used as a defining criterion, and can therefore not be considered a subject property at that stage.

In Old Norse, the finite verb is found in first or second position in declarative main sentences. The element preceding or immediately following the finite verb is often a nominative NP.

(3a)   Hálfdan   hvítbein var   konungr ríkr
        Halfdan-N Whiteleg was-3S king   powerful
        'Halfdan the Whiteleg was a powerful king.' (Heimskringla)
  b)   hafi   þit   verit hér um hríð   með mér
        have-2P you-N   been here for while with me
        'You have stayed here with me for a while.' (Egils saga)

However, we also find other case forms, so this position is not uniquely a nominative position. In (4), the finite verb is followed immediately by a dative phrase.

(4)   var   þeim   gefinn dagverðr
        was-3S them-D given   lunch-N
        'They were given lunch.' (Heimskringla)

Thus, if this position is reserved for a certain type of NP, then that NP cannot be defined only as being in the nominative. The constituent order in (4) is, however, in accordance with the information structure: the dative phrase is an anaphoric pronoun and thus carries given information; whereas the nominative NP carries new information and comes at the end of the sentence. This is not only a question of placing pronouns before full NPs. Observe sentence (5) with two unstressed pronouns in the order dative-nominative.

(5)   þótti   honum hon   vel hafa gert
        seemed-3S him-D she-N well have done
        'It seemed to him that she had done well.' (Heimskringla)

What this seems to show, then, is that either the order of NPs has nothing to do with subjecthood at all, or that there are NPs other than nominative phrases which can have subject properties.

2.1.2 Dispensability

Tensed sentences (except imperative, see below) in Modern Norwegian have an obligatory subject.

(6)   *Såg ikkje skipet
        saw not   the-ship

In Old Norse, on the other hand, a nominative NP is not obligatory in every sentence.

(7a)   Ekki sá   skipit   fyrir laufinu
        not saw-3S the ship-A for   the-foliage
        'The ship was invisible because of the foliage.' (Olafs saga ins
        helga)
  b)   þegar er   lýsti
        then when brightened-3S
        'As soon as it dawned.' (Olafs saga ins helga)
  c)   hér hefr   upp sǫgu   Heiðreks   konungs (Herv. 203,1)
        here lift-3S up saga-A Heidrek-G king-G
        'Here starts King Heidrek's saga.' (Hervarar saga ok Heiðreks)

2.1.3 Verb agreement

In Modern Norwegian, verbs do not agree with the subject, since finite verbs have only one form for each tense.

In Old Norse, the finite verb has a neutral form which is used when there is no nominative phrase in the sentence, see (7), or when the nominative is in the third person singular, see examples (3a), (4), and (5). If the sentence has a nominative phrase in the plural or one that refers to the speaker or the hearer, one of the marked forms of the finite verb will be used, see for example (3b) or (8).

(8)   þú   skalt   fara með mér á Stiklastaði
        thou shall-2S go   with me to Stiklastad (Heimskringla)

The main rule seems to be that only nominative phrases can trigger verb agreement. As it happens, however, nominative phrases that lack other subject-like properties do not always affect the form of the finite verb.

(9a)   í þann tíma fannst   í Danmǫrk kvernsteinar tveir
        at that time found-3S-REFL in Denmark millstones-N two
        'At that time there were (found) two millstones in Denmark.'
        (Snorra Edda)

   b)   mér þótti   vit   vera   í hellinum
         me-D seemed-3S we-N be-INF in the-cave
         'I thought we were in the cave.' (Flateyjar bók)

In (9a) the nominative NP fails to trigger verb agreement since it is rhematic and comes at the end of the sentence. In (9b) the most thematic element is the first person singular *mér*, rather than the dual *vit*.

It is true that there is a high degree of correlation between nominative and verb agreeeement, but it is not absolute, as we have seen. In any case, verb agreement is a very superficial feature; one which strictly belongs to morphology rather than to syntax.

2.1.4 Reflexive

The rules for the use of the reflexive in Norwegian are rather complex, as they presumably are in most Germanic languages. But although there are regional and individual variations and conflicting acceptability judgments, the main rule seems to be that the reflexive has to be controlled by an NP which is a subject at some level of analysis.

(10)   Han kjøpte   seg   ein hatt
        he   bought himself a   hat

Similarly, in Old Norse the reflexive may be controlled by a nominative phrase.

(11)   Flosi   bjó   sik   austan
        Flosi-N prepared himself-A from-east
        'Flosi got ready to go west.' (Njals saga)

Other NPs, however, also control reflexive pronouns, as in (12), where the reflexive possessive adjective has as its antecedents the immediately preceding dative phrase.

(12) Ólafr   konungr þakkaði henni vel orð   sín
      Olaf-N King   thanked herᵢ-D well words-A hersᵢ-REFL
      'King Olaf thanked her very much for her words.' (Heimskringla)

Again we see that a property usually thought of as a subject property is
not a unique property of nominative phrases. It may be that a further
investigation of reflexives in Old Norse will show that reflexivization
works more or less mechanically, with the most immediately preceding
NP as the antecedent.

2.1.5 Imperative

In Modern Norwegian, the subject is regularly deleted in imperative
sentences.

(13) Gjer det no!
      do   it now

Nygaard (1906: 8) in his discussion of the Old Norse imperative states:
"Ved imperativ udelades ofte subjekt af 2den pers. ent. og flertal (In the
imperative the subject in the 2nd person singular and plural is often
omitted.)" In the plural, for all verbs except *vera* 'be', the imperative is
identical to the indicative and the subjunctive. Therefore, a missing
nominative NP would be the only formal criterion of an imperative
plural; and all the examples of imperative plural cited by Nygaard also
lack a nominative NP. In the singular, however, the imperative has
separate forms, and of the eleven sentences in Nygaard 1906 with the
verb in the imperative singular, ten have a nominative NP. Only one is
'subjectless'. It therefore seems that deletion of the agent of imperative
verbs in Old Norse is just an instance of a more general rule of deletion
of unstressed pronouns. The nominative phrase in (14a) is therefore
deleted for the same reason as the nominative phrase in (14b), the
accusative phrase in (14c), and the dative phrase in (14d).

(14a) gakk [-] ok bið hann bíða úti
       go [-N] and tell him wait outside (Egils saga)
   b) var þat ráð   konungs at rjúfa leiðangrinn, ok gaf
       was it council king's   to abolish the-fleet   and gave
       [-] þá   hverjum manni heimleyfi
       [-N] then each   man   leave

'The King gave orders to abolish the fleet and gave all the men a leave.' (Olafs saga ins helga)

c) þá   er þú skyldi leysa nestbaggan, þá   hafðak bundit
   when   you should loosen the-bag   then had-I   tied
   [-]   með gresjarni
   [-A] with spell-bound-iron
   'When you wanted to untie your bag, I had tied it with spell-
   bound iron ropes.' (Snorra Edda)

d) var sá vatni   ausinn, ok [-] nafn gefit, ok kallaðr
   was he water-D poured and [-D] name given and called
   Egill
   Egil
   'Water was poured over him, and he was given a name and called
   Egil.' (Egils saga)

2.1.6 Conjunction deletion

Modern Norwegian has a rule that deletes an NP which is coreferential with an NP in a preceding coordinated sentence, but only if the identical NPs are both subjects.

(15a) Dei flytte   liket   og [-] grov   det ned
       they moved the-corpse and   buried it   down
       (subj-subj)

  b) *Dei flytte   liket   og dei   grov [-] ned.
      they moved the-corpse and they buried down
      (obj-obj)

  c) *Liket   vart flytt og dei   grov [-] ned.
      the-corpse was moved and they buried down
      (subj-obj)

  d) *Liket   skremde dei   og [-] grov   det ned
      the-corpse frightened them and   buried it   down
      (obj-subj)

In Old Norse, NPs can be deleted in this way regardless of case or grammatical relation, even if the coreferential phrases have different case forms, different semantic roles, and (seemingly) different grammatical relations in the two sentences.

(16a) þá   brá   hann sverðinu hart ok   títt   ok   hljóp [-]
       then struck he-N sword-D hard and often and ran [-N]
       í   stofuna
       into the-room
       'Then he struck hard and often with the sword and rushed into
       the room.' (Olafs saga ins helga)

   b) þá   lét Óðinn bera inn í hǫllina sverð,   ok   váru [-]
       then let Odin bear into the-hall swords-A and were [-N]
       svá bjǫrt
       so bright
       'Then Odin ordered swords to be brought into the room, and
       they were so bright ...' (Snorra Edda)

   c) síðan fluttu þeir þorgils   líkit   upp með
       then moved   they Thorgils-N the-corpse-A up   along
       ánni   ok   grófu [-]   þar niðr
       the-river and buried [-A] there down
       'Then Thorgils and his men moved the corpse up along the river
       and buried it there.' (Heimskringla)

   d) honum var fengin leynilega harpa, ok   sló   hann [-]
       him-D was got   secretly harp-N and struck he [-A]
       með tánum
       with the-toes
       'He was given a harp secretly, and he played it with his toes.'
       (Snorra Edda)

   e) Einarr þambarskelfir fór   með líki   Magńuss
       Einar Thambarskelfi went with corpse-D Magnus'
       konungs ok   með honum allr þrœndaherr
       King's and with him   all Thronderarmy
       ok   fluttu [-]   til Niðaróss
       and moved [-A] to Nidaros
       'Einar Thambarskelfi travelled with King Magnus' corpse and
       with him the whole army of the Thronders, and they moved it
       to Nidaros.' (Heimskringla)

In (16a — b) nominative phrases are deleted, and the one in (16b) is deleted
under coreferentiality with an accusative phrase in the preceding sentence.
In (16c — e) accusative phrases are deleted; in (16d) under coreferentiality
with a preceding nominative phrase, and in (16e) under coreferentiality
with a preceding dative phrase. These deletion rules, therefore, do not
seem to be constrained by subjecthood or by nominative case.

2.1.7 Subject control

In subordinate sentences the verb may be in the infinitive and the subject represented by an empty category controlled by a phrase in the matrix sentence. The sentences in (17) are from Modern Norwegian.

(17a)   Eg håpar å   komma
         I-N hope   to come
   b)   Ventar du   å   bli trudd?
         expect you-N   to be believed
         'Do you expect to be believed?'

In Old Norse only nominative NPs seem to be able to be represented by an empty category in this way.

(18a)   hann heitr   at gefa þeim bæði ríki   ok fé
         he   promises to give them both power and wealth
         (Heimskringla)
   b)   Kjartan kaus heldr at vera með konungi en   fara til
         Kjartan chose rather to be with king   than go   to
         Íslands
         Iceland (Laxdoela saga)

No example of a similar omission of other cases is found in the attested Old Norse literature. At this point in the argument, this is the only certain syntactic property associated with nominative NPs.

2.1.8 Summary

Modern Norwegian may be characterized as a language with a clearly identifiable subject. The subject in Modern Norwegian can be identified on the basis of its position in the sentence and on the basis of a set of properties which all uniquely select the same phrase. Even without any trace of a case inflection in any lexical category, the subject would be easily identifiable.

In Old Norse, only subject control and perhaps verb agreement are clearly connected with the nominative case. Other subject properties may select NPs of various case forms, and no unique definition of 'subject' is possible on the basis of these other criteria. Therefore it seems hard to find good syntactic arguments for an analysis of Old Norse sentences whereby S branches into a separate NP node which is the sister of a VP node.

2.2 Semantics

A necessary prerequisite for a description of semantic properties of subjects and nominative NPs is a fairly precise notion of 'logical subject'. As part of its semantic specification, each verb is marked in the lexicon for the number of arguments it takes and what semantic roles it distributes to those arguments. For the purpose of a syntactic description of Old Norse and Modern Norwegian, it seems that a distinction of three 'emic' roles will suffice (Faarlund 1980 a: 25−28). They can be organized in a hierarchy as follows:

(19)   SOURCE > GOAL > OBJECTIVE

SOURCE includes such roles as agent and instrument, GOAL includes recipient (benefactive) and location, and OBJECTIVE (for lack of a better term) includes patient and result (that is, *a book* both in *read a book* and in *write a book*). For a given verb, the 'logical subject' is the argument which receives the semantic role which is highest in the hierarchy. Instead of the somewhat misleading term 'logical subject', I will henceforth use the notation A1 (for 'First Argument').

A characteristic feature of Modern Norwegian syntax is the relatively high number of both sentence types and sentence tokens with another subject than A1. Surface subjects do not express a particular semantic role in Modern Norwegian. Constructions with other subjects than A1 are of four different kinds: *passive* (20b), *'impersonal' passive* (21b), *existential* sentences (22b), and *subject-to-subject raising* (23b). The a-sentence in each pair is the non-derived counterpart with an A1 subject.

(20a)   Nokon   åt   kaka
       someone ate the-cake
  b)   Kaka   vart eten
       the-cake was eaten

(21a)   Nokon   åt   kaker
       someone ate cakes

b)   Det[4] vart   eti   kaker
      there was eaten cakes
      'Cakes were eaten.'

(22a) ?Ei kake er på bordet
       a   cake is on the-table
  b)   Det   er ei kake på bordet
       there is a cake on the table

(23a) *At kaka   er muggen, ser ut til
       that the-cake is moldy,   seems
  b)   Kaka   ser ut til å   vera muggen
       the-cake seems   to be moldy

According to what has been said above about nominative and subject in Old Norse, the equivalent of a non-A1 subject would be an NP which has acquired nominative case through some morphosyntactic process. The way to look for such processes and constructions, would be to look for Old Norse counterparts to (20b – 23b).

Old Norse has passive constructions formed with the auxiliary verbs *vera* 'be' or *verða* 'become'.

(24a) fjórir hleifar   brauðs   eru honum fœrðir   hvern dag
       four   loaves-N bread-G are him-D brought each day
       'He was brought four loaves of bread every day.'
       (Olafs saga ins helga)
  b)   af   því varð   bœn   hans heyrð
       from that became prayer-N his heard
       'Therefore his prayer was heard.' (Old Norwegian Book of Homilies)

Only accusative objects correspond to nominative subjects in the passive. The sentences in (24) are thus the passive versions of (the constructed) (25). Alternative passive constructions like the one in (26) are not found in Old Norse.

(25a) fœrði   honum fjóra hleifa   brauðs   hvern dag
       brought him-D four loaves-A bread-G each day
  b)   af   því heyrði boen   hans
       from that heard prayer-A his

(26)   *hann var fœrðr   fjóra hleifa   brauðs hvern dag
         he-N was brought four loaves-A bread-G each day

Data like those illustrated in (25) and (26) provide evidence against
passive as a result of a syntactic movement rule, since there is no non-
arbitrary way of preventing a transformation from deriving (26) from
(25a) once it is allowed to derive (24a). If, on the other hand, passives
are taken to be base-generated, as assumed by Dyvik 1980, then case is
assigned separately in active and passive sentences, and in *hann var fœrðr*
the nominative *hann* would be interpreted as objective, not goal.

Furthermore, there are no passive constructions where the subject NP
has left a 'visible' trace, for example by stranding a preposition.

(27)   *hon var tǫluð   við
         she-N was spoken to

Since we cannot point to any certain case where the passive construction
interferes with any other syntactic process, we must conclude that in Old
Norse passive constructions are not the result of a process, but base
generated structures with a copula verb (*vera* 'be', *verða* 'become') and a
participle. The past participle in Old Norse is morphologically an adjective. There is thus no syntactic difference between (28a), where *fœddr* is
the past participle of *fœða*, and (the constructed) (28b), where *dauðr* is
an adjective with no derivational relationship to a verb.

(28a)   þá   er   vesall maðr   er fœddr
         then when poor   man-N   is born-MASC-N-S
         (Old Norwegian Book of Homilies)
   b)   vesall maðr   er dauðr
         poor   man-N   is dead-MASC-N-S

Modern Norwegian passive constructions show several properties that
are different from those of Old Norse. There is a distinct difference
between the use of the copula verb *vera* 'be', and the verbs used as passive
auxiliaries *verta* or *bli*.[5] The former, when used with a past participle,
always yields a stative, resultative meaning, and may thus function as the
perfect of the passive.

(29)   Huset   er   måla
         the-house is/has been painted

Real passives with a dynamic reading and verbal content must be expressed by means of the auxiliary *verta/bli*, which, when used with pure adjectives, always have an inchoative meaning.

(30a)   Huset   vart   måla
         the-house was (being) painted
   b)   Huset   vart   vakkert
         the-house became beautiful

Modern Norwegian has passive sentences where the subject may correspond to an indirect object in the active sentence.

(31a)   Eg vart vist   alle dokumenta
         I   was shown all   the-documents
   b)   Dei viste   meg alle dokumenta
         they showed me   all   the-documents

Passive subjects also correspond to active prepositional objects.

(32a)   Ho vart tala   om
         she was talked about
   b)   Denne stolen har aldri vorti seten på
         this   chair has never been sat   on

These differences between Old Norse and Modern Norwegian passives are accounted for if we assume that while nominative NPs in Old Norse passive sentences are non-derived, bearing an A1 role with regard to the verb 'be', subjects in passive sentences in Modern Norwegian are derived, bearing a non-A1 role with regard to the main verb.[6]

Existentials (22b above) are another type of non-basic subject in Modern Norwegian. In Old Norse, we do not find existential sentences with dummy subjects, that is, sentences with a dummy element in the nominative and A1 in a non-nominative case. First of all, the dummy subject does not exist for Old Norse, and secondly, in existential sentences A1 is still in the nominative:

(33)   kastali   var fyrir austan sundit
         castle-N was for   east-of the sound
         'There was a castle to the east of the sound.' (Olafs saga ins helga)

For more examples of Old Norse existential sentences, see the a-sentences in (37—42).

The lack of a dummy subject and a 'de-nominativizing' process in existential sentences also erases any distinction between 'impersonal' passives (21b above) and other passives. The closest we would get to an impersonal passive would be sentences like (4), repeated here as (34):

(34)   var   þeim   gefinn   dagverðr
        was-3S them-D given-MASC-S-N lunch-N
        'They were given lunch.' (Heimskringla)

The only difference between (34) and a regular passive sentence is the word order. The direct object of the corresponding active sentence is in the nominative, and the finite verb and the adjectival participle both agree with this nominative NP.

Subject-to-subject raising results in the construction known as 'nominative with infinitive'.

(35a)   þótti   honum hon   vel   hafa   gert
         seemed him-D she-N well have-INF done
         'He thought she had done well.' (Heimskringla)
    b)   þóttu   þeir   mjǫk hafa   spottat sik
         seemed they-N much have-INF mocked him-REFL
         '(He) thought they had mocked him much.' (Heimskringla)
    c)   mér   þótti   vit   vera   í   hellinum
         me-D seemed we-N be-INF in the-cave
         'I thought we were in the cave.' (Flateyjar bók)

The question is whether this is a 'nominativizing' process, or whether it is a general raising process which in these instances just happens to raise a nominative NP. An answer to this question would be found if we were able to determine whether other NPs than nominatives can be raised in this way. If a sentence with two accusative NPs and no nominative, such as e. g. (36a), is embedded under the verb *þykkja* 'seem' (past tense *þótti*), there are two conceivable results of raising, (b) or (c). Neither (b) nor (c) (nor any equivalent construction) seems to be attested.

(36a)   þik   hefir mikla úgiptu   hent
         you-A has great accident-A happened
         'A great accident has happened to you.' (Fornsǫgur Suðurlanda)

b)   ?þykkir mér   þik   mikil úgipta   hafa   hent
     seems   me-D   you-A great accident-N have-INF happened
     'It seems to me that a great accident has happened to you.'
c)   ?þykkir mér þik mikla úgiptu hafa hent
                                accident-A

It may be concluded that Old Norse shows no clear instance of a
(morpho-)syntactic process whereby an NP acquires nominative case
without being A1. If that is so, there is a one-to-one relationship between
morphological surface case and rank on the semantic role hierarchy as
far as the nominative case is concerned.[7]

2.3 Pragmatics

In Old Norse the nominative NP is not characterized by any particular
pragmatic or contextual properties. In Modern Norwegian, on the other
hand, the subject is almost always definite in some (specifiable) sense, cf.
(22a). (Faarlund 1980 a). In the a-sentences below, the nominative NPs
are indefinite both morphologically and semantically. The sentences are
excerpted from the first seven chapters (eight pages) of the 'Gylfaginning'
in the *Snorra Edda* (Holtsmark and Helgason 1968). For comparison I
have cited the corresponding sentences (the b-sentences) from a Modern
Norwegian translation (*Yngre Edda* 1967), where we see that the translator
has used the dummy subject *det*, instead of translating the indefinite
nominative NPs of the original as subjects.

(37a)   fyrst vil hann spyrja ef nǫkkvorr er fróðr maðr   inni
        first will he   ask   if some   is wise man-N in
        'First he will ask if there is a wise man in there.'
   b)   fyrst vil han spørja om det   er nokon kunnig mann der
        first will he ask   if there is some wise   man there
        inne
        in

(38a)   Hvernig óxu ættir   þaðan
        how   grew families-N thereof
   b)   Korleis kom det   ætter   frå han
        how   came there families from him

(39a)   þá   óx   undir vinstri hǫnd honum maðr   ok   kona
        then grew under left   arm his   man-N and woman-N
        'Then a man and a woman grew up under his left hand.'

   b)   Då   voks det   fram under den venstre armen hans ein
        then grew there out under the left   arm   his a
        mann og ei kvinne
        man and a woman

(40a)   en   fjórar miólkár   runnu ór   spenum hennar
        and four   milk-rivers-N ran   from teats hers
   b)   og   or   spenane hennar rann det   fire mjølkeelvar
        and from teats   hers   ran there four milk-rivers

(41a)   Ok hinn fyrsta dag er   hon sleikti steina,
        and the first day when she licked stones
        kom ór   steininum at kveldi   mannz hár
        came from the-stone at evening man's hair-N
        'And the first day when she licked the stones, a man's hair came
        out of the stone in the evening.'

   b)   og fyrste dagen   som   ho sleikte steinane,
        and first the-day when she licked the-stones,
        kom det   om kvelden   mannehår ut or steinen
        came there in the-evening man-hair out of the-stone

(42a)   en er   han fell, þá   hlióp svá mikit blóð   ór
        and when he fell then ran   so much blood-N from
        sárum   hans
        wounds his

   b)   Og då   han fall, rann det   så mykje blod ut or
        and when he fell ran there so much blood out of
        såra   hans
        wounds his

In the same text excerpt we also find a large number of nominative NPs
without the definite article, but with a postposed demonstrative func-
tioning as the head of a relative clause. Many of these NPs introduce
new information, which is also unusual for Modern Norwegian subjects,
and accordingly these NPs are likewise not translated as subjects.

(43a)   þat hugsaði hann hvárt   þat myndi vera af   eðli
        that wondered he   whether that might be   from power

siálfra þeira, eða myndi því valda goðmǫgn-N þau   er
self   theirs or might it cause godstrengths those which
þeir blótuðu
they worshipped
'He wondered whether it came from their own strength, or
whether it was caused by the power of the gods that they
worshipped.'

b)   han undrast   på om   dette kom av   evner hjå
     he wondered   whether this came from powers in
     dei sjølve eller frå   overnaturlege makter som   dei
     them selves or   from supernatural powers which they
     dyrka
     worshipped

(44a) í honum miðium liggr bruðr sá   er   Hvergelmir
       in its   middle lies well-N that which Hvergelmi
       heitir
       is-called
       'In the middle of it is the well which is called Hvergelmi.'

b)   Midt   i den ligg det   ein brunn som   heiter
     middle in it lies there a   well   which is-called
     Kvergjelme
     Kvergjelme

These examples, which could easily be multiplied from any Old Norse
text, should suffice to show that the Modern Norwegian subject has to
obey pragmatic and contextual requirements that are not associated with
the Old Norse nominative.

2.4 Summary of observed contrasts between Old Norse and Modern Norwegian

Modern Norwegian has a positionally and otherwise syntactically well-
defined subject. In Old Norse such a definition of the subject independent
of case form does not seem feasible. If the term 'subject' is to be used in
a syntactic description of Old Norse at all, it can only be defined as a
referring nominative NP. The nominative NP in Old Norse sentences has
only a few of the relevant subject properties.

Modern Norwegian has passive constructions where the subject is promoted from some other relation and position (not only direct object) in the corresponding active sentence. Old Norse has passive constructions which are grammatically indistinguishable from regular copula constructions with an adjectival predicate, and where the subject always corresponds to an accusative object in the active counterpart.

In Old Norse, the nominative NP always bears the A1 role with regard to the main verb in the sentence. This is also true of passive sentences, since the past participle is an adjective, and the main verb therefore is 'be'. In Modern Norwegian the main verb is not 'be', and the subject bears some non-A1 role with regard to the main verb.

3. Changes in the grammar

3.1 Introduction of NP movement

The term 'NP movement' is used here to refer to any type of movement of an NP into an argument position. NP movement thus implies not only a change in linear position, but primarily a change in grammatical relation.

As we have seen, one difference between Old Norse and Modern Norwegian is the absence vs. presence of a passive as a result of movement of a non-subject NP into the subject role. In languages where 'subject' is defined positionally or structurally, this involves movement to a designated position in the sentence structure. In order for a language to have NP movement as part of its syntax, it must have syntactically defined grammatical relations. If grammatical relations are identified by morphological case only, the closest we would get to NP movement would be some morphosyntactic relation changing process.

The non-A1 subjects in Modern Norwegian (cf. 20−23) are all the results of NP movement, whereby an NP has been moved into a position where it acquires the syntactic and pragmatic subject properties, while maintaining its semantic properties (non-A1). If the moved NP belongs to a category that shows morphological case, it also acquires the nominative case.

3.2 Effects of NP movement

As an illustration of the kinds of effects the introduction of NP movement has on the syntax, consider the change from what is traditionally called 'impersonal' to 'personal' constructions, discussed by numerous linguists.[8] The very misleading term 'impersonal' is used to refer to constructions where verbs typically denote some kind of emotion or experience, yet where the human experiencer is not expressed in the nominative. Such constructions are said to become 'personal' when the human experiencer begins to be expressed as the subject. Using the verb 'like' as an example, we may sketch the development in the following way: the grammar of Old Norse generates strings like (45a). Topicalization of a given NP yields (45b), and subsequent inversion (45c).

(45a) [[at frialsa með miskunn] líkaði   guði]
       to   save   with mercy   pleased god-D
   b) [guði [at frialsa með miskunn] líkaði]
   c) guði líkaði at frialsa með miskunn
       'God preferred to save with mercy.' (Barlaams saga ok Josaphats)

After the introduction of NP movement and the appearance of a structurally defined subject position (which could be underlyingly empty), the grammar of Modern Norwegian generates the string (46a). At a derivational level where no NP has been moved to subject position, there is no difference between a predicate meaning 'like' and one meaning 'please'; the lexical meaning depends on the syntactic roles of the respective arguments. The recipient is most typically a human with a high degree of empathy, and therefore the most thematic argument with this verb, so for pragmatic reasons this NP will be chosen as a subject of *lika*. The verb is then reinterpreted from denoting 'sympathy emanating from something/somebody to somebody' to denoting 'somebody having certain sentiments about something/ somebody'. NP movement then yields (46b), where *barnet* receives subject properties at surface structure.

(46a) lika   barnet   soga
       liked/pleased the-child(GOAL) the-story(OBJECTIVE)
   b) Barnet lika soga

This account also explains why constructions with a nominative (objective) argument and a dative (goal) argument denoting the human

experiencer would change into constructions with the human experiencer
as the subject rather than the original nominative NP. An example would
be the Middle English (47a) (from Seefranz-Montag 1983), which changed
into (47b) rather than into (47c), which would also be in accordance with
Modern English word order patterns and syntax in general.

(47a)   non other good of thee me nedeth
  b)   I need no other good of yours
  c)   *No other good of yours needs me

4. Causes

The question now is why NP movement was introduced at this particular
stage. This question is linked to the question of how and why the
structural subject arose.

4.1 Thematic position

In case-marked Indo-European languages, including Old Norse, the order
of NPs in terms of cases is relatively free. A nominative NP, for example,
can precede or follow a dative NP. So there is no 'nominative position'.
On the other hand, certain positions make their occupants more thematic
than others, in the sense that elements in such positions are interpreted
as having a specific reference or being existentially presupposed. Such
positions are the ones to the left in the sentence, in Modern Germanic
languages typically the ones surrounding the finite verb in declarative
main sentences. Everything else being equal, a constituent far to the left
is more thematic than one far to the right. Thus in (48a) the theme of
the sentence is the daughter, whereas the king is new information. In
(48b) the nominative phrase carries new information and comes at the
end. In (48c) the dative pronoun is naturally more thematic than the
nominative phrase.

(48a)   Ásu   dóttur   sína gipti   hann Guðrøði   konungi
        Asa-A daughter-A his   married he-N Gudrød-D king-D
        'He married his daughter Asa off to King Gudrød.'
        (Heimskringla)
   b)   þá   óx   undir vinstri hǫnd honum maðr   ok   kona
        then grew under left   arm his   man-N and woman-N
        'Then a man and a woman grew up under his left hand.'
        (Snorra Edda)
   c)   var þeim   gefinn dagverðr
        was them-D given lunch-N
        'They were given lunch.' (Heimskringla)

Any syntactic process which moves constituents from one part of the
sentence to another consequently affects the thematicity of that constituent. We may for example posit a topicalization rule for Old Norse which
moves a constituent towards the left, into a position where it receives a
thematic interpretation. This rule is different from the modern NP movement, which gives the moved NP a certain grammatical function, complete
with its syntactic properties. By topicalization no properties of the constituent except its position and pragmatic interpretation will be affected
by the movement. If it is a nominative NP, it will still be a nominative
NP after the movement.

4.2 Semantic role

The nominative case in Indo-European is the case that encodes the
semantic role highest in the semantic role hierarchy (cf. (19) above).
Whenever there is an agent expressed, it would then be in the nominative.
In the typical instance the agent, being animate, would also be most
thematic. Topic position and nominative case would therefore often
coincide. A syntactic property originally associated with the nominative,
such as sensitivity to a certain rule, might therefore be reinterpreted as
being associated with a certain position.

4.3 Grammatical relation

Positions can be defined either linearly or hierarchically. A transformation may therefore 'find its victim' by counting, say, from the left, or by scanning the phrase structure looking for a certain configuration. If we assume that transformations are subject to Boolean conditions on analyzability, which means that their structural description cannot contain quantifiers, only the structural procedure is available to the transformation. The set of elements that are subject to a syntactic rule must of course have something in common, and if the rule is no longer associated with case, it has to be associated with a structural position. New generations of speakers then may interpret a certain position in the sentence as being structurally defined.

In the final stage a discourse function has acquired the character of a grammatical relation. Movement rules that move elements into this kind of position are now rules that affect grammatical relations, and subjects are therefore the result of syntactic derivations. This is what underlies the main differences between the old nominative and the modern subject. Since subjecthood is associated with a certain structural and linear position, subjects carry certain pragmatic features that nominatives do not.

5. Further development

Subject requirements may be strengthened through history. Through analogy, construction types with a non-A1 subject may become more and more frequent. Middle English, for example, seemed to have a structural subject, and the dummy subject *there* had been in use since Old English times; still we find sentence (49a) (quoted from Breivik 1983), with an indefinite subject in the Middle English Wyclif-Purvey version of *The Nativity of Christ*. In the early Modern English Tyndale version we find (49b), where it seems that the indefinite NP no longer qualifies as a subject.

(49a)   and scheepherdis weren in þe same cuntre
   b)   and ther were in the same region shepherdes

As the NP in subject position acquires more and more subject properties, it may also have a more and more remote origin. We may for example observe today how the Scandinavian languages are in a process of expanding the range of prepositional objects that are available for NP movement. In Norwegian, NP movement rather freely moves NPs from a PP which is the sister of V, see (32a) (repeated here as (50)), although certain restrictions seem to apply when the preposition is less predictable on the basis of the verb, as in (51).

(50a)   Ho vart tala   om
        she was talked about
   b)   Denne stolen har aldri vorti seten på
        this   chair has never been sat on

(51a)   ?Denne brua   blir ofte   gått   over
        this   bridge is   often walked across
   b)   *Denne byen vart ofte reist   til
        this   city   was often travelled to

In Modern Icelandic we also find sentences with fronted prepositional objects like:

(52)   Vigdísi   er oftast   talað   vel um
        Vigdis-A is most-often spoken well of

Since Icelandic may have non-nominative subjects, we cannot immediately tell whether *Vigdísi* in (52) is a topicalized NP or a subject. On closer investigation, however, it turns out, as shown by Maling and Zaenen (1985), that it does not have the usual subject properties, such as subject-to-object raising.

(53)   *Eg tel   Vigdísi   vera oftast   talað   vel um
        I   believe Vigdis-A be   most-often spoken well of

Since (53) is ungrammatical, *Vigdísi* cannot be the subject in (52), and Modern Icelandic therefore does not seem to allow the same extent of NP movement from PP as Modern Norwegian does.

But this expansion also seems to be quite recent in the other Scandinavian languages. In their description of late 19th century Dano-Norwegian, Falk and Torp (1900: 23) state that "Dog befinder denne konstruktion sig endnu i sin vorden og er langt fra saa vidt fremskreden som i engelsk. Man skriver således ikke:[9] han blev følt sympati med; han blev ikke mere hørt til (engelsk: he was heard of no more). (This construction [i. e. the prepositional passive] is, however, still in its inception and is far from being as widely used as in English. Thus, one does not write [the Dano-Norwegian equivalent of]: he was felt sympathy with; he was heard of no more)."

Even contemporary Swedish and Danish seem to be less liberal than Norwegian in this respect. Maling and Zaenen (1985) star the Swedish (54a) and the Danish (54b) (with reference to native linguists), whereas the Norwegian counterpart, (54c), is perfectly acceptable.

(54a) *Hon skrattades   åt
       she   was-laughed at
  b) *Hun blev leet   ad
       she   was laughed at
  c) Ho vart ledd av

The transitional character of these construction types becomes evident when we see that Platzack (1985) — a native Swede — presents both the sentences in (55) as acceptable. ((55a) is Danish, (55b) Swedish).

(55a) Du skal tas   på med fløjelshandsker
      you shall be-taken on with kid-gloves
      'You ought to be treated with kid gloves.'
  b) Hon blev bytt   på för fem minuter sedan
      she   was changed on for five minutes ago
      'She was changed diapers on five minutes ago.'

6. Conclusion

In Medieval Norwegian (Old Norse) as in other older Indo-European languages, the NP bearing the highest ranking semantic role (A1) is in the nominative (but see note 7). Most nominative NPs are thematic, which in Modern Norwegian is a typical subject property. Being a subject is therefore not only associated with a high rank in the semantic role hierarchy (19), but also with a high degree of thematicity. This of course creates a problem whenever a different NP than the highest ranking one is most thematic.

The origin of NP movement may be found in general pragmatic principles of distribution of discourse functions in the sentence. The effects of NP movement are also partly pragmatic and partly syntactic, as can be seen from a study of pragmatic and syntactic properties of subjects in Modern Norwegian and other contemporary Germanic languages.

Notes

1. For further documentation and support of this view, see Faarlund 1985.
2. Under certain circumstances a sentence adverbial may intervene between the verb and the subject.
   Det   kunne   ikkje   Eva   gjera
   that   could   not   Eva   do
3. The term 'topic' is not synonymous with 'theme'. The former is a syntactic term denoting an element in a syntactically defined topic position, such as the first position in declarative main sentences in Germanic languages. 'Theme' is a pragmatic term used about an element with certain pragmatic properties, such as givenness, specific reference, existential presupposition, empathy, etc.
4. In Modern Norwegian, *det*, the neuter singular of the personal pronoun, is used as a dummy subject, equivalent to English *there* and *it*.
5. *verta* and *bli* are as close to a synonymous pair as one can get. The latter — a Low German loan word — has replaced the former in many dialects, and both are used in the standard language.
6. This contrast between passives in Old Norse and Modern Norwegian corresponds roughly to Wasow's (1977) distinction between lexical and transformational rules. Wasow argues that the grammar of English includes both a lexical passive and a transformational passive. Lightfoot (1979) ascribes certain differences in the passive constructions in Old and Modern English (similar to the differences in Norwegian) to the lack of a transformational passive in Old English.
7. Weather verbs and other verbs that never take a nominative, e. g. *syfja* 'become sleepy', *þyrsta* 'be thirsty', *dreyma* 'dream', may be considered predicates where an agent is understood, but never expressed. In the cosmology of our ancestors the rain and the snow certainly had an agent; and there was 'somebody/something' that made you sleepy or thirsty, or who was the author of your dreams. The agent of such verbs never needed to be mentioned. There is in other words an understood, unexpressed A1 with such verbs.
8. For example Gaaf 1904, Jespersen 1927, McCawley 1976, Butler 1977, Tripp 1978, Lightfoot 1980, Elmer 1981, Fischer and Leek 1983, Seefranz-Montag 1983, 1984, Faarlund 1983, 1985.
9. The course of syntactic history has been meticulously recorded by an anonymous previous reader of my second-hand copy of Falk and Torp's book: With a pencil he has deleted the word *ikke* 'not' here and replaced it with *nu* 'now'.

References

Breivik, Leiv Egil
1983   *Existential THERE: a synchronic and diachronic study* (Bergen: Department of English, University of Bergen).
Butler, Milton C.
1977   "Reanalysis of object as subject in Middle English impersonal constructions", *Glossa* 11: 155–170.
Dyvik, Helge J. Jakhelln
1980   *Grammatikk og empiri. En syntaktisk modell og dens forutsetninger* (Bergen: University of Bergen).
Elmer, Willy
1981   *Diachronic grammar: the history of Old and Middle English subjectless constructions* (Tübingen: Max Niemeyer).
Faarlund, Jan Terje
1980 a   *Norsk syntaks i funksjonelt perspektiv* (Oslo, Bergen, Tromsø: Universitetsforlaget).
1980 b   "Subject and nominative in Old Norse", *Scripta Islandica* 31: 65–73.
1983   "Explaining syntactic change", in: *Papers from the Seventh Scandinavian Conference of Linguistics*, vol. 1, edited by Fred Karlsson, 150–162 (Helsinki: University of Helsinki, Dept. of General Linguistics).
1985   "Pragmatics in diachronic syntax", *Studies in Language* 9: 361–393.
Falk, Hjalmar – Alf Torp
1900   *Dansk-norskens syntax i historisk fremstilling* (Kristiania: Aschehoug).
Fischer, O. C. M. – F. C. van der Leek
1983   "The demise of the Old English impersonal construction", *Journal of Linguistics*, 19: 337–368.
Gaaf, W. van der
1904   *The transition from the impersonal to the personal constructions* (Heidelberg: Carl Winter).
Holtsmark, Anne – Jón Helgason
1968   *Snorri Sturluson Edda* (København: Munksgaard).
Hopper, Paul J.
1975   *The syntax of the simple sentence in Proto-Germanic* (Den Haag: Mouton).
Jespersen, Otto
1927   *A modern English grammar on historical principles*, vol. 3 (London: Allen & Unwin).
Keenan, Edward L.
1976   "Towards a universal definition of 'subject' ", in: *Subject and topic*, edited by Charles N. Li, 303–333 (New York: Academic Press).
Lightfoot, David W.
1979   "Rule classes and syntactic change", *Linguistic Inquiry* 10: 83–108.
1980   "The history of NP-movement", in: *Lexical grammar*, edited by Teun Hoekstra, Harry van der Hulst, and Michael Moortgat, 255–284 (Dordrecht: Foris).
Maling, Joan – Annie Zaenen
1985   "Preposition-stranding and passive", *Nordic Journal of Linguistics* 8: 197–209.
McCawley, Noriko A.
1976   "From OE/ME 'impersonal' to 'personal' constructions: what is a subjectless S?", in: *Papers from the Parasession on Diachronic Syntax*, edited by Sanford

B. Steever, Carol A. Walker, and Salikoko S. Mufwene, 192−204 (Chicago: The Chicago Linguistic Society).

Nygaard, Marius
1906   *Norrøn syntax* (Kristiania: Aschehoug).
Platzack, Christer
1985   "The Scandinavian languages and the null subject parameter", *Working Papers in Scandinavian Syntax* 20 (Trondheim: University of Trondheim).
Seefranz-Montag, Ariane von
1983   *Syntaktische Funktionen und Wortstellungsveränderung* (München: Fink).
1984   " 'Subjectless' constructions and syntactic change", in: *Historical syntax*, edited by Jacek Fisiak, 521−553 (Berlin: Mouton de Gruyter).
Tripp, Raymond P.
1978   "The psychology of impersonal constructions", *Glossa* 12: 177−188.
Wasow, Thomas
1977   "Transformations and the lexicon", in: *Formal syntax*, edited by Peter W. Culicover, Thomas Wasow, and Adrian Akmajian, 327−360 (New York: Academic Press).
Yngre Edda
1967   *Snorre Sturlason Den Yngre Edda*, translated by Erik Eggen (Oslo: Det Norske Samlaget).

Language planning and language change

Ernst Håkon Jahr

1. Deliberately planned changes

Linguistic changes discussed in the literature are almost without exception unconscious and unintended changes, changes that have occurred without deliberate actions or motivations on the part of the speakers/users to change the language or part(s) of the language. Here, I want to draw attention to some changes that are consciously and deliberately initiated by language users, or rather, by the speech community through planning. Language planning can be said to be the only activity in which a language community takes action actively and intentionally in order to obtain a linguistic change.

In earlier periods language planning did not play any part in linguistic change, since, of course, language planning was non-existent. Only from the time of the founding of the first language academies, as in France in 1635 and in Sweden in 1786, can we begin to discuss the possibility of influence of language planning on language change. Up till the present century, however, the academies had very limited possibilities for directing language development.

With the development of a compulsory school system in most European countries over the last two centuries, and with a school period of up to 9 or even 12 years in some countries, the political authorities now have a powerful instrument which enables them — in principle — to reach the whole population with language planning.

In this paper, then, I will focus on the role of language planning in language change. By 'language planning' I understand 'a deliberate effort by political authorities, some institution or prescriptive linguists to change a spoken language or a spoken variety of a language in a certain defined direction'. Adopting this definition I exclude, of course, that type of language planning which deals with the relationships between different languages within an area or country, e. g. the relationship between English and indigenous languages in former British colonies, or the relationship between the two Norwegian written standards *Bokmål* and *Nynorsk*. I also exclude examples of the reviving of entire languages, such as modern Hebrew in Israel, as well as languages of communities with very few speakers, where it is possible for a small group or even individuals to bring about major linguistic changes. Melanesia has many such communities with less than 500 speakers (cf. Peter Mühlhäusler's paper in this volume).

What I want to look at are cases where (small) parts of actual languages have been changed through means controlled by political or administrative bodies, mainly, it turns out, through the compulsory school system and broadcasting. Actions taken by individual schoolteachers to correct the speech of their pupils are also excluded, unless such corrections are motivated by and are part of a wider language planning policy.

Most of the language planning around the world is concerned with functional, legal, or other relationships between different languages within a region – or with cultivation of or changes in written languages. Language planning concerning speech is much rarer, and, it seems, most often unsuccessful. However, it can be and has been done, and I will present three examples, from Norwegian and Icelandic, which will illustrate different effects of language planning on Norwegian and Icelandic speech.

There are at least three possible ways in which language planning can cause changes in speech in a given language:

1. *By introducing a new feature into the language in question.* A feature not previously found in the language is either just added, or – and this is, I think, in most cases the objective of the language planners – this new feature replaces an old one, which then disappears. To obtain a complete substitution in this way seems to be extremely difficult. But I will give one rather surprising example from Norwegian which shows how language planning has added an important feature to the core lexicon of practically every Norwegian, and thereby created an area of linguistic variation which did not exist before and which can be studied and described within a sociolinguistic framework.

2. *By removing a feature from the language in question, most often by halting and reversing an ongoing (and spreading) change.* This is, then, a type of anti-change, where language planning engages in maintaining the linguistic state prior to a change that is not favoured by the language planners. I shall report on one successful and illustrative example of this type, from Icelandic, where a phonological feature found in almost 40% of the capital's inhabitants in the early 1940s was removed and today is almost non-existent in Reykjavik.

3. *By changing the written standard of a language and through this, as a side effect, influencing the speech variety most closely connected with this written standard.* This third type is, obviously, of a somewhat different kind than the first two. Here, there is no conscious wish on the part of the language planners to actually change the spoken language. But if a change nevertheless occurs as a result of a conscious change in the written standard, language planning is of course responsible, and, consequently, the cause of the change. I will discuss some changes in upper-class Oslo speech from about 1880 onwards as a possible example of this type.

2. Counting two-digit numbers over 20 in Norwegian

In 1950−51, the Norwegian Government as well as Parliament set out to change the pronunciation of every two-digit number over 20 in Norwegian. Although Norway has a long history of language planning, this was the first, and up till now, the only time that the spoken language has been dealt with specifically. Language planning in Norway has otherwise been exclusively preoccupied with the written language.

The modern Germanic languages have two distinct methods of compounding numbers from 21 to 99, including cases where these are expressed as part of a higher number, as in 243 for example. Modern German, Dutch, Danish, and Faeroese place the units before the tens, as in German 'einundzwanzig'. Modern English, Swedish, and Icelandic, however, put the tens first, as in English 'twenty-one'.

Before 1951, Norwegians − without exception − counted with the units before the tens, as in German, Dutch, Danish and Faeroese. The reform of 1951 introduced the English, Swedish and Icelandic method, with tens before units. This new method was made compulsory in schools and broadcasting, and the Norwegian population was urged to change to the new method.

The language planners were quite optimistic about the reform, expecting the new method of counting to replace the old one completely after a few years. Those in favour of the change claimed that the new method was more logical and more international (!) than the old method. In this context, then, 'international' means in line with English and Swedish, departing however from Danish and German.

Today every Norwegian uses both methods, units before tens as well as tens before units. A recent sociolinguistic study of 30 informants from Northern Norway yielded these results (Mercer 1986):

Table 1. % Usage of old and new method of counting. Age and formality.

Age Group	Reading				Informal interview, conversation	
	Formal text		Informal Text			
	Unit-tens	Tens-unit	Unit-tens	Tens-unit	Unit-tens	Tens-unit
11 – 12	0.0	100.0	0.0	100.0	14.3	85.7
17 – 18	0.9	99.1	1.8	98.2	85.7	14.3
19 – 35	0.9	99.1	0.0	100.0	51.2	48.8
36 – 55	55.6	44.4	52.1	47.9	73.5	26.5
> 55	60.2	39.8	50.0	50.0	90.2	9.8

These results can be visualized by means of the following chart:

Chart 1.   % of new forms.

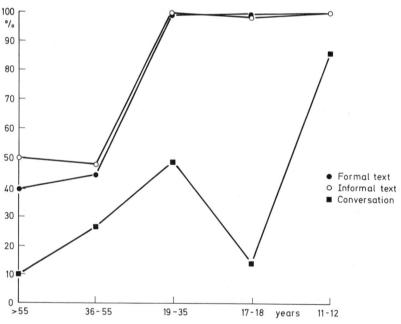

It turns out that age and formality are important factors: the younger the informant and the more formal the situation, the higher the frequency of the new forms. The variation ranges from the youngest group (11 – 12

year-olds) who had no occurrences of old forms in the reading tests, to the oldest group (above 55 years old) who had 90.2% occurrences of the old forms in informal conversation. There seems to be a clear difference between those born before and those born after the introduction of the new forms in 1951. (The exceptionally low proportion of new forms used in conversation by the age group 17−18 may be a result of few occurrences of compound forms − only 14 were recorded.)

These results − from 1986 − can be compared with a study done in Oslo ten years ago (Kvifte 1978):

Table 2. % Usage of tens-unit counting (48 informants: 24 males, 24 females, aged 11, 14, and 17).

	11 year-olds		14 year-olds		17 year-olds	
	Reading	Informal interview	Reading	Informal interview	Reading	Informal interview
West	85.6	52.8	66.7	32.4	60.7	35.7
East	68.9	41.4	34.5	20.6	29.8	10.7

West is a middle and upper-class area, *East* is a working class area.

These figures correspond to the following columns:

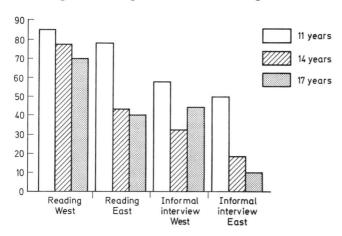

Here, we observe a fall in frequency of new forms from the youngest to the oldest group, both in the reading test and in the informal interview, but in this study the oldest informants were only 17 years old. Especially low was the frequency in the informal interview in the 17 year-olds from the eastern part of Oslo (10.7%).

These results from young Oslo speakers can be interpreted in two very different ways: (1) the use of new forms seems to be increasing since they are more frequent among the very young than in the groups of teenagers, or (2) young speakers tend to decrease the use of new forms when they become teenagers.

Without a new study today, it is impossible to decide which one of these interpretations is correct. However, when the figures from the Oslo study are compared with the results reported in Table 1, it seems most plausible that the use of new forms is increasing.

Furthermore, if we can apply the usage by youngsters in Kvifte's 1978 study to the population in Oslo in general, it seems that social class is also a factor involved in variation between new and old forms. New forms were more frequently used by the young informants from the middle and upper-class West area than from the working class East area.

Table 1 and Table 2 show that the language planning reform of 1951 has created an area of variation within Norwegian today which did not exist before, and the frequency of occurrence of units-ten forms now seems to depend on such sociolinguistic factors as social class, age, and formality of context.

The reform of 1951 has not, however, succeeded completely, since the old method of counting is still very much alive, especially in casual everyday speech. I will mention only one important linguistic factor that could be claimed to work against the reform.

The new forms which were introduced by the reform were in conflict with a trochaic stress pattern which is usual in Norwegian. The trochaic Norwegian stress pattern has been referred to in order to explain why Norwegian developed units-ten counting in the first place (Liestøl 1910: 23). The new forms with tens first mostly had a strong stress on the final syllable, since only two of the nine Norwegian words for the units have two syllables — *fire* 'four' and *åtte* 'eight'. This strong word-final stress often produced a clash with the word-initial stress of the following word. If, however, units are used first — as in the pre-1951 method of counting — this problem does not arise, since all the words for tens have the stress-pattern strong-weak. The problem of having two strong stresses within the compound number is then resolved by insertion of a stressless *og* 'and' between the unit and tens numbers. This important prosodic factor was not fully appreciated in the debate prior to the reform.

This stress pattern must also be the reason why Mercer in his study (1986) found more occurrences of units-ten forms when the number was followed by a noun (with first syllable stress) than when it occurred alone;

thus they were more likely in phrases such as 25-*watts pære* '25 Watt bulb' or 25 *prosent* '25 percent' than in the year '1925' or a telephone number '25 35 25'.

What we have seen here, then, is a change in the *core lexicon* of a spoken language. When we take that into account, I think it is fair to conclude that the result of the 1951 reform is quite remarkable. Most, perhaps all, Norwegians use both tens-unit and units-ten forms in their speech. The occurrence of a units-ten form as opposed to a tens-unit form depends on several factors, such as age, style, and context: the less formal the style, the more likely is the use of a units-ten form, and the older the speaker, the more likely the occurrence of units-ten forms. In addition, social class also seems to play a part.

The 1951 reform has had an effect on everybody's speech, though only in the most formal style of the older generation. Before 1951, nobody used tens-unit counting and now everybody does to a certain degree. And the reform can be the only and exclusive reason for the change.

3. *Flámæli*: The merging of /ɪ/ with /e/, and /ʏ/ with /ø/ in Icelandic

In his paper 'The vowel system of Icelandic' (1959), Hreinn Benediktsson showed how the Icelandic vowel system has developed and has been reduced in terms of distinctive features from Old to Modern Icelandic (Benediktsson 1959). The last step in this long historical development of the vowel system is the merging of /ɪ/ with /e/, and /ʏ/ with /ø/, which is manifested by a lowering of /ɪ/ and /ʏ/ and a raising of /e/ and /ø/, yielding a vowel of intermediate quality, or a concomitant diphthong:

Figure 1. Flámæli: The merging of /ɪ/ with /e/, and /ʏ/ with /ø/ in Icelandic.

This process makes homophones out of words like *viður* 'wood' and *veður* 'weather', and *flugur* (plur. of *fluga* 'fly') and *flögur* (plur. of *flaga* 'slab, flake'). This last step in the development of Icelandic vowels originated among the common fishermen in the 19th century, and spread rapidly in the west, east, and north of the country.

There are no dialects in the traditional sense in Iceland. But speakers of Icelandic have different linguistic features to a variable degree. There is also no sharp contrast between a standard spoken language and other varieties of Icelandic. Most variable features are considered equally 'good' and 'correct' socially. But there is one important exception to this: the vowel merging just mentioned. The Icelandic name given to this feature suggests a low social reputation. In Iceland it is called *flámæli* 'slack-jawed speech'. (The opposite of *flámæli* is *réttmæli* 'correct speech'.) Its origin among common fishermen, who were the first proletarians in Iceland, may account for the low social status of this specific feature.

Around the time of World War II, Björn Guðfinnsson conducted the largest dialect survey investigation ever in Iceland. He interviewed about 10,000 subjects, mostly school children. The purpose of the project was to map recent phonological innovations in order to establish a basis of knowledge for intensive planning of the spoken language through the school system.

In his investigation in the early 1940s Björn Guðfinnsson found *flámæli* present in 38.55% of all his informants in the capital Reykjavik (Guðfinnsson 1964: 84). He also claimed that it was spreading rapidly (Guðfinnsson 1947: 27). After that, however, *flámæli* was systematically opposed on all levels of instruction and education. Guðfinnsson himself published a normative guide in pronunciation where several pages were dedicated to the fight against the 'slack-jawed speech' (Guðfinnsson 1947: 41−48).

The scenario we have here, then, is a conflict between a sound change that is the last step of a long historical development of the Icelandic vowel system, a change that is clearly in line with the preceding development, and, on the other hand, the extra-linguistic factor of social evaluation. The language planners of Iceland found the outcome of this particular sound change unacceptable and took action against it.

Twenty years after Guðfinnsson's survey investigation, Hreinn Benediktsson (1961−62: 95) reported that as a result of the intensive campaign against *flámæli* it was said to be losing ground among the youngest generation. According to Benediktsson, however, the outcome was still not certain at that time.

Then, after another twenty years, in the early 1980s, Höskuldur Þráinsson and Kristján Árnason did a new survey investigation in Reykjavik in order to compare it with Guðfinnsson's of the early 1940s. Their results show a quite dramatic change in the use of the *flámæli* feature. While Guðfinnsson found – as already mentioned – that 38.55% of the Reykjavik speakers in his investigation had this feature in their speech, Þráinsson and Árnason (1984: 123, cf. also Árnason 1987: 89) found the same feature in only 2.6% of their informants. Among the younger generation they did not find it at all. Linguistically speaking the Icelanders had reversed the last step in the historical development of their vowel system.

Since the campaign for the eradication of *flámæli* in Icelandic could draw to a considerable extent on the low social value of this particular phonological feature, one important question arises. Is it the low social status that is responsible for the result now reported from Reykjavik by Þráinsson and Árnason, or is the action taken by normative linguists and the schools responsible?

In Jahr 1988, I have tried to show how the parameter *urban – rural* plays a decisive part in the halting of a sound change in Oslo Norwegian. A recent change in the system of laterals in Oslo Norwegian, where an alveolar or retroflex *l*-allophone replaced a dental allophone, has been stopped before reaching completion, i. e. after the vowels /a/ and /ɔ/ we still find a dental allophone. The reason for this linguistically uneconomical situation is that a pronunciation of alveolar or retroflex *l* after /a/ or /ɔ/ sounds extremely rural to the inhabitants of Oslo.

Now, could this also apply to the Icelandic example, and perhaps explain why *flámæli* is non-existent among the younger generation of the capital Reykjavik? I believe not. The main difference here is that *flámæli* was well established among young people in Reykjavik 50 years ago, while alveolar/retroflex *l* after /a/ or /ɔ/ never entered Oslo speech. It seems that the parameter urban – rural is not as important in Iceland as it is in Norway.

Another possible explanation for the eradication of *flámæli* could perhaps be this: the vowel phonemes that were the outcome of the lowering of /ɪ/ and /ʏ/ and the merger with /e/ and /ø/ became functionally overloaded. This functional overload then created a reaction, yielding again the older system.

This system-internal explanation is, however, contradicted by the fact that Þráinsson and Árnason in their study (1984: 125) found a slight tendency among young people in the direction of a new merging process,

i. e. the merging of /ø/ with /ʏ/ by a *raising* of the /ø/. This tendency has also been observed by Blöndal (1984). This indicates that instead of reacting against simplification, the vowel system seeks new ways of obtaining reduction (by raising the /ø/), since the first attempt (starting with the lowering of /ɪ/ and /ʏ/) has been stopped.

Language planning, then, with steps taken against the *flámæli* feature from the late 1940s onwards is responsible for the decline of *flámæli* in Icelandic.[1]

4. The changes voiced > unvoiced stops after long vowels in some words in upper-class Oslo Norwegian

Around 1880, the spoken language of the upper classes in Norway was greatly influenced by the written standard of the 19th century, which was predominantly Danish. When Norway got her political independence from Denmark in 1814, after a 400-year-union, the Norwegians continued to use the Danish standard which had been the common written medium during the period of the union. Upper-class speech in the 19th century was strongly influenced by this written standard, often reflecting a near spelling pronunciation.

In an attempt to nationalize the written standard the Norwegian authorities have engaged heavily in language planning and have succeeded in changing the written standard from being Danish to being predominantly Norwegian. The transformation from Danish to Norwegian has been completed through a step-by-step Norwegianization. By including more and more elements from spoken Norwegian in the written standard and at the same time removing salient Danish features, the language planners have been able to change the written standard quite dramatically.

By means of three language reforms in this century (1907, 1917, 1938), the orthography and word forms of the written standard changed from the Danish forms to a way of spelling which, to the language planners, reflected a more 'Norwegian' pronunciation. But since upper-class speech to a considerable degree was influenced by Danish spelling, several important features of this spoken variety were not regarded as sufficiently national. Thus, the language planners turned to other spoken varieties, considering them to be more genuinely Norwegian. To the language planners this followed logically from and was merely a consequence of the desire to nationalize the written standard. But members of the upper classes regarded this as an impairment and vulgarization of the written standard. Being upper class they were used to considering their own spoken variety 'correct', 'nice', and 'educated', and why, they asked, should not the written standard reflect this?

Thus, the upper classes have on the whole been extremely negative to the official planning of the written language. Generally speaking, we may say that as long as changes in the standard were made within, and could be motivated by, upper-class pronunciation, they were reluctantly accepted after a few years. This applies especially to the 1907 changes. However, when popular and dialectal pronunciation was taken account of in the reforms of 1917 and 1938, this initiated a most active and organized resistance. Nevertheless, upper-class speech has not been unaffected by the changes made in the written standard.

The changes in upper-class speech which I want to focus on here is the development of /b/, /d/, /g/ to /p/, /t/, /k/ after long vowels in words like

Danish *skaber* — Norwegian *skaper* 'creator'
Danish *vide* — Norwegian *vite* 'know'
Danish *rige* — Norwegian *rike* 'realm'

A major aim of language planning in Norway was to replace *b, d, g* by *p, t, k* in all words having the Danish form.

Upper-class speech, however, had long ago adopted a pronunciation with voiced stops after long vowels in many of these words, in line with the Danish orthographic system. But with the orthographic changes in these words in the written standard, upper-class speech also changed, as can be seen in Table 3. The use of /p/, /t/, and /k/ after long vowels has increased in the words in question and is now predominant even in this high prestige spoken variety of Norwegian. In terms of Norwegian language planning, we may say that upper-class speech, too — along with the written standard — has been 'Norwegianized'. Subsequently, the fierce opposition to the official spelling with *p, t* and *k* has declined.

The question is, then, whether we can count these changes in upper-class Oslo speech as an example of language change caused by language planning.

In the upper-class speech of 1880 there were in fact some tendencies to move away from the use of voiced plosives after long vowels in some of the words in question (cf. Table 3). It is therefore legitimate to ask

Table 3. The changes from *b, d, g* to *p, t, k* in spelling and upper-class pronunciation. (From Jahr 1986)

Written form 1880 Dano-Norwegian	Pronunciation 1880	Written form 1907 ('—' means no change)	Pronunciation 1910	Written form 1917	Pronunciation 1925	Written form 1938 Bokmål	Pronunciation today
sæbe 'soap'	seːbə	*såpe*	seːpə/sɔːpə	—	sæpə/sɔːpə	—	sɔːpə/sɛːpə
råbe 'call'	rɔːbə/ruːbə	*rope*	ruːpə	—	ruːpə	—	ruːpə
dåb 'baptism'	dɔːb	—	dɔːb	*dåp/dåb*	dɔːp/dɔːb	*dåp*	dɔːp
skaber 'creator'	skaːbər	—	skaːbər	*skaper*	skɑːpər/skɑːbər	—	skɑːpər
håbe 'hope'	hɔːbə	—	hɔːbə	*håpe/håbe*	hɔːbə	*håpe*	hɔːbə/hɔːpə
læbe 'lip'	leːbə	—	leːbə	*lepe/lebe/leppe*	leːbə/lepə	*leppe/lepe*	lepə/leːbə
skib 'ship'	ʃiːb	—	ʃiːb	*skip/skib*	ʃiːb	*skip*	ʃiːb/ʃiːp
våben 'weapon'	vɔːbən	—	vɔːbən	*våpen/våben*	vɔːbən	*våpen*	vɔːbən/vɔːpən
-hed (suffix)	-heːd/-heːt	*-het*	-heːt	—	-heːt	—	-heːt
båden 'the boat'	bɔːdn̩	*båten*	bɔːtn̩	—	bɔːtn̩	—	bɔːtn̩
foruden 'without'	fɔruːdn̩	*foruten*	fɔruːdn̩	—	fɔruːtn̩	—	fɔrɑːtn̩
udgjøre 'constitute'	uːdjøːrə/-t-	*udgjøre*	uːtjørrə	—	ɛːrøːɾɑ	—	ɛːrøːɾɑ
vide 'know'	viːdə/viːtə	*vite*	viːtə	—	viːtə	—	viːtə
ved 'know' pres.	veːd/veːt	*vet*	veːt	*vet/veit*	veːt	—	veːt
vidende 'knowing'	viːdə	—	viːdn̩ə/viːtn̩ə	*vitende/vidende*	viːtn̩ə/viːdn̩ə	*vitende*	viːtn̩ə/viːdn̩ə
viden 'knowlege'	viːdn̩	—	viːdn̩	—	viːdn̩	*viten*	viːdn̩/viːtn̩
pigen 'the maid'	piːgən	*piken*	piːkən	—	piːkən	—	piːkən
tilbage 'back' adv.	tilbaːgə/-k-	*tilbake*	tilbaːkə	—	tilbɑːkə	—	tilbɑːkə
rige 'realm'	riːgə/riːkə	*rike*	riːkə	—	riːkə	—	riːkə
sprog 'language'	sprɔːg	—	sprɔːg	*språk/sprog*	sprɔːg	*språk*	sprɔːg

whether this 'Norwegianization' of upper-class speech would not have taken place anyway, without the reforms of the written language. It is not easy to reject this objection totally, since – of course – there is no possible way of finding out whether the observable development in upper-class speech would have occurred regardless of the language reforms.

A cautious conclusion about the influence of the language planning on upper-class Oslo speech would be that the changes in the written standard have at least *stimulated tendencies* within upper-class speech itself, and that they have caused an acceleration of the general shift to unvoiced plosives after long vowels.

5. Conclusion

The three examples of language change discussed above are all caused by language planning, but to a varying degree. The first change is the only one about which we can say with absolute certainty that without language planning this change would not have taken place. A decision was made by Parliament stating that a language change was to be implemented, and the political authorities acted accordingly using the means at their disposal: the school system and the radio (there was no television in Norway in the early 1950s). The outcome can be studied today: Norwegians use both the old and the new method of counting, and the variation can be studied and described in well-known sociolinguistic terms, taking into account, among other things, age, social class, formality, and linguistic context. It is reasonable to assume that level of education may be an important factor here as well.

The *flámæli* example is also fairly certain, although it is different from the first one in many respects. First, it concerns the eradication of a phonological feature, not the establishment of something new. The objective was to preserve the state of development of the Icelandic vowel system referred to by the Icelanders as *réttmæli* 'correct speech'. But there was no vote in the Icelandic Allting or a decision by the Icelandic government behind the action taken against *flámæli* from the 1940s onwards. It was a tacit decision made by everyone who had to do with the study and cultivation of Icelandic, based on the view that it was important to preserve the opposition in the phonological system between the vowels involved in *flámæli*. The low social reputation of this feature in Icelandic society helped support this decision. There was a consensus among linguists, school teachers, and the cultural establishment in general that the *flámæli* feature ought to be obliterated, and they worked together to reach that objective. I have, however, no hesitation in calling this also 'language planning', in line with the first Norwegian example. Although there was no decision made by a language planning body, or Parliament, as in the Norwegian example, a clear goal was defined that meant a linguistic change for a large part of the Icelandic population. A phonological feature that was already well established in the speech of nearly half the population first had to be stopped from spreading any further, and then done away with.

The third example, from upper-class Oslo speech, is of course more dubious, since the changes, on the basis of tendencies within upper-class speech itself, might have occurred regardless of the planning of the written standard. It is, however, difficult to imagine that the changes would have happened as rapidly as they have without the support of the changes made in the written standard. Around 1880, pronunciation with unvoiced stops in many of the words in question was considered utterly vulgar by the upper classes. However, when codified in the written standard with *p, t,* or *k,* some of these words lost the vulgar stigma that was associated with a pronunciation with unvoiced stops, and could then be more easily accepted also in upper-class speech. Therefore, we may conclude, language planning has also played a role in these changes in upper-class Oslo speech, although the effect of language planning in this example is more indirect than in the first two.[2]

Notes

1. The fate of *h*-dropping around the English speaking world provides a possible parallel example to the Icelandic *flámæli*-example. There is a lot of documentary evidence to suggest that, just as in England and Wales, *h*-dropping was very common in the U. S. and in Australia and New Zealand in the 19th century. Certainly in the U. S. and in New Zealand it has died out altogether. Elizabeth Gordon (1983) quotes an interesting report from a school inspector of the 19th century in New Zealand complaining about *h*-dropping in the speech of the school children. But in the 100—150 years which have elapsed since then, *h*-dropping has disappeared; even in very colloquial speech in New Zealand today we do not find it. It seems to have been a joint effort on the part of school inspectors and presumably also of other people in the cultural establishment to get rid of it. However, in this process in New Zealand — contrary to what was the case in Iceland — the influence of Standard English and the influence of immigrants from Scotland and Ireland, which did not have *h*-dropping, probably combined with the

efforts by the school inspectors to get rid of the *h*-dropping. In Iceland there is no single speech variety with an influence comparable to that of Standard English in the English speaking world, and there was, of course, no immigration like that in New Zealand. Still, the fate of *h*-dropping in New Zealand provides a case rather similar to the Icelandic example described in this paper. (I thank Peter Trudgill for informing me about *h*-dropping in New Zealand, cf. Trudgill 1986: 138−139.)

2. I thank Leiv Egil Breivik and Toril Swan for correcting my English.

References

Árnason, Kristján
    1987   "Icelandic dialects forty years later: the (non)survival of some northern and south-eastern features", in: *The Nordic languages and modern linguistics 6*, edited by Pirkko Lilius−Mirja Saari, 79−92 (Helsinki).
Benediktsson, Hreinn
    1959   "The vowel system of Icelandic: a survey of its history", *Word* 15: 282−312.
    1961−62 "Icelandic dialectology: methods and results", *Islenzk Tunga / Lingua Islandica* 3: 72−113.
Blöndal, Þórunn
    1984   "Flámæli. Nokkrar athuganir á framburði Reykvíkinga fyrr og nú", Unpublished thesis, Háskóla Íslands, Reykjavík.
Gordon, Elizabeth
    1983   "New Zealand English pronunciation: an investigation into some early written records", *Te Reo* 26: 29−42.
Guðfinnsson, Björn
    1947   *Breytingar á framburði og stafsetningu* (Reykjavík: Ísafoldarprentsmiðja H. F.).
    1964   *Mállyzkur II Um íslenzkan framburð* (= Studia Islandica 23). Reykjavík.
Jahr, Ernst Håkon
    1986   "The influence of a century's language planning on upper-class speech in Oslo", in: *Linguistics across historical and geographical boundaries. Vol. 1: Linguistic theory and historical linguistics*, edited by Dieter Kastovsky−Aleksander Szwedek, 397−408 (Berlin: Mouton de Gruyter).
    1988   "Social dialect influence in language change: the halting of a sound change in Oslo Norwegian", in: *Historical dialectology, regional and social*, edited by Jacek Fisiak, 329−337 (Berlin: Mouton de Gruyter).
Kvifte, Bjørn Harald
    1978   "Den nye tellemåten − departementalt påfunn eller språkforbedring? Søkelys på tallreformen av 1951", Unpublished thesis, University of Oslo.
Liestøl, Knut
    1910   "Nynorsk maalføring i tale og skrift samanlikna med gamalnorsk", in: *Maal og Minne* 2, 18−36 (Kristiania (Oslo): Bymaalslaget).
Mercer, David
    1986   "Can Norwegians count? An investigation into the conflict in the Modern Norwegian counting system", Unpublished paper, University of Tromsø / University of Reading.
Þráinsson, Höskuldur−Kristján Árnason
    1984   "Um reykvísku", in: *Íslenskt mál og almenn málfræði* 6, 113−134 (Reykjavík).
Trudgill, Peter
    1986   *Dialects in contact* (= Language in Society 10). (Oxford: Blackwell).

The origin and function of switch reference in Green Hmong[1]

Charles N. Li

0. Introduction

This paper addresses two related issues. The first one is the diachronic development of switch reference in Green Hmong. To date, switch reference has been found exclusively in inflectional and polysynthetic languages. Green Hmong, however, is a prototypal isolating language without inflection, case, agreement, number, and gender markings. The emergence of switch reference in such a language is intriguing for both typological and diachronic reasons. The second issue is the function of switch reference. The Green Hmong evidence suggests that switch reference is not restricted to tracking the reference of subjects. Partly due to its diachronic origin, switch reference in Green Hmong may also have the function of presenting two clauses with different subjects in weak contrast. This additional function poses a challenge to the standard interpretation of switch reference: is it possible that in other languages where switch reference occurs in coordinate constructions it may also have some other function besides referential tracking?

1. The Hmong language

Hmong is a branch of the Hmong-Mien language family of East Asia. The vast majority of the Hmongs, approximately six million, is scattered among various mountainous enclaves in South China. They speak a great variety of dialects which differ from each other primarily in phonology[2].

About two centuries ago, some of the Hmongs began migrating from China to Southeast Asia. Several hundred thousands of them now live in Thailand, Vietnam, and Laos. After the Vietnam war, nearly one third of the Hmongs of Laos left for the United States, Thailand, China, Australia, and France. Nearly all of the Hmong immigrants in the United States are speakers of Green Hmong and White Hmong.

The genetic relations between Hmong-Mien and other language families of East Asia is indeterminate. A variety of claims have been made linking Hmong-Mien with Sino-Tibetan, Mon-Khmer, or Austronesian, e. g. Benedict (1975), Diffloth (1985), Haudricourt (1954), and Wang (1986). None of the claims, however, can be shown to be unequivocal and definitive.

The Hmong languages are characterized by two salient features: (1) A large number of lexical tones. It has been reported that the Hmong dialect of Zongdi in Guizhou Province of Southern China has twelve lexically contrastive tones including five level tones and four falling tones of different pitch registers (Li et al. 1959). In addition, tones are often correlated with phonation types such as breathiness and glottalization (Ratliff 1986). (2) All Hmong languages are prototypal isolating and monosyllabic languages. They have neither inflectional nor derivational morphology. Their strategy of forming sentences is the simple concatenation of nouns and verbs with few functor words. Their sentences taken out of discourse context are more likely to be ambiguous than those of a language with a rich morphology.

2. Canonical switch reference

Canonical switch reference is considered a category of verb inflection which marks the co-referentiality or the non-co-referentiality between the subject of a verb and the subject of another verb in a difference clause. A typical example is given by Gordon (1983):
(Maricopa, a Yuman language)

(1)   Nyaa ′-ashvar -k   ′-iima -k
       I   1-sing -SS 1-dance -aspect
       'I sang and I danced.' (SS = same subject)

(2)   Bonnie -sh   0-ashvar -m   'iima   -k
         Bonnie -subj. 3-sing   -DS l-dance -aspect
         'Bonnie sang and I danced.' (DS = different subject)

The general characteristics of switch reference are discussed in several articles in Haiman and Munro (1983). I will summarize them as follows:

(1) With the exception of Lenakel, an Austronesian language of Papua New Guinea, and Gokana, a Niger-Congo language of Nigeria (2), languages displaying the switch reference phenomenon are verb-final (Lynch 1983 and Comrie 1983).

(2) Only one of the two clauses involved in switch reference in a language is marked for the same-subject vs. different-subject distinction. If one of the clauses is subordinate, it will be the clause bearing the switch reference marking.

(3) The same-subject and different-subject markers typically appear as verb affixes. In a few languages such as Pima (a Uto-Aztecan language), the markers are independent morphemes.

(4) The diachronic origin of switch reference markers could be deictics, case suffixes, subordination markers, temporal markers, and causative markers.

3. Switch reference in Green Hmong

Switch reference in Hmong is an exception to all of the general characteristics of canonical switch reference. First, Hmong is a verb-medial language. Second, the same-subject vs. different-subject distinction is not marked on a clause in Hmong. The distinction is indicated by the coordinator. Thirdly, since Hmong is an isolating language without inflection, Hmong switch reference cannot be an inflectional category. Finally, the diachronic origin of Hmong switch reference markers are coordinators which have changed their grammatical function. In this section I will present data illustrating switch reference in Green Hmong.[3]

Each of the sentences in (3) contains two conjoined clauses with different subjects. Sentence (3a) uses the coordinator, *huas*. Sentence (3b), which is ungrammatical, uses the coordinator, *hab*:

(3a)   Tuam sab huas Tub muaj-zug
       Tuam tall and Tub strong
       'Tuam is tall and Tub is strong.'
  b)   *Tuam sab hab Tub muaj-zug
       Tuam   tall and Tub strong

Each of the sentences in (4) contains two conjoined clauses with the same subject, an understood second person pronoun. Sentence (4a) uses the coordinator, *hab*, and sentence (4b), which is ungrammatical, uses the coordinator, *huas*:

(4a)   nqeg   lug   hab nyob quas-tsawg
       descend come and stay   sit
       'Come down and sit!'
  b)   *nqeg   lug   huas nyob quas-tsawg
       descend come and   stay   sit

Sentences (3) and (4) strongly suggest that *hab* is a coordinator for clauses with the same subjects and *huas* is a coordinator for clauses with different subjects. This distinction between *hab* and *huas* is further supported by the referential property of the third person pronominal subject of the second clause of two conjoined clauses in sentences (5) and (6). In (5), with the coordinator, *huas*, the third person pronominal subject of the second clause cannot be co-referential with the subject of the first clause. In (6), with the coordinator, *hab*, the third person pronominal subject of the second clause is obligatorily co-referential with the subject of the first clause.

                            − coref

(5)   Tuam moog kawm-ntawv huas nwg moog yuav zaub   noj
       Tuam go   school   and 3sg. go   buy   grocery eat
       'Tuam went to school and he bought grocery to eat.'

                            − coref

+ coref

```
          ┌─────────────────────────────────┐
(6)    Tuam moog kawm-ntawv hab nwg moog yuav zaub   noj
       Tuam go   school      and 3sg. go   buy  grocery eat
       'Tuam went to school and he bought grocery to eat.'
       └──────────────────────────────┘
```

+ coref

In the case of overlapping reference between the subjects of two conjoined clauses, e. g. 'I' and 'we', 'they' and 'he', the same-subject and different-subject distinction is not maintained. In sentences (7) and (8), where the subjects of the clauses in each sentence have overlapping reference, the clauses may be conjoined by either *huas* or *hab*. In sentence (7), the reference of the subject of the second clause is included in the reference of the subject of the first clause. In sentence (8), the reference of the subject of the first clause is included in the reference of the subject of the second clause.[4]

```
(7)    puab yuav ib   lub tsev   huas/hab nwg muag ib   lub tsheb
       3pl. buy  one  CL house    and      3sg. sell one  CL car
       'They bought a house and he sold a car.'
         ↑──────────←──────────┘
```

```
(8)    kuv yuav ib   lub tsev   huas/hab peb muag ib   lub tsheb
       1sg. buy  one  CL house    and      1pl. sell one  CL car
       'I bought a house and we sold a car.'
       └──────────→─────────↑
```

The neutralization of switch reference coding in the case of overlapping reference does not reduce the significance of switch reference in Green Hmong. Comrie (1983) noted that the same phenomenon may be found in languages considered to have prototypal switch reference.

4. Other properties of *huas* and *hab*

The syntactic properties of *huas* and *hab* presented in this section will be relevant to the reconstruction of the diachronic development of switch reference in Green Hmong.

4.1 Conjunction of constituents other than clauses is the exclusive domain of *hab*. Sentences (9) − (14) illustrate different types of conjoined constituents. In all of these sentences, the coordinator must be *hab* not *huas*, and *hab* functions as a symmetric coordinator.

Conjoined NPs

(9)   Tuam hab Tub sab-sab
        Tuam and Tub tall-tall
        'Tuam and Tub are quite tall.'

(10)   kuv nyam tug txiv-neej kws   ncaws pob hab tug txiv-neej
        1sg. like   CL man   REL kick   ball and CL man
        kws   moog rua Fresno
        REL go   to Fresno
        'I like the man who plays soccer and the man who went to
        Fresno.'

Conjoined VPs

(11)   Tuam sab hab muaj-zug
        Tuam tall and strong
        'Tuam is tall and strong.'

(12)   kuv muag ib   lub tsheb hab yuav ib   lub tsev
        1sg. sell one CL car   and buy one CL house
        'I sold a car and bought a house.'

Conjoined adverbials

(13)   naag-mo hab nub-nua Tuam nkeeg-nkeeg
        yesterday and today   Tuam weak-weak
        'Yesterday and today, Tuam is rather weak.'

Conjoined modifiers

(14)   lub tsev   nruab hab dlawb yog kuv -le
        CL house green and white be 1sg. -GEN
        'The green and white house is mine.'

4.2 Only *hab* not *huas* can be used to list or enumerate multiple events. In listing multiple events, *hab* is used only to link the final two events.

Sentence (15), which is an answer to the question posed below illustrates the listing function of *hab*:

Question: Tell me about the stars, the sun, and the moon!

(15)   lub nub kub, lub hli   txag hab cov nub-qub ci
         CL sun hot CL moon cold and PL star   bright
         'The sun is hot, the moon is cold, and the stars are bright.'

Sentences (16) and (17) demonstrate that *huas* cannot be used for listing multiple events, and *hab* can occur only once between the final two events in a list of multiple events:

(16)   *lub nub kub, lub hli   txag huas cov nub-qub ci
          CL sun hot, CL moon cold and PL star   bright

(17)   *lub nub kub hab lub hli   txag hab cov nub-qub ci
          CL sun hot and Cl moon cold and PL star   bright

4.3 In addition to its function as a coordinator, *hab* also performs the grammatical function of 'too'. When *hab* is used to denote 'too', however, it must be in sentence-final position. Sentences (18) and (19) illustrate this function of *hab*.

(18)   Tuam moog rua suav-teb hab
         Tuam go   to China   too
         'Tuam went to China too.'
         (Presupposing the fact that other people went to China)

(19)   Tuam yog ib   tug tub-kawm-ntawv huas Paaj yog ib   tug
         Tuam be one CL student   and Paaj be one CL
         tub-kawm-ntawv hab
         student   too
         'Tuam is a student and Paaj is a student too!'

4.4 The different-subject coordinator, *huas*, may also serve as a coordinator with a weak contrastive function. In sentences with *huas* as a contrastive coordinator, the contrast may be signified by *huas* as well as special intonation and special word order. Sentence (20) is an example:

(20)   Paaj, kuv nyam, huas Tuam, kuv tsi   nyam
        Paaj, 1sg. like,   and Tuam, 1sg. NEG like
        'Paaj, I like, and Tuam, I don't like.'

As it is in English, the object noun of the two clauses in (20), *Paaj* and *Tuam*, is fronted and stressed. Fronting and special intonation pattern, however, is not obligatory in Green Hmong contrastive constructions. Sentence (21), for example, shows two clauses with the normal verb-medial word order and normal intonation conjoined with the contrastive coordinator, *huas*. It should be noted that the best approximation to the meaning of sentence (21) is to render the coordinator into an expression such as 'and instead':

(21)   kuv tsi   moog *Nebraska* huas kuv moog *Hawaii*
        1sg. NEG go   Nebraska   1sg. go   Hawaii
        'I didn't go to Nebraska and instead, I went to Hawaii.'

With regard to contrastive coordination, Green Hmong has another coordinator, *tab-sis*, which is equivalent to 'but' in English. The difference between *huas* and *tab-sis* is that the latter is stronger in its contrastive function. In addition, the usage of *huas* as a contrastive coordinator seems to be vanishing among the Hmong speakers according to the native language consultants with whom I have worked. Sentences such as (20) and (21) rarely occur in the speech of contemporary Green Hmongs. For such sentences, they prefer to use *tab-sis* instead of *huas* as a clause linker.

4.5 The same-subject coordinator, *hab*, is semantically neutral in the sense that it does not signify or imply any semantic relation between the clauses conjoined by it. It functions as a symmetric coordinator. Green Hmong has other coordinators signalling specific semantic relationships between the conjoined clauses. One of those coordinators is *ces/tes* which conjoins sequential events. It can be most suitably translated as 'and subsequently'. Sentence (22) is an example illustrating the function of the coordinator, *ces/tes*:

(22)   khi tug dlev ces tug miv lug
        tie CL dog   CL cat come
        'Tie up the dog and subsequently the cat will come!'

Another coordinator, *es*, signals a causative relation between the conjoined clauses.[5] Its most accurate English equivalent is: 'and consequently'. Sentence (23) is an example:

(23)   Tuam tsi   sab es Tub tsi   sab hab
        Tuam NEG tall   Tub NEG tall also
        'Tuam is not tall and consequently, Tub is also not tall.'
        (Inference: Tuam is Tub's father.)

5. The origin of switch reference in Green Hmong

The evidence presented in the preceding sections shows that (i) *hab* is the semantically neutral and symmetric coordinator whose function is to conjoin words, phrases, and clauses with the same subject, (ii) *huas* is a weak contrastive coordinator as well as a coordinator for clauses with different subjects. The link between "weak contrast" and switch reference should be self-evident. In fact, two conjoined clauses with different subjects can always be seen as weakly contrastive. Consider sentence (24):

            − coref

(24)   Tuam sab huas nwg muaj-zug
        Tuam tall and 3sg. strong
        'Tuam is tall and s/he is strong.'

            − coref

On the one hand, it is distinct from sentence (25) which conveys a strong contrastive sense because of the presence of the contrastive coordinator, *tab-sis* 'but',

(25)   Tuam sab tab-sis nwg muaj-zug
        Tuam tall but   3sg. strong
        'Tuam is tall but s/he is strong.'

            ± coref

On the other hand, it is impossible to exclude a weak contrastive reading of (24). Thus, *huas* seems to have a dual function: it signals that the subject of the second clause is not co-referential with the subject of the first clause, and it implies a weak contrast between the first and the second clause. In Hmong, the weakly contrastive function of the switch reference coordinator can be traced to the diachronic origin of the coordinator. The diachronic scenario leading to the displacement of *huas* as a full-fledged contrastive coordinator and the development of the Green Hmong switch reference involves a jostling of three coordination particles and a re-organization of the functional domain of each of them:

hab, huas, tab-sis

The entire diachronic process appears to be triggered by the introduction of the strong contrastive coordinator, *tab-sis* 'but'. There is a good deal of evidence indicating that *tab-sis* was borrowed into Hmong through contact:

(i) The fact that *tab-sis* is a bisyllabic morpheme, not a compound composed of two indigenous morphemes, makes it a suspect as a native word. Native Hmong morphemes are nearly without exception mono-syllabic, and bisyllabic words are either loan words or compounds composed of indigenous monosyllabic morphemes.

(ii) *tab-sis* has the same form in both Green Hmong and White Hmong. This identity violates a sound correspondence between two Hmong dialects: Green Hmong /a/ corresponds to White Hmong /ia/ except after the post-velar stop /q/ and /h/ where Green Hmong /a/ corresponds to White Hmong /ai/. The following cognate pairs illustrate this sound correspondence between Green Hmong and White Hmong:

Table 1. Green Hmong /a/ and White Hmong /ia/

	'skirt'	'liver'	'monkey'	'new'	'bee'
Green Hmong	tab	sab	lab	tshab	cab
White Hmong	tiab	siab	liab	tshiab	ciab
	'chicken'	'meat'	'speak'	'to weave bamboo'	
Green Hmong	qab	nqaj	ha	qhab	
White Hmong	qaib	nqaij	hai	qhaib	

(iii) The Hmongs of Southeast Asia migrated there from China during the past two centuries. Before their migration, their primary contact would be with speakers of southern Chinese dialects. The Mandarin Chinese word for 'but' is *dan-shi* [tan-ṣi] which is sufficiently similar to *tab-sis* [ta-ṣi] for one to suspect that *tab-sis* has its origin in Chinese. There remain, however, two problems. One is the final nasal in the first syllable of the Mandarin Chinese word for 'but', and the other is that the tones of *tab-sis* are not in agreement with the normal tonal correspondence between the original Chinese words and the Chinese loan words in Green Hmong.[6] I cannot offer any solution to the second problem concerning the tonal correspondence. With regard to the first problem concerning the final nasal in the first syllable of the Chinese word, I believe that it is highly likely that the southern Chinese dialect which was in contact with the speech of the ancestors of the Southeast Asian Hmongs did not have the final nasal. The reason behind my assumption is that the final nasal of the word *dan-shi* is dropped in a southern dialect which I speak: the dialect of Shanghai, and in a number of other dialects, the final nasal is dropped but the preceding vowel is nasalized.

(iv) In a folk tale narrated by a Green Hmong elder in the "old" language,[7] the form *tab-sis* is not found. The contrastive coordinator is *huas* instead of *tab-sis*. In two narratives in contemporary Green Hmong, *tab-sis* is the exclusive contrastive coordinator and *huas* is not found.

The introduction of *tab-sis* as the contrastive coordinator displaced *huas*. Instead of disappearing from the language, *huas* continued the diachronic process in the fashion of a push chain, becoming a weak contrastive coordinator before assuming the role of a switch reference coordinate marker. This is a reasonable and smooth diachronic transition for the displaced contrastive coordinator, *huas*, because two conjoined clauses with different subjects unavoidably imply weak contrast. One might suppose that *huas* was all along serving two functions in the language: switch reference coordinator and contrastive coordinator, but that scenario would necessitate the postulation of two highly unlikely events. One such event would be that at some point in time, the following sentence would be ambiguous with two readings: "Tuam is tall but Tub is weak" and "Tuam is tall and Tub is weak".

(26)   Tuam sab huas Tub nkeeg
         Tuam tall   Tub weak

The other unlikely event would be that when *tab-sis* was borrowed from Chinese, it would have to replace *huas* in sentence (26) only for the contrastive reading but not for the switch reference reading. The first event is unlikely because it is rare for a language to use the same morpheme for both the contrastive coordinator and the neutral coordinator. The second event is unlikely because *huas* would have to lose one coordinative function while retaining the other. There is nothing unusual for a grammatical morpheme to lose one function while retaining another, provided the two functions involve different syntactic constructions. Such a diachronic process in syntax is equivalent to the diachronic process in phonology where one phoneme loses one allophone while retaining another. But the diachronic event necessitated by postulating *huas* being both the contrastive coordinator and the switch reference coordinator would involve *huas* performing two functions on the same syntactic construction, namely, conjoined clauses. It would be highly unusual for *huas* to be replaced by *tab-sis* only when it had a reading of contrastive coordinator but not when it had the reading of a switch reference coordinator in sentences such as (26).

We now have reasons to postulate that a new negative contrastive coordinator, *tab-sis*, was borrowed from Chinese, and the borrowing of *tab-sis* initiated a push chain event among three coordinators in Green Hmong: *tab-sis, huas, hab. tab-sis* displaced the original contrastive coordinator, *huas*, and *huas* in turn displaced *hab* in a part of its functional domain, namely, the conjunction of clauses with different subjects. The diachronic pathway that *huas* has undergone may be summarized as: strong contrastive > weak constrastive > neutral connective for clauses with different subjects. Given that *huas* took on its new role only after it was displaced by *tab-sis* for its erstwhile function, we can assume that before the appearance of switch reference, there was no formal distinction between the conjunction of clauses with the same subjects and the conjunction of clauses with different subjects in Hmong. At that point in time, beside the coordinators with the meaning of 'subsequently' and 'consequently', Hmong must have had a neutral coordinator for all clauses whether they had the same subjects or different subjects. It is easy to infer that this neutral coordinator for all clauses was *hab*, since *hab* remains the neutral coordinator with the largest functional domain in contemporary Green Hmong. Section 4 contains evidence showing that *hab* not only conjoins clauses with the same subjects but also conjoins all constituents within a sentence.

6. Conclusion

The exercise in syntactic reconstruction of the switch reference in Green Hmong has several general implications. First, the Green Hmong data demonstrate that switch reference can occur in a prototypal isolating language which is verb-medial. Second, owing to its diachronic origin, the switch reference coordinator in Green Hmong might signal both referential tracking and weak contrast. This possibility raises the question: could switch reference in coordinate structure of other languages have any other function besides referential tracking? For instance, consider sentence (2), a different subject coordinate construction of Maricopa:

(2)   Bonnie-sh   0-ashvar -m   'iima   -k
        Bonnie-subj. 3-sing   -DS 1-dance -aspect
        'Bonnie sang and I danced.' (DS = different subject)

Is it possible to exclude a weak contrastive reading of such a Maricopa sentence?

Third, the diachronic reconstruction of the Green Hmong switch reference shows that a push chain process can occur in syntactic change as well as in phonological change. Examining clusters of interrelated syntactic changes may shed more light on the cause and process of syntactic change than delving into isolated instances of syntactic change. Fourth, while grammaticization is a major vehicle for the emergence of new grammatical devices, reinterpretation of grammatical markers as illustrated by the realignment of the functional domains of *huas* and *hab* may also be an important source of new grammatical devices.[8]

Notes

1. The preparation of this paper was supported in part by NEH grant RT-20756-87. The data in this paper were obtained from five native speakers of Green Hmong: Jeu, Ar Vang, Jim Saylue, Ar Vang's aunt, and Ko Vang. I wish to thank them for their patience and cooperation. I also wish to thank Elizabeth Traugott, Marianne Mithun, Brenda Smith, David Strecker, and Sandra Thompson for their suggestions and criticism as I was working on this paper. Finally, I wish to thank Ar Vang and Don Litton for assisting me in transcribing and translating the folk tales of Green Hmong.
2. Wang (1979) provides a comparative dictionary of Hmong dialects which is a good source for investigating the phonological differences among Hmong dialects in China. The Hmong-Mien language family bears the name of Miao-Yao in China.

3. The data in this paper are presented in the Hmong writing system devised by western missionary linguists after the Second World War. This writing system has been adopted by all people working on Hmong in the United States. In this writing system, tones are represented by syllable-final consonants:

-b   =   high level tone
-0   =   mid level tone
-s   =   low level tone
-v   =   rising tone
-j   =   falling tone
-g   =   breathy tone
-m   =   glottalized tone

Aside from syllables with the glottalized tone which ends in a glottal stop, the only syllable-final consonant in Green Hmong is the velar nasal. It is represented in the writing system by reduplicated vowel, e. g. *aa* = /aŋ/.

4. Sentences such as (7) and (8) where the references of the subjects overlap are probably rare in natural discourse. I did not find any instances of this construction in the discourse data I have. Sentences (7) and (8) were elicited specifically for the purpose of investigating the way Green Hmong speakers cope with switch reference in case of overlapping reference.

5. It should be noted that a consequential event is normally also a subsequent event, and a subsequent event may easily be interpreted as a consequential event. In my experience of working with Green Hmong native speakers, the distinction between *es* and *tes/ces* is often confused in the process of translating between Green Hmong and English. But there is a formal difference between *es* and *tes/ces*. *es* may optionally co-occur with *txhaj* in the conjunction of an antecedent event and a consequential event, while *tes/ces* may not co-occur with *txhaj* in the conjunction of an antecedent event and a subsequent event. For instance, sentence (23) may have *txhaj* added in without a change of meaning:
Tuam tsi   sab es Tub txhaj tsi   sab hab
Tuam NEG tall   Tub   NEG tall also
'Tuam is not tall and consequently, Tub is also not tall.'

6. For loan words from Mandarin Chinese to Green Hmong, the Mandarin falling tone is typically changed into the glottalized tone in Green Hmong, and the Mandarin high level tone typically remains as the high level tone in Green Hmong. In this case, the first syllable of the Green Hmong word *tab-sis* 'but' has a high level tone, but the first syllable of the Mandarin Chinese word *dan-shi* 'but' has a falling tone.

7. The folk tale is entitled "The little buffalo". It is part of an oral tradition of Green Hmong told in formulaic language and passed on from generation to generation.

8. There is an increasing body of literature demonstrating the reinterpretation of grammatical markers as a course of syntactic change in many languages. I will not cite them here.

References

Benedict, Paul K.
  1975   *Austro-Thai language and culture with a glossary of roots.* (New Haven: Human Relations Area Files Press).
Comrie, Bernard
  1983   "Switch-reference in Huichol: a typological study", in: Haiman and Munro (eds.), 17−38.

Diffloth, Gerard
1985   "What happened to Austric?", paper presented at the 18th International Conference on Sino-Tibetan Languages and Linguistics, Bangkok.
Gordon, Lynn
1983   "Switch-reference, clause order, and interclausal relationships in Maricopa", in: Haiman and Munro (eds.), 83–105.
Haiman, John and Pamela Munro
1983   Switch reference and universal grammar (= Typological Studies in Language 2). (Amsterdam: Benjamins).
Haudricourt, André
1954   "Introduction à la phonologie historique des langues miao-yao", Bulletin de l'Ecole Francaise d'Extrême-Orient 44: 555–574.
Li, Yung-sui, Ch'en K'o-chung, and Ch'en Ch'i-kuang
1959   "Some problems concerning initials and tones in the Miao language", *Yuyan Yanjiu* 4: 65–80.
Lynch, John
1983   "Switch-reference in Lenakel", in Haiman and Munro (eds.), 209–222.
Ratliff, Martha
1986   *The morphological function of tone in White Hmong.* Ph. D. dissertation, Department of Linguistics, University of Chicago.
Wang, Fushi
1979   *Comparison of initials and finals of Miao dialects.* (Beijing: Central Nationality Institute).
1986   "A preliminary investigation of the genetic affiliation of the Miao-Yao languages", paper presented at the International Symposium on the Minority Nationalities of China, Santa Barbara, California, January 27–29, 1986.

Invisible-hand processes and the universal laws of language change

Helmut Lüdtke

Phenomenological considerations

The notion of language *change* ought to be kept distinct from that of shift, switching or conflict between different norms current among a population. The illustrative studies carried out by Labov (1965: 102−110) on the pronunciation of vowels in New York City are good examples of the latter (i. e. switching), though not for language change proper, since they will not help us explain long-term events such as the phenomena that lead from Latin to modern Romance dialects and languages.

We should furthermore distinguish between external interference (such as loan, syntactic or semantic calque etc.), internal interference (e. g. spelling pronunciation; banning or recommendation of words or constructions), and the "normal course", i. e. the set of language-changing events that would happen anyway, even if the linguistic community in question were left in isolation. The latter phenomena are the *natural outcome of normal speech activity*, as stated by Paul (1920: 32) followed by Hall (1962: 50) and Coseriu (1980: 135).

Our linguistic behaviour is goal-directed, i. e. governed by principles or "maxims" (see Keller 1982: 13, 15, 21 − 26; 1984: 67 − 72, 76 − 78) that guarantee successful performance. This behaviour, however, has *unintended side effects* (Lüdtke 1980: 8 − 14; 1986: 5 − 7) comparable to similar phenomena in other fields of human activity. They are neither "natural" in the sense of "independent of human action" (such as a mountain range or an earthquake) nor due to man's intent and purpose (like a game or a cathedral); they constitute a *third set* of phenomena which is metaphorically called "invisible-hand processes": not planned or intended as such, but nevertheless due to man's activity; more specifically, to the involuntarily combined effect of a great number of single individual acts.

It should be clear that language change — as far as it consists of invisible-hand processes — happens continually and inevitably. It has neither to be actuated nor can it be resisted.

Variation

Language change is a subset of variation. A prerequisite of variation is redundancy in performance (cf. Lüdtke 1980: 11—13; 1986: 17—21). While distinguishing diatopic, diachronic, diastratic, idiolectal variation, we easily forget the widest of all variations, viz. that which occurs within a speaker's performance. To give an anecdotic example: when a group of Germans are eagerly trying to find a lost object, one of them may suddenly exclaim: "/çaps/" and be immediately understood, because /çaps/ is quite normal slur from (*ich habe es*) /ʔIç haːbə ʔɛs/. Given the proper circumstances, phonic shrinkage from four syllables to one is quite acceptable and adequate to the purpose (for a fuller treatment as far as German is concerned, see Kohler 1977: 207—230; generally, Lüdtke 1980: 185—195; 1986: 17—19).

Quantity vs. quality

In traditional diachronic (allegedly "historical") linguistics there is a certain propensity for qualitative statements: some item X "becomes Y" or "is replaced by Y". Nothing seems to be wrong if we find that in Late Antiquity Lat. *urbs* was replaced by *civitas*, *vir* by *homo*, and that in Old French syllable-final *-l* was vocalized to *-u̯* (*multum* > *mout*). And yet, is "otherness" the appropriate label for the processes in question? For superficial understanding, for comparison, for classification — yes; not so, however, if we earnestly endeavour to explain language change events. There is a quantitative side to the above examples. While *homo*, *hominem* and *civitas*, *civitatem* are "longer" than *vir*, *virum* and, respectively, *urbs*, *urbem* (which means that they require more time and effort to pronounce) — a semi-vowel or glide after a vowel needs less articulatory effort than a liquid. The above processes are thus at the same time of both qualitative and quantitative nature.

This finding, so often overlooked, has important consequences. While man's qualitative decisions depend on his/her free choice (it does not matter whether free will is regarded as reality or as "mere" consciousness) and are, therefore, haphazard or random, statistically speaking — these same decisions, if taken on the same issue, by a huge mass of people, become subject to calculation. Let us take an example from what happens at the polls in the Federal Republic of Germany. After all the offices have closed at 6 p. m., in less than half an hour, on a basis of only 1% of the votes having been counted, the final result is predicted with no more than 1% uncertainty. This is clear evidence for the contention that human behaviour can be calculated (and hence predicted, in spite of undeniable free will!), provided it can be made into, and processed as, a statistical sample. This should be true for linguistic behaviour, too. It seems worthwhile, then, to extract the quantitative content from language change phenomena.

Irreversibility

Empirical studies of both present speech and long-term language change such as that from Latin to Romance or from Classical to modern dialectal Arabic or Maltese reveal the existence of three obviously universal quantitative processes that nearly always follow a given direction (cf. Lüdtke 1985: 358 – 362), viz.: items (= meaningful elements) growing shorter and shorter, as regards their phonic representation (or exponence); longer items replacing shorter ones, and optionally added items becoming necessary; syntactically adjacent items getting merged or fused. This triple of processes may be represented by the schema in Figure 1.

Although each of these processes (which belong to the "invisible-hand" set) can be separately derived from man's normal linguistic behaviour, they nevertheless compensate each other as to the impact they will exert upon any language; the result of which is *homeorhesis* (cf. Lüdtke 1980: 15; 1986: 31).

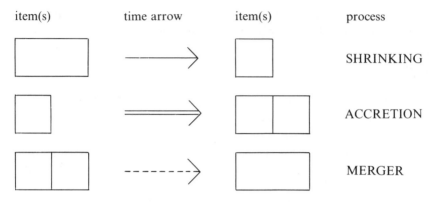

Figure 1. Quantitative processes in language change

Process vs. result

To describe change in a given language over a stretch of time as a set of events is a rather sketchy and superficial procedure. On the one hand, speech is a continuum, and so is change in speech; it is, therefore, highly artificial to mark the beginning or the end of a process, i. e. to establish what is "*a* change". On the other hand, it is crucial to distinguish between the following classes of facts: features we can observe in speech performance (e. g. instances of slur and of prolixity), changes happening to single linguistic items (due to the combined effects of millions of individual speech acts), and such overall results as — in the course of centuries or millennia — alter the state of a language in a significant way.

Processes may be irreversible, like the triple indicated above; their bearing on a given language state, however, need not be irreversible, speaking in quantitative terms. Colloquial French *ça* 'that' not only conveys the same meaning as Latin *hoc* but is also its descendant, in a way, i. e. if we take descendance as an instance of the triple of irreversible processes schematized above: through semantactic accretion *hoc* became *ecce-hoc*, and *ce* (which in the meantime had evolved, through phonic shrinkage, from *ecce-hoc*) later became *cela*, which in turn shrank to *ça*; given the appropriate situation, a Frenchman might point to an object saying: "*ça, là-bas!*" So there is no end to the story of language change.

Etymologically speaking, French *ça* has as its ancestor *ecce-hoc-illac*, a monster, from a Latin point of view. In the minds of French speakers, of course, *ça* is an unanalysed item. In this sense, *ça* and *hoc* are not identical (as French *terre* 'land' and Lat. *terra* are); we may say that there has been some (qualitative) change. Quantitatively speaking, however, from *hoc* to *ça*, there has been no appreciable change in phonic size (or articulatory effort). That is what is meant by homeorhesis.

Change vs. innovation

This is another important distinction. There is so much room for creativity in languages that innovations abound; many of them are *hápaks legómena*, nonce expressions. Others may remain for a while until they disappear. Some may enter into serious competition with established rivals and eventually oust them. We should reserve the term "change" for those phenomena which consist in the *abolition* of something that had been current in a language; such change is much rarer, indeed, than the creation of something new. And, last but not least, lost stages are irretrievable.

Change vs. necessity

Change in the sense of abolition is a chance event. Full pronunciation of German *'-en* as /ən/ in words like *kommen singen* may be expected to give way — sooner or later — to its rival /kɔm:/ /zɪŋ:/ which already is by far more frequent. What we cannot predict is when this change will take place, although — on the other hand — the direction of change is practically certain: /kɔm:/ /zɪŋ:/ will not be abandoned in favour of /kɔmən/ /zɪŋən/; why, indeed, should people refrain from slurring?

If chance events follow a pre-established course, chance turns into necessity (Monod's principle, cf. Lüdtke 1980: 13; 1986: 23). The presence of chance accounts for the fact that languages change at varying rates.

References

Coseriu, Eugenio
1980   "Vom Primat der Geschichte", *Sprachwissenschaft* 5: 125—145.
Hall, Robert, A., Jr.
1962   "Il perché del mutamento linguistico", *Ricerche linguistiche* V: 49—54.
Keller, Rudi
1982   "Zur Theorie sprachlichen Wandels", *Zeitschrift für germanistische Linguistik* 10/1: 1—27.
1984   "Bemerkungen zur Theorie des sprachlichen Wandels", *Zeitschrift für germanistische Linguistik* 12/1: 63—81.
Kohler, Klaus
1977   *Einführung in die Phonetik des Deutschen.* (Grundlagen der Germanistik 20) (Berlin: Schmidt).
Labov, William
1965   "On the mechanism of linguistic change", *Monograph Series on Languages and Linguistics* (Georgetown University, Washington) 18: 91—114.
Lüdtke, Helmut
1980   "Sprachwandel als universales Phänomen" and "Auf dem Weg zu einer Theorie des Sprachwandels", in: *Kommunikationstheoretische Grundlagen des Sprachwandels*, edited by H. Lüdtke (Grundlagen der Kommunikation) (Berlin: de Gruyter), 1—19, 182—252.
1985   "Diachronic irreversibility in word-formation and semantics", in: *Historical semantics/Historical word-formation*, edited by Jacek Fisiak, 355—366 (Berlin: Mouton de Gruyter).
1986   "Esquisse d'une théorie du changement langagier", *La Linguistique* 22/1: 3—46.
Paul, Hermann
1920   *Prinzipien der Sprachgeschichte*[5] [Reprint Tübingen 1966] (Halle: Niemeyer).

On the causes of accelerated linguistic change in the Pacific area

Peter Mühlhäusler

> The fundamental problem for linguistic theory is to understand (explain and predict) how linguistic structures come into being and change into new (sub) systems — and thereby to learn what the true nature of language is.
>
> (Bailey 1982: 25)

1. Introduction

Accelerated linguistic change has been reported in many parts of the Pacific area, both in the more distant past, where it is typically associated with taboo (cf. Dyen 1963), and more recently, as a consequence of modernization (cf. Mühlhäusler 1987). Regarding the latter period, reports of dramatic structural changes exist for the entire area from the Pacific rim countries of South-East Asia and Australia to the coast of the Americas, though the changes appear to be particularly striking in highly multilingual areas such as Australia and Melanesia.

As I have reviewed some existing findings in Mühlhäusler 1987 and since my brief for this paper is to discuss the causes rather than the consequences of language change, I shall not go into linguistic detail here. Instead, I would like to suggest the following very general characterization of the changes that seem to have affected the languages of the area following contacts with Europeans from the 18th century onward. Very similar structural consequences have been reported for smaller languages which have come under the influence of larger non-European languages, such as the minority languages of Thailand (see Bradley 1981, 1987) or East Timor (Carey 1986).

Thus, the salient changes include:

i) Rapid loss of inflectional and derivational morphology, a particularly striking feature being the loss of noun class marking. Polysynthetic languages appear to be particularly susceptible to this process (e. g. Tiwi as described in Lee 1983);
ii) A general narrowing of the stylistic range of languages manifested, for instance, in the loss of registers, special languages, and styles;
iii) A gradual westernization of semantics, even in core areas such as the kinship and metaphorical systems;
iv) Phonological convergence with prestige languages;
v) Overall reduction in derivational complexity.

Thus we can observe the dual trends of impoverishment (both referential and stylistic) and lexicalization (replacing previous greater reliance on regularities of grammar). The resulting new systems are more exocentric, easier to acquire for outsiders, and often similar to the koinés and pidgins spoken around them. This, however, does not render them socially any more viable than earlier, more complex systems. Progress in understanding the rapid changes in the languages of the area has been hampered by a number of factors, not least the very limited monetary and manpower resources available for their study. Once a grammar and lexicon had been compiled for one of the many thousands of languages of the area it was not seen as a priority to carry out linguistic description at a later date. For many languages, longitudinal evidence thus remains very sketchy. Moreover, and in spite of some early warning voices, most changes remained unnoticed almost to the point of the structural collapse of some languages. A widely held view was that the languages of the area were alive and well. This optimistic and simplistic view is summed up in the following quotation:

> Where a population remains stable, indigenous languages will survive and even flourish under considerable adverse pressure; where a population is transferred to a new terrain, languages will wither even in the face of positive efforts to keep them alive (Bickerton 1977: 57).

Laycock (1979: 81−97) provides a discussion of traditional multilingualism in New Guinea which appears to bear out Bickerton's view. However, not many years later we find some dramatic linguistic changes in the same area which cannot be explained by physical mobility or displacement.

In my view, the main obstacle to obtaining explanatorily more powerful models of language change in the Pacific has been that European and European-trained linguists have approached the problem through unsuitable metaphors. The reification metaphor portrays languages as entities, the container metaphor provides places in time for them. Common to all of these visions is that languages are seen to be more or less self-contained and amenable to study in isolation from other languages and other factors.

However, the Pacific is not a sea speckled with small isolated islands, each of them with its own small language; nor are the larger land areas of this part of the world (such as Australia or New Guinea) covered in geographically neatly separated linguistic entities. Rather (to borrow a metaphor from Australian Aborigines), it is like a field of mushrooms where the visible individual mushrooms above ground are linked by a complex network of underground roots. Changes in the ecology cannot be explained by studying the growth and decay of individual mushrooms but rather by paying attention to the complex underground life-lines and the environmental factors maintaining them. In a similar fashion, an understanding of the changes that have occurred in the languages of the Pacific region is best achieved not by generalizing from case studies of individual instances of accelerated change or death but by studying panregional or even global developments. Thus, my paper is inspired by the following assumptions:

i) The linguistic and sociolinguistic fate of individual languages depends on the ecological changes in a wider area.
ii) The best way to reveal causes of change is to work one's way down (rather than up, as has been customary) the following hierarchy of units of different rank: language area − repertoire of communication communities − languages − varieties of languages.
iii) The parameters defining a language area as well as units of lower rank comprise both linguistic and extralinguistic factors.

It should be clear by now that the task that I have set myself is one that cannot be performed satisfactorily within the confines of a short paper. Among the many obstacles is the absence of information on language ecology and change in many parts of the area, the lack of a sociolinguistic theory and the inaccessibility of some of the information.

However, it may be profitable to look at the language situation in the Pacific and changes within it from the point of view of an approach that makes available a large number of etic labels, thus forcing the observer to consider a multitude of factors, only some of which will turn out to be emically relevant in the ultimate analysis. The approach I refer to is that of Hymes, i. e. the ethnography of communication. My hope is that at least some of the many parameters considered by ethnographers of communication will turn out to be causally related to structural changes and to one another.

2. The Pacific as a communication area

Before the arrival of Europeans in the area, numerous trade and linguistic links existed between different groups of inhabitants of the Pacific area. Much of this trade was conditioned by the uneven distribution of economic commodities. Thus, salt, pottery, sago, or meat were found in some parts of New Guinea and absent in others, leading to regular intergroup communication over both shorter and longer distances. Many groups were capable of long-distance travel, enabling contacts such as those between Polynesia and South America or Micronesia and Melanesia among others. The linguistic consequences of such contacts, namely trade languages, pidgins, bilingualism, and other solutions are the current concern of the "Atlas of Languages for Intercultural Communication in the Pacific Area" (Mühlhäusler 1987 b, c). Leaving aside the details, intergroup communication of many types was firmly established. What characterizes most instances examined so far is that the linguistic solutions to intercultural communication tended to be compatible with the prevailing linguistic egalitarianism and diversity of the area. It is not possible to speak of superstrate languages in the majority of interface languages; nor do we find many large vernaculars in the area.

A second important aspect of the linguistic situation in the Pacific area is the gradient and transitional character of the vernaculars of the area. Thus, dialect and language chains cover large areas, and small differences between languages are felt to be sufficient for the purposes of social indexicality; indeed linguistic and social identity very often do not coincide.

In an important paper on the historical linguistics of Melanesia, Grace (1981) illustrates the special character of the languages with the example of New Caledonia. His research was triggered by his failure to reconstruct an immediate proto-language for two languages of New Caledonia, as the application of the usual method of cognate identification and establishment of regular sound correspondences would have forced him to set up a proto-language with 36 consonant and 28 vowel phonemes, even if he eliminated all correspondences that occurred less than 10 times in his sample. Applying the same method to a larger set of languages, for example in the reconstruction of Proto-New Caledonian, would have resulted in even less plausible reconstructions and would have left many ambiguities and inconsistencies.

Grace argues that part of the problem lies with "our traditional approach to linguistic diachrony (which) has given a central position to the individual language" (261) whereas in Melanesia, at least, we are dealing with a situation where "each individual conceives of the immediate linguistic reality in terms of pools of linguistic resources" (263), such that the difference between translation and synonymy becomes blurred. Individuals have a number of words for concepts, some of them felt to be their own, others seldom used and felt to belong to others, though there are numerous reports of "individuals being unable to say which words properly belong to their language and which do not" (266). Speakers thus operate in more than one tradition at the same time, which, in turn, leads to large-scale dialect-level borrowing and complication of sound correspondences. One is reminded of Boretzki's general remarks on sound change in exotic languages (Boretzki 1984) which provide some interesting suggestions as to factors causing Melanesian languages to have an 'aberrant' history.

Grace concludes that data such as those just mentioned call for considerable reorientation in historical linguistics. The tentative model he alludes to suggests "that we might attempt to develop a second, complementary, model of linguistic diachrony – one in which a community of languages is seen as the entity undergoing change" (266). Finally, he suggests that, in the long run, we should be looking for a new metaphor – one which does "not require us to see diachrony in terms of internal changes in structured entities which maintain their identity over time" to which he adds "but that may take time" (267).

Such a view coincides with my own that we should move from larger units to languages and sublanguages and that consequently the question as to what causes languages to change is not a very felicitous one. It is like asking "why do fir trees die?" when almost the entire natural environment is under threat. Thus, as well as asking "how are patterns of intercultural communication changing?" we shall direct our attention to changes in the repertoire of groups of speakers.

3. Components of language use and language

Malcolm (1982) has made one of the few large-scale attempts to present an inventory of components of speech events for a large area, Aboriginal Australia, using Hymes' model as an etic grid for listing components identified by numerous researchers in the area. Although I would very much like to extend his collection of data to the entire Pacific area, this would clearly be beyond the aims of this paper. All I can do here is to isolate such components that would seem to be particularly relevant to the question of language change. These will relate to both the *situation* (about which Malcolm has very little to say) and the rank of *event*.

My general view is that it is the advent of European colonialism that brought about the most dramatic, even catastrophic, changes in the components of traditional speech situations and events and I shall therefore be particularly concerned with the effects of Westernization and modernization.

3.1 Changes in situation

By situation, in its broadest sense we understand the material and human setting of communication. In both respects, the Pacific has been drastically changed. I can only give a very brief summary of the kind of changes portrayed by Moorehead (1966), Clerk (1984), and Crosby (1986):

i) The introduction of new plants, animals, and diseases caused a very rapid change in the physical world. The disappearance of indigenous flora and fauna was accelerated by indiscriminate exploitation of natural resources by consecutive groups of whalers, sandalwood collectors, beche-de-mer fishers, and others. In areas such as Australia, land that had previously been used for indigenous crops (e. g. yam plantations in Western Australia) was seized by the colonial agriculturalists. In other areas, tropical plantations were established, thus putting an end to pre-existing 'coral gardens and their magic'.

ii) Introduced human diseases, drink, and drugs rapidly decimated the population of most islands. The loss of life was accelerated by genocide, deportation, and labour recruiting, which led to the total destruction of many traditional societies.

iii) European colonization promoted the influx of large groups of outsiders which either replaced (as in Australia) or severely affected the previous indigenous population (as in Fiji or New Caledonia).

iv) The pre-existing material culture was replaced rapidly by a heavily westernized culture, iron tools replacing stone and bone tools, firearms, traditional weapons, and European forms of transport replacing indigenous ones. The Westernization of the material culture has accelerated greatly in recent years and has led to the disappearance or virtual disappearance of pre-existing forms in many areas.

v) Existing communication networks were destroyed by a) the imposition of arbitrary colonial boundaries and b) the reorientation of the communication from a horizontal (inter-indigenous) to a vertical (master-dominated group) process, c) bringing groups into contact that had not communicated previously.

vi) Much of the spiritual culture was destroyed (deliberately or accidentally) by intensive missionization, education programmes, and other forms of colonial social control. In the process, many domains of traditional discourse simply disappeared.

vii) An aspect which is often overlooked is that the social and residential groups encountered today are not a continuation of pre-contact patterns in many cases. In the area of New Guinea, for instance, successive governments have discouraged semi-nomadic groups and groups living in small hamlets and vigorously promoted larger villages in order to facilitate the administrative process. Very much the same goes for residence groups in Australia and elsewhere. Consequently, the notion of speech community or communication community has a very different meaning today from that which it had 200 years ago.

viii) In the more recent past, the new factors of overpopulation and urbanization have led to renewed large-scale regional mobility and the further erosion of traditional forms of settlement.

It would be easy to continue listing such changes. The outcome, as regards our specific question, is a cataclysmic change in the situational context of language in many (and in the meanwhile, most) parts of the area.

ix) The formerly egalitarian status of the languages of the region was changed to a hierarchical one with the metropolitan expatriate languages occupying top position, followed by a smaller number of languages which were lucky enough to be singled out for mission and government purposes, followed by the pidgins derived from the metropolitan languages, with a large number of local languages and language varieties at the bottom of the hierarchy. Status changes in areas with changing colonial administrations complicate the picture, as pointed out by Solenberger (1962) for Micronesia. Note that the concept of 'a language' is brought into existence by this process, as are those of 'minority language' and 'dialect'. "Structured entities which maintain their identity over time" (Grace) begin to exist with the setting up of administrative and mission centres and the description of the variety of speech used there.

x) The usefulness of many local languages to their speakers is greatly reduced as former communication partners become inaccessible. Small local trade languages, for instance, give way to large cross-regional pidgins that give access to imported Western goods. The structural dependency of the pidgins on outside languages mirrors the economic dependency of their users on outside providers.

xi) The indexical function of the numerous small languages of the area as markers of local group membership becomes attenuated as geographic mobility, life in non-traditional settlements and marriages outside the traditional exchange patterns become common. Very often, being a speaker of a small local language carries negative indexicality, marking users as underdeveloped, country-bumpkins.

xii) Pre-existing multilingualism is changed in character. Instead of being proficient in several local languages and trade languages, bilingualism today typically involves the local vernacular, a metropolitan language (English, French, Thai, Bahasa Indonesia) and, sometimes, a Pidgin derived from the metropolitan language.

Thus, the first part of my argument on the causes of language change in the Pacific area is that, over the last 200 years, the speech situation in which these languages and their speakers are embedded has changed very dramatically; speakers now find themselves in a radically changed physical and cultural environment and have to adapt their linguistic resources to numerous new requirements. In terms of our mushroom metaphor, the network that has linked the individual mushrooms has been disrupted in places, altered in others and destroyed in yet others. This process has led to an acceleration in the rate of language disappearance. Many languages that seemed viable only a decade ago are now on the verge of extinction. The number of languages unaffected by the situational changes (still several hundred 25 years ago) is now probably only a handful.

3.2 Changes in speech events

It stands to reason that the situational changes have had similar dramatic consequences for the linguistic events that can occur in the languages of the region. Of the many events provided for in Hymes' model and in the somewhat smaller collection of events I have presented for the Pacific, I shall single out only a few components.

3.2.1 Message form

This category is concerned with the means of expression in a community for the performance of speech events such as greetings, addressing, thanking, conveying news, joking and so forth. It should first be noted that different cultures attach different values to such forms (verbal means for thanking may be highly developed in one culture and absent in another) and that, furthermore, situational factors govern some aspects of this fact. One of the most striking aspects of many traditional language communities is the relative lack of new information (i. e. information that is not available or known to every member of a community). With limited communication with the outside world and with closed (homodynamic) communication networks within small self-contained communities, the function of language which in modern Western linguistics is taken to be the primary one, the cognitive or informative one, plays a relatively subordinate role. This fact was initially commented on by Malinowski (1937) and, more recently, beautifully illustrated for Malagasy by Keenan and Keenan (1971).

The creation of new communication networks with the outside, the introduction of new media, and the process of religious and educational/ political conversion have greatly enhanced the role of the cognitive function of language and the need for message forms appropriate for it.

Table 1. Cardinal number sets in languages of Micronesia

number	humans	taro
1 tang	tang	tëluóng
2 orúng	tërúng	ëruóng
3 odei	tëdei	ëdeiuóng
4 oáng	tëoáng	ëuáiuóng
5 oím	tëím	ëimuóng
6 malóng	tëlólom	a lolom uóng
7 uíd	tëuid	ëuíd uóng
8 iái	tëái	ëáiuóng
9 ítiu	tëtíu	ëtiuuóng
10 mágod	tërúiug	ëtrúiug

fish	coconuts	trees, leaves
	money, stones	boards
tang	geimóng	tegetóng
gërúng	tëblóng	gëregetóng
gëdei	kedei	gëdeiegetóng
gëoáng	klaoáng	gëodiegetóng
gëim	kleím	gëimegetóng
gëlólom	klólom	gelólomegetóng
gëuíd	kleuíd	
gëái	kleai	
gëtíu	kltíu	
telbúdok	tágar	

Let us briefly consider some other forms. Several observers have remarked on the absence of verbal forms for thanking (which, of course, is not to be confused with the absence of gratitude) and on European efforts to introduce local equivalents to English 'thank you'.

Naming and calling someone by their name in the languages of the Pacific (for the language of Manus see Nevermann 1934: 305 ff.) used to be associated with giving power and/or having power over the named person. Both the practice of missionaries to give people Christian names (even adults after baptism) and that of governments to take down the names for census purposes drastically altered existing practices of naming. Most people in the area now have — like their SAE (Standard Average European) model — a Christian name and a surname rather than a name derived from the often extremely complex traditional naming practices (as described for instance by Wassmann 1982). Counting, again, is an area where there are numerous practices that are radically different from SAE ones. The most comprehensive general discussion is Laycock (1975) who analyses a large number of non-decimal counting and tallying systems in Melanesia. With the latter, parts of the body are used as reference points such that, for larger numbers, more than one person is needed for the counting process. Even those languages employing a decimal system may differ from European counting practices. An interesting example is provided by some of the languages of Micronesia, where different cardinal number sets are chosen for counting different entities, as in the following Palauan data adapted from Kraemer (1919: 331): (see Table 1).

Ray (1907: 86) reports that the Miriam speakers in the Torres Straits had adopted the decimal system and the process has subsequently accelerated. It will soon have reached completion with schooling becoming increasingly common, to the exclusion of other systems.

Closely related to counting are the processes by which the year is subdivided into smaller sections. In most instances the solar calendar of SAE speakers has replaced indigenous methods. An example is that of Micronesian Kusaiean (Lee 1975: 393)

> It is also true that many words become obsolete. In Kusaiean there are the following words which refer to different phases of the moon:

maspang 'full moon'	luhlti
mesalem	kowola met
alwat	kowola tyok
mesohn	sropahsr ahpnak
mesait	sropahsr
	srohsluhn
me saul	suhan kusahf
lohtlohtoh	kusahf suhnak
sriafong	srohmpahr
arfohkoh	arpi
seken par	li 'moonless night'
sohfsen	sripuhp
aohlwen	linguli
fahkfong	lingalang
mesr '14th phrase	
el '15th phrase	

Except for the four words meaning 'full moon', '14th phrase', '15th phrase', and 'moonless night', most Kusaiean speakers cannot associate the words with particular phases of the moon. Before the solar calendar was introduced to Kusaiean culture, the lunar calendar must have been closely related to Kusaiean culture, especially as it related to fishing. But since the introduction of the solar calendar, the lunar calendar was less frequently used. As a result, some of the words are becoming obsolete.

Finally, the message form of 'joke' was widely absent in the Pacific area in 'prehistoric' times, though the culture was rich in humour and funny tales. However, jokes of a Western type together with cartoons and comic strips are becoming widespread among the indigenous speakers of the area.

3.2.2 Message content

The principal effect of contacts between the Pacific area and Europeans is a large-scale change in the range of topics featuring in conversations. On the one hand, numerous new topics have been added to the traditional inventory. Malcolm (1982), for instance, reports motorcars, pushbikes and motorbikes, and the future as topics in addition to old established ones such as witch doctors, spirits of deceased persons, strife in camp, and hunting. With the spread of a cash economy, money, betting, and gambling have also become important topics. With increasing urbanization some of the traditional topics have declined, with traditional myths and oral history dying out at an ever faster rate. Perhaps even more drastic than the changes in the inventory of message content are changes in the patterns of access to and use of it. In many traditional societies knowledge of and talk about topics were restricted to subgroups according to sex, age, or other social parameters. Thus, talk about menstruation, birth, and pregnancy in many Aboriginal societies tended to be reserved for women. With governments promoting birth control programmes, missionaries instructing males about the birth of Jesus, and, most recently, government sponsored campaigns against sexually transmitted diseases those topics are now open to men as well.

3.2.3 Setting

The component of setting is concerned with time, place, and physical circumstances of speech events. Regarding the first factor, one can observe a widespread changeover from traditional concepts of time and use of time to a European style, characterized by instruments for measuring time and school and work routines prescribing, for example, when it is appropriate to talk and when it is not. The general effect of such routines has been to silence numerous groups and individuals. It is interesting to note, for instance, that the introduction of pastoralism in the 'Neo-Europes' of the Pacific (Australia and New Zealand) created the need to employ indigenous shepherds, boundary riders and station hands who very often were on their own for prolonged stretches of time. The introduction of electricity, as in Europe, had a very considerable influence on the time available for communicative events for which light was required.

Moving on to place, we find that, generally speaking, most speech events in pre-contact days took place in the open, whereas the fast conversion of many areas into built-up zones, the introduction of prisons, dormitories, church buildings, libraries, schools, offices, and hotels has changed this, particularly among urban inhabitants. It would seem that one consequence has been the increase in private and semi-private conversation and the decrease in public discussion. Changes have also taken place in the proxemics of interaction. (For remarks on these among Australian Aborigines see Malcolm 1982: 63.)

Surprisingly little is known about this aspect in traditional societies and the changes it underwent after contact. However, we have numerous anecdotes of Europeans preventing indigenes getting close to them, touching them or sitting at the same level. We also have reports of the gradual replacement of various forms of greeting involving touching the genitals or other (Western) taboo areas by either handshaking or simply verbal greetings.

There are many reports of a close association between traditional and non-traditional settings on the one hand and use of a traditional or imported language on the other. Thus, the metropolitan languages in many areas were rarely spoken outside the school precinct and certain mission lingue franche were restricted to mission stations and church buildings. As the setting of speech events is becoming more and more westernized, the physical context appropriate to the use of traditional languages is shrinking.

3.2.4 Scene

By scene we understand the psychological context of speech events, such as the human context (e.g. are children and adults part of the same scene?), or degree of formality, comfort, or discomfort. Also of great importance is the question of whether indigenes and expatriates are regarded as being factually or potentially members of the same scene or not. Thus, one can expect quite diverse linguistic consequences from the Dutch policy up to about 1860 of preventing indigenes from learning and using Dutch, French assimilation policies in New Caledonia or Tahiti, and a sequence of different policies ranging from separation to assimilation with regard to Australian Aborigines. As regards the place of children, European presence has in many instances led to a separation of age groups. Thus, boarding schools, mission reserves, special centres for children of the indigenous workforce and so on have left few of the pre-existing traditional patterns of language transmission between the generations intact (cf. Hockett 1950). Again, fathers and members of secret men's clubs who acted as primary linguistic socializers for the 'high' varieties of speech in traditional societies lost their role as men were absorbed in the workforce, recruited to workplaces far away, or stripped of their authority in favour of government-appointed officials. The setting up of larger settlements made it possible for larger viable groups of children to become involved in their own linguistic socialization. To what extent adult norms can disappear in the process is illustrated by Schmidt (1985).

As long as most indigenes found themselves at the bottom of the colonial hierarchy, many aspects of traditional scenes were not under direct threat. However, with increasing social mobility, new differences between groups are created, changes in status initiated, and new definitions of formality and deference needed. Victims in such circumstances are the very widely distributed respect languages of the area. Whereas in some instances (e. g. Japan) the old honorific system has been adapted successfully to changed social circumstances, in most other areas surveyed respect language is either lost or restricted to traditional contexts. Thus, Javanese faced with new social distinctions will adopt the neutral language of Bahasa Indonesia rather than mapping former distinctions onto the new situation.

3.2.5 Sender

By sender we mean the actual source of information which may but need not be identical with the addresser. Thus, ambassadors speak on behalf of their governments, solicitors on behalf of their clients and so on. A brief survey of the literature of the area suggests a number of dramatic changes in the wake of European penetration. First and foremost, a number of new distant senders are added including the Christian god, the Queen, the Kaiser, the French Emperor, and the American government, followed by directors of trading companies, big bosses, and many other senders far away in the metropolis. They all write letters and send messages through their various representatives in the Pacific area. At the same time, the role of at least some local senders decreases; traditional chiefs, spirits, gods, and ancestors and the special forms of speech they may have employed (cf. Sankoff 1976) diminish in importance. The colonial governments also institute new rules for who can speak for a group, often bypassing traditional solutions. The role of intermediaries between members of different groups is changed by both the development of pidgin languages and the mixing of members from many different backgrounds on ships, plantations, and in camps.

3.2.6 Addresser

Addressers are speakers who communicate their own message. Neither in traditional nor in Western societies is it possible to address whoever one likes, though the restrictions in different societies can vary greatly.

A widespread feature among the languages of the area is ownership of words and expressions, i. e. the utterance (but not understanding) of forms is restricted to members of a particular social group. The rules regulating this phenomenon depend on the viability of those groups and with a rapid breakdown in social structures the rules of linguistic use have also disappeared.

In many documented instances, even such basic rights as the right of the parents to address their children were interfered with by the colonizing powers, principally by a number of mission organizations who took children away from their parents to educate them in Christian doctrine. As late as 1973 I participated in a church service in New Guinea where the converted members of church were warned against talking to their non-converted relatives. Some of the political boundaries established in the Pacific (e. g. that between the western and eastern halves of New Guinea) also restricted the right of individuals to address former addressees.

Many traditional societies were characterized by taboo practices which prevented direct talk between groups and subgroups such as different kinds of relations. Missionization and government regulations have removed many of these previous restrictions.

As with other components, there have been significant changes in the regularities governing addressers and consequently in the flow and transmission of linguistic material.

3.2.7 Hearers and addressees

The distinction between hearer and addressee parallels that between speaker and addresser. One particularly important effect of European colonization is the establishment of a hierarchical society with numerous mediaries between the source and destination of a message. Thus, the appointment of government translators is an important stage in the spread of both the message and the code of the external seat of power, often by complex chains of translation, such as those discussed by Voorhoeve (1979).

Equally important has been the introduction of mass media such as radio (which is now universal in the area) and television (which is becoming so), by means of which the number of hearers as well as addressees has multiplied. One effect has been the rapid decrease in restricted information, i. e. information accessible only to a certain class of hearers or addressees. Michaels (1986: 153) illustrates some of the potential consequences of this with the following scenario, following the introduction of Aboriginal television in Central Australia:

> This report has presented alarming evidence in relation to this question. For example, the probability of national broadcast of Aboriginal material without Aboriginal control by agencies such as the ABC, assures disaster for the Aboriginal tradition. The single most certain act of culturecide that I could imagine would be the public airing of a secret ceremony. If the ABC's archives (or the Institute's) were transmitted on AUSSAT, it seems likely that no tribal elder would be left standing within a week. This scenario seems entirely plausible, encouraged by an Aboriginal Affairs media policy which will "embed" Aborigines in the mass media in ways that are intended to make them more attractive to Europeans, rather than to assure their own cultural survival. "We use media to destroy cultures, but first we use media to create a false record of what we are about to destroy."

The invasion of previously taboo areas is not restricted to the media, however. The right not to reply or respond, a widespread feature in the languages of the area, is being diminished by the growing power of government agencies that have the right to expect a reply or justification.

The range of addressees appears to have shifted gradually from the traditional one which may have included animals, objects, spirits, or natural forces to that prevailing in European societies, a process which is being accelerated by the schooling through metropolitan languages, as shown in detail by Milner (1984). As a result, many special forms of speech and the belief that "a great deal of the vocabulary of magic, its grammar and its prosody ... must be cast in another mould, because it is derived from other sources and produces different effects from ordinary speech" (Malinowski 1925: 218) are beginning to give way.

3.2.8 Purposes

Speech events can have a number of purposes. It has already been said that the transmission of new information is one which was not very important in many traditional societies of the area. Apart from the absence of new information, a second reason for this lies in differences between culture-derived learning practices. Learning by explicit verbalization was not common in the traditional past where learning in informal situations was the preferred type. Formal schooling modelled along western lines has changed this process greatly.

The use of language for social control is probably a sociolinguistic universal, though the types of control that can be exercised differ from society to society. In traditional Melanesian societies, for instance, political power at village and regional level was associated with multilingual skills. The traditional big men, as described by Sankoff (1976: 290 ff.) were skilful rhetoricians. However, their linguistic skills were drastically reduced in value with the introduction of government-appointed village leaders whose main linguistic asset was typically a knowledge of an English-derived pidgin, and with the realization of the villagers that access to political power meant playing a game defined by outside government, and that even this only gave very limited power. With decolonization and increasing social mobility the metropolitan languages have increasingly become the tool for social advance and participation in modern society. Such patterns of multi- and bilingualism that have existed in the past are rapidly disappearing.

At the level of individual languages, the phenomenon of mission languages illustrates how social control can be shifted through carefully designed changes in the lexicon and grammars of vernaculars. This is done mainly by accelerating amelioration and pejoration of existing lexical items in conformity with the requirements of the Christian missions, or word-formation emphasizing or de-emphasizing meanings. Whilst there are many isolated studies of how this was done for individual languages (e. g. Renck 1978 for Yagaria or Schütz 1976 for Hawaiian, Mosel 1980 for Tolai), only a few writers discuss the wider implications (e. g. Lynd 1975).

Missionization often also implies the obsolescence of pre-existing functions. Thus, in the case of the Ilongot of the Philippines, traditional oratorical skills used for negotiating personal, economical and political advantages were given up from one generation to the next in a deliberate break with the past.

Rosaldo (1984: 159) describes this process as follows:

Thus, Christianity, opposed to headhunting, came to be seen as incompatible with a style of verbal art that construed persons in ways alien to the national legal system. Young men, knowledgeable in national speech and ways, could then invoke their newfound faith in the defense of their desires for law or power. And persons who defined their claims in terms of goods (and threatened the supportive intervention of police) could understand and argue for their style and stance with reference to an opposition between things made by men (betar) − the customary ways of "anger" − and Catholic Filipino norms of "order", understood, ironically enough, as those dictated by a Protestant God.

In brief, for Ilongots a set of verbal skills that once were used to balance and display the "passion" held by would-be equal men came to be seen as fundamentally disruptive because the sociocultural world that they portrayed and shaped had lost its sense. The convergent power of an end to headhunting, a rise in Christian faith, and almost simultaneous change in the material nature of their concrete daily interactions led Ilongots to come to understand their art and politics primarily as a negation of the art and politics of their past. For Ilongots in 1974, it was because their art made social sense that there was "Christian" reason to deny it.

It was because aesthetics was so intimately bound up with practical and ethical concerns that Ilongot oratory came to be seen at once as socially and emotionally disruptive − unworthy both as politics and as art.

A last goal to be considered here is that of marking identity. As has been illustrated by a number of writers (e. g. Laycock 1981) the multiplicity of languages and sublanguages in the Pacific often served the primary purpose of marking speakers as belonging to different social groups. In many languages, this is no longer possible for one or more of the following reasons:

i) Standardization and graphicization of languages have led to a significant decline in non-prestige varieties. Speakers prefer language forms indexical of status to those indexical of location.
ii) Traditional settlement and marriage patterns have broken down.
iii) The linguistic socialization of new generations of speakers is only partial — indexical aspects are no longer transmitted.

That many linguistic rules are cultural rules brought into being by acts of identity of the type described by Le Page and Tabouret-Keller (1984) has seldom been considered by linguists working in the Pacific area and many aspects of their special and personal indexicality remain unexplored. However, it seems reasonable to assume that a rapid change in the personal identity of many of their speakers will result in certain structural changes in these languages.

3.2.9 Key

This parameter is concerned with the tone, manner, and style of speech events. For the Pacific area, we have only scattered observations, in addition to a number of shorter summaries such as that by Fisher (1971).

Some aspects of key are closely bound to the medium of speech and it is here that some of the greatest changes have taken place. The literary revolution of the Polynesian languages in the 19th century (Parsonson 1967) was followed by similar literary revolutions in Micronesia and Melanesia in the 20th century, mainly as a consequence of missionary efforts to provide Bible translations. New standardized written forms of the language, often exhibiting structural influence from the languages of expatriate translators, exist for a substantial proportion of the languages of the area. This new literary style tends to exercise very considerable influence on other styles as it is the most prestigious one. It is well known that graphicization is more than simply "a method for reducing a spoken language to writing" and can have numerous repercussions in phonology and other levels of grammar (see Ong 1981).

Many languages of the area have special styles of indirect and metaphorical use of language and/or conventions for reducing conflict by allowing a greater degree of semantic indeterminacy than is tolerated in modern SAE languages. An interesting example of language being used in this way is found in Bilmes (1975) for Thai.

The threat to such styles is provided by three factors:

(a) The disappearance of suitable settings for their use. Voorhoeve (1977) comments on the loss of the ceremonial houses in the Asmat community of New Guinea which "were at the same time dormitories for boys and bachelors, training school, club house and feast house... Nowadays, warfare and headhunting have stopped; most of the ceremonial houses have disappeared; the cycle of feasts has collapsed, and with it the exuberant expression of much that was meaningful in the life of the Asmat" (1977: 19). Particularly important in this quotation is its indication of the former role of the ceremonial houses as centres where knowledge of special styles was explicitly taught and learnt.

(b) The belief, widely found among missionized and westernized indigenes, that talk should be 'straight'. For the Ilongots, Rosaldo (1984: 132) reports:

> But what is clear is that from at least the mid-1960s the art of traditional oratory was increasingly called into question. Ilongots argued about whether to conduct debate in the elaborate oratocial style or, instead, in the manner of lowland authorities. They criticized metaphorical turns of phrase in the name of a Christian God who desires "straight speaking". And, in response to my disappointment at the lack of artful speech in a bridewealth meeting recorded, men told me that talk in the "old style" would have bred conflict. Concerned to display their "new knowledge", they all had, as Christians, submitted to the dictates of a pistol-waving young "Captain", who directed participants to eschew "curvy speech", "name" their objects, and follow the way of "the law".

(c) The complimentariness of stylistic diversification and multilingualism. As the functional range of traditional languages is taken over partly by new intrusive languages, there is a tendency for their stylistic diversity to shrink. One of the most important aspects of key is its social institutionalization. Linguistic diversity in itself is not an index of stylistic or key resources unless such diversity is associated with clear social functions. This is an important consideration, for a number of writers have drawn attention to the growing diversification of some languages of the area prior to their demise. An example is the dying Koko-Bera language of the Cape York Peninsula of Queensland (Black 1982: 18—19):

> Nowadays Koko-Bera is spoken a bit differently by each different speaker — even brothers and sisters talk it a bit differently. Some of the differences are in phonology — the sounds of the language. For example, some speakers have all three of the sounds n, ny, and nh, but even one of the best speakers had only two, n and ny. This old man would thus say *nay* instead of *nhay* 'see' and *pany* instead of *panh* 'body'. Another difference between speakers is whether they say rr or t at the beginnings of some words, such as *rrikepir* or *tikepir* 'small'. Different speakers also pronounce some words in rather different ways: e. g. *yipel* or *yupel* 'you two', *chekont* or *thekont* 'head', and even *kunmarrp* or *kurrmap* 'belly'.
>
> Some differences in pronunciation are clearly due to the fact that some words are hardly ever used these days, so that people don't remember them very well.

New socially meaningful types of key have also emerged, particularly those associated with social stratification. Thus, many indigenous users of metropolitan languages distinguish between basilectal (heavy) and acrolectal (light) varieties, the latter being used in the presence of or in communication with Europeans. Similarly, some mission lingue franche now possess special registers used in the discussion of religious affairs. A systematic survey of the gains, losses, and changes for the languages of the Pacific is badly needed.

3.2.10 Channels

By channels we mean the verbal, non-verbal, and other semiotic systems for communication. A first observation is that the communicative load of individual channels may differ from society to society. Thus, singing, writing, or gesture may have different functions across languages. Related to this is the principle that the communicative force of different channels can also differ. All things being equal, non-verbal messages tend to be more important in human communication than verbal ones. In many parts of the Pacific the status of written communication is considerably higher than in Western societies. The written word, particularly in the first decades of literacy, is associated with power and truth to an extent that the spoken word is not.

One of the main effects of European penetration of the Pacific area is the spread of literacy and the closely-related disappearance of indigenous non-verbal forms of communication such as drum languages, tally sticks and message sticks, tattoos, and pictograms.

The channel or medium through which information is transmitted is differentially suited to variability of the codes employed. Thus oral communication can occur in a vast variety of languages and sublanguages and, in the case of face to face contacts, differences in the verbal code used can be made up by extra-linguistic and non-linguistic clues, an important factor in successfully communicating across a dialect or language continuum.

Western technological media tend either to reduce the amount of redundancy in communication by filtering out clues (e. g. the visual ones and certain auditory ones in the case of the telephone) or, in the case of mass media, to require standardization of the codes. Printing is expensive for different dialects and very small languages, television programmes are really only feasible for a small number of large languages, and computers and associated technology tolerate English and hardly anything else. As a consequence, the introduction of new channels will lead to a change in the status of languages as well as to a reduction in linguistic diversity.

It would be wrong to regard the new media simply as alternatives to pre-existing forms of communication. Rather, the introduction of English language television changes the very speech and communicative events at issue. In addition to increasing the amount of new information available, it increases the role of one-way communication, shifts bilingualism in favour of metropolitan languages, introduces new genres (soap opera, weather forecast etc.) and reduces the importance of old ones (e. g. story telling or communal singing). More recently, the rapid introduction of video technology has triggered off new changes. Morgan (1986: 12) reported to the Canberra Conference on International Communication in the Pacific:

> Video hire shops jostle one another on the streets of townships all over the Pacific. There are video replay machines in seventy thousand homes in Fiji and ninety per cent of those in Raratonga. There are some exceptions, such as the copies of vintage Truffaut and Chabrol films in Noumea and Vila, and the tapes of traditional ceremonies

and living arts in Vila and Majuro. Generally however the tapes are copies of cinema films and television soap-opera, frequently pirated and often labelled with photocopies of the newspaper program guides from the places where the tapecopies were made. Rambo, Schwarzenegger and Playboy bunnies prevail apparently free from either copyright or censorship or any other control.

Whilst the pros and cons of introducing new channels of communication are still debated by some governments, they have become a de facto part of the overall speech situation in most areas, with consequences that are difficult to assess. A pessimistic stance is taken by Gilliam (1986) and Michaels (1986: 154): the latter suggests that for Aborigines, European television may well prove an additional and unbearable strain on an already threatened cultural autonomy. Others, including Morgan (1986), take a much more positive view, pointing out the adaptive capacity of local cultures.

3.2.11 Forms of speech

By forms of speech we understand varieties indexical either of the language used to address certain groups (e. g. baby talk, mother-in-law languages) or varieties associated with certain social groups (e. g. hunters, females, initiated persons, old people). Few comprehensive inventories of the speech forms of the languages of the area exist, and there remains a dearth of information about the metalinguistic labels used to describe them. One of the exceptions is a paper by Franklin (1977) which gives an exhaustive account of the speech forms of Kewa, a non-Melanesian language of Papua New Guinea. Among the numerous named forms, we find

tata ne agaa	'baby talk, the first words a baby may use'
ona rumaa pe agaa	'marriage talk, referring to the specific bartering exchange of fathers or brothers of prospective couples'
rumula agaa	'pandanus language consisting of a special vocabulary used to "ritually protect people who travel in pandanus swamp forest areas where ghosts and wild dogs are present"' (p. 6)

yaini pi agaa   'bespelling talk or ritual speech used to cure
                              sicknesses or warding off an unwanted situ-
                              ation'

It would seem that the last two of these forms are particularly sensitive
to change, as they depend on a situation which is threatened by the
introduction of new cultivated plants and a cash economy or medical
services consisting of aid posts and hospitals staffed by outsiders.

A widespread phenomenon is the growing importance of young people's speech (cf. Romaine 1987: 8−9), typically forms stripped of much
of their morphological complexity and mixed with material borrowed
from the metropolitan culture. The transition from traditional to young
people's speech has been described for a number of Australian languages
(e. g. Donaldson 1985, Douglas 1968, and Schmidt 1985). These changes
reflect the position of the younger generation as increasingly socially
mobile and dominant as well as its rejection of or lack of opportunity
for learning traditional forms of speech. The typological changes that
occur in the grammar of the affected languages involve a change from
polysynthetic or inflectional languages to isolating ones, together with
the replacement of traditional contact languages by English or other
metropolitan languages as a source for new structures.

3.2.12 Norms of interaction and interpretation

By this parameter we understand socially sanctioned conventions for the
use of speech and speech forms, and the attachment of social meaning
to actually occurring forms. A reasonable body of literature exists to
suggest that such norms can be widely different in areas such as conventions for questions and answers, asking favours, distancing, and fluency,
and that, moreover, such norms tend to be more resistant to external
pressure than rules of grammar. Thus, Eades (1982, 1983) has illustrated
the survival of numerous Aboriginal norms in Black Australian English
as spoken in South East Queensland, and future studies of the emerging
new Englishes in the Pacific will in all likelihood demonstrate similar
developments.

Not all norms are equally likely to survive, as there is considerable
pressure from the educational system to impose new external norms. The
norms for the interpretation of speech in actual situations would seem to
provide an excellent field of inquiry for speech act theoreticians and those
interested in conversational maxims.

It must be noted that communal norms depend on the survival of communities. As members of smaller communities are dispersed into towns and new settlements, at least some of their local norms will disappear.

4. Analysis

We have now come to the end of our pre-theoretical tour of some of the principal components of speech events. The tentative character of my remarks should again be stressed. It is simply beyond the resources of a single investigator to survey communicative events in a third of the world's languages and to carry out the basic research needed to fill the many serious gaps in information. What I have presented thus remains anecdotal and incomplete, though not necessarily irrelevant.... My main point has been that the proliferation of languages and sub-varieties of languages in the Pacific area has been the response to a highly complex web of environmental factors, with the environment possessing both a natural and a man-made dimension. An understanding of the ecology of individual languages can be achieved only when the linguistic ecology of larger communication areas and, ultimately, the entire region has been understood.

At no point have I accepted the view that traditional societies or languages were static, nor have I suggested that their rate of change was slower than is posited, for instance, by advocates of the glottochronological method. What I would conclude, however, is that the changes following contact with European explorers, traders, and colonizers were different qualitatively and in order of magnitude from the changes that took place in 'prehistoric' times.

The difference in quality is not, as might be suggested, one between internal development and contact-induced changes. Language contacts were a pervasive feature of the Pacific linguistic scene a long time before the arrival of Europeans. However, most of these contacts tended to take place within a framework of highly institutionalized trade cycles, exogamy, or gradual internal colonization. Thus, the kind of language contacts that led to the interpenetration of languages in areas such as Arnhemland (Heath 1978) or language chains in the New Hebrides (Tryon 1979) are qualitatively different from the encounter of Aboriginal languages or Arnhemland with English in the last century. This difference between the two contact situations is not, however, explained by reference to the typology of the languages involved, for contacts between historically unrelated and typologically dissimilar languages took place in numerous areas of the Pacific, those between Austronesian and non-Austronesian languages being the most important.

I would not wish to argue that catastrophic and indeed accelerated change did not occur in the past. Invasions, raids, natural catastrophes, and diseases played an important part in the history of many languages, as has been very lucidly illustrated by Thurston (1982) for some languages of New Britain. However, such catastrophes as occurred remained local and their effects were often attenuated by local resources. Languages in the past died out, were dislocated or changed beyond recognition in many instances, more often perhaps than is admitted by those trying to fit the linguistic history of the area into a family tree model. It might be useful here to appeal to a biological analogy, namely the change and/or loss of species in phylogenesis. The disappearance of dinosaurs and many other species is an indisputable fact. However, what distinguishes their disappearance from the loss of hundreds of species subsequent to the industrial revolution is the order of magnitude; present-day ecological changes occur at a vastly accelerated pace, processes that took millions of years in the past now take only decades.

To return to linguistics and languages; human settlement of Australia dates back 40,000 years or more. During this time, older languages (of the Tasmanian type?) may have been replaced by one or more ancestral language of the present day Aboriginal languages. These proto-Aboriginal languages developed through diversification and convergence as well as through occasional contacts with the outside world. In the course of 40,000 years of linguistic history their number has probably varied, but may have remained at the level of about 250 languages, as was the case when the first white settlement was established 200 years ago. The subsequent fate of Aboriginal languages is qualitatively very different:

a) An average of one language per year was lost, with the result that only about 50 Aboriginal languages are spoken today. There are no signs that this process is decelerating.
b) Many languages were cut off from former sources of lexical and structural enrichment as a result of resettlement, dispersal, diseases, and killings (cf. Evans et al. 1975). Most of them have now become dependent on English as their contact language.

c) Typological changes that took centuries in the past now occur at a very fast rate.

Thus, the argument that all languages change misses the point. This also goes for a second, frequently heard, argument that all languages change in such a way as to meet their speakers' changed communicative needs. Even the most superficial look at the Pacific linguistic scene will reveal a very different picture. Among the observations that can be made, the following seem to be the most pertinent:

a) Many languages of the area have acquired new lexical material through borrowing and internal word-formation, enabling speakers to cover non-traditional areas of discourse. Typically, internal solutions appear before borrowing (cf. Fischer 1962), and tend, eventually, to be replaced by borrowings.

b) In many instances access to modern technology is not available to speakers of small languages and many of them have therefore remained fairly unmodernized. We can note a wide gap, well known to those in the language planning business, between what these languages express and what they need to express.

c) More frequent than the modernization of indigenous vernaculars is their being supplemented by 'modern' languages, particularly Western metropolitan ones and the pidgins derived from them. However, instead of a situation of stable bilingualism and diglossia, we often encounter 'galloping diglossia' of the type in which the functional range of the traditional vernacular diminishes with every subsequent generation, as is stated in Table 2, which refers to the Australian Aboriginal Language Ngiyampaa (according to Donaldson 1985: 128):

Table 2.

Date	Where the Ngiyampaa lived	In whose country (by language)
1900	Their ngurrampaa 'camping about' on pastoral stations	Ngiyampaa
1926	Carowra Tank 'isolated mission'	Ngiyampaa
1933	Menindee 'mission' near town	Paakantji
1949	Marrin Bridge, outside town (Lake Cargelligo)	Wiradjuri

Table 3. Ngiyampaa institutionalization and the transition to English

Date	Use of Ngiyampaa	Use of English
1900	First and main language	With pastoralists
1926	*lingua franca* between Aborigines (mainly Ngiyampaa)	And with 'mission' management
1933	Domestically among Ngiyampaa	And *lingua franca* between Ngiyampaa and Paakantji and in town
1949	Privately among oldest Ngiyampaa	Main or first language of all Ngiyampaa. Paakantji and Wiradjuri descents and at town school

d) There is a considerable division of opinion as to whether traditional languages should be modernized or should be used in new media among their speakers. A case study illustrating this with regard to graphicization is that by McKay (1982).

I am not arguing that the languages of the Pacific cannot, in principle, adapt to new circumstances. Indeed, languages such as Tagalog, Bahasa Indonesia, Samoan, or Japanese have demonstrated this capacity. My observation is, however, that the ecological conditions and speakers' preparedness to do so simply do not exist. Moreover, as has been discussed by McConvell (1987), the very modernization of languages may be a factor contributing to their accelerated demise. Whereas bilingualism involving a traditional and a modern language can persist for a considerable time, that involving a modernized and a modern language leads to overlap in function and domains and thus reduces the usefulness of the traditional language to its speakers. The question of modernization has, like that of language death, often been asked for individual isolated languages without regard to the wider language ecology of the region. Modernizing all of the hundreds of languages of a country like Papua New Guinea, for instance, would put an impossible strain on the economy of the country, whilst providing only marginal communicative advantages to their speakers and perhaps accelerating their takeover by Tok Pisin or English. Languages may all be equal naturally, but they certainly are rendered most unequal by cultural and sociohistorical forces of the type that have occurred in the Pacific over the last 200 years. A return to the egalitarian linguistic status quo ante must remain a utopian dream.

5. Focus on causes

In an important recent paper on the Australian Aboriginal linguistic situation, McConvell (1987) contrasts (or 'caricatures', as he puts it) two approaches to the rapid changes in the languages of the fifth continent:

Language death studies by and large consider only what is happening to one of the languages in the language situation. They assume that this language is going to die out, and study changes in it as a reflection of the hypothesized or assumed end-point of the process.
Language shift studies do not look at individual languages, but at entire bilingual or multilingual situations, seeing the functions of each language as fitting together to make a whole. Changes in one language's use are seen as related to changes in the use of other languages, and not necessarily to a particular end-point. The future development is to be predicted from the state of the whole situation and the theory, and not to be assumed.

I agree with McConvell's sentiment that language death studies tend to focus much too narrowly on certain structural happenings in isolated (and often idealized) linguistic systems. In my view, those in the business of explaining language change with reference to language death studies have deprived themselves of a large number of explanatory parameters of a non-structural type and are thus as unable to come forward with explanations as Lass's various types of historical linguists (cf. Lass 1980).

McConvell (1987) goes on to examine a number of approaches to language shift, namely the 'Domain theory', the 'Variationist theory' and the 'Adaption theory'. He points out a number of shortcomings of each of them and proposes what he labels a 'Functional Choice Theory' of language shift which integrates the effects of the basic communicative, social, and cultural functions of language into a comprehensive theory.

My own aims, I am afraid, have been somewhat more modest. Given the ease with which previous accounts of language shift can be falsified with evidence from 'exotic' languages, I hold out little hope for a global theory at this stage. Instead, I have suggested that we can do two things:

a) continue collecting and classifying data from as many different contexts as possible;

b) be guided in our collection and interpretation by a holistic, ecological metaphor; a linguistic area is like a forest of mushrooms and fungi, interrelated and mutually dependent.

That languages have communicative, social, and cultural functions is only part of the picture; they also have speakers, and media, and are located in a partially man-made and partially natural environment.

What I have tried to show is that of the numerous etic parameters which make up the overall linguistic situation in the Pacific, hardly one has remained unaffected by the advent of European colonization and subsequent Westernization. True, in some quiet backwaters the processes that have affected the local ecology of languages in a catastrophic (in the technical sense) way have occurred later and/or with less force, but there are few places today where rapid change is not taking place.

Finally, I would like to mention a few factors which appear to be particularly pertinent to the question of accelerated language change:

i) Many of the languages of the area are of an esoteric type, i. e. their most important function is that of excluding outsiders and expressing cultural independence and group identity. Many of the grammatical complications (e. g. complex classificatory markers or honorific systems) are man-made, and transmitted in a formal fashion by teachers in long-houses, schools, or secret clubs. In as much as such marked grammar is cultural grammar, its loss is unavoidable if the cultural institutions for its transmission are removed.

ii) European penetration of the Pacific interrupted both transmission of languages from one generation to the next (through boarding schools, blackbirding, murder, or resettlement) and the channels by which languages could grow and enrich themselves, such as borrowing from related varieties or from more distant languages through networks of exogamic practices.

iii) In most parts of the area under discussion, the status of different languages did not differ greatly. One of the most immediate consequences of colonization was the creation of a hierarchy of languages of differential status, by which previously non-existent concepts such as 'minority language' or 'dialect' came about.

iv) New media were introduced at a much greater rate than in Europe. Some languages in the area underwent a development from spoken language in a stone-age society to written, broadcast, and televised language in little more than a generation. Increasing changes in communication technology seem to threaten small languages more and more, and will continue to do so unless a stable traditional-modern language bilingualism can be maintained.

v) New values, religions and forms of behaviour have disoriented many of the inhabitants of the area, causing the breaking up of societies and social norms and their replacement by new ones. Language as a marker of traditional identity has become less important, whereas its function in urban ethnogenesis and marking of rapidly changing identity has increased in significance. This, it appears, has caused rapid changes in the indexical dimensions of language.

6. Conclusion

I have tried to argue that the investigation of the causes of structural change in individual linguistic systems is not a viable approach to explaining language change. The independence hypothesis, which has been fashionable throughout most of 20th century linguistics is thus rejected. I have argued implicitly against other mainstays of traditional and modern historical linguistics, particularly their dependence on a uniformitarian view of language change.

Implicit in much of what I have said has been the fact that most causes of change are person-made changes in linguistic ecology and that, moreover, what are affected are predominantly man-made, cultural aspects of language (culturally made structures as well as cultural rules for their use and interpretation). I reject the widespread view that languages such as English, French, Samoan, or Motu are 'natural languages'. For those interested in the details of my argument I would like to draw attention to Mühlhäusler 1987 c.

Man in the Pacific has caused language change in a way similar to culture change. Only in a few individual cases are we dealing with well thought out deliberate and successful planning. In the vast majority of cases, the consequences were neither intended or foreseen. Even today, in the days of intensive language and educational planning, most of the consequences of human interference in language ecology are ill understood.

Accelerated language change in one language or one area tends to have repercussions on the next one. Thus, as well as accelerating structural changes in individual systems we are concerned with an accelerating overall rate of change.

I have commented on some of the moral and philosophical consequences of accelerated change elsewhere (Mühlhäusler 1987). Firth, the first holder of a chair of Linguistics in the United Kingdom, is reported to have said (Milner, personal communication 1987) on being told that a language was dying fast and should be recorded: "Let it die. It is already recorded in the mind of God." Such a view may be compatible with other views widely held among linguists, e. g. the view that 'linguistics should be concerned with language, not with languages', but it is certainly not one that I would wish to encourage or even condone. Rather, I would like to emphasize again the urgency of studying as many languages of the Pacific area in as much detail as possible before it is too late, paying particular attention to those areas of structure and use that seem to be most under threat.

What I have said in this paper should also be of interest to those concerned with the future of the languages in the Pacific area. Language planners should pay particular attention to the problem of directing change into channels compatible with the needs and aspirations of the inhabitants of the area and to the need to understand and control wider situational factors if their corpus or status planning is to meet with success.

References

Bailey, Charles-James N.
   1982   *On the yin and yang nature of language* (Ann Arbor: Karoma).
Bell, Jeanie (ed.)
   1982   *Language planning for Australian aboriginal languages* (Alice Springs: Institute for Aboriginal Development).
Bickerton, Derek
   1977   "Pidginization and creolization: language acquisition and language universals", in: Albert Valdman (ed.): *Pidgin and creole linguistics*, 49–70 (Bloomington: Indiana University Press).
Bilmes, J.
   1975   "Misinformation and ambiguity in verbal interaction: a Northern Thai example", *Linguistics* 164: 63–75.

Black, Paul
1982   "Why and how languages change", in: Bell (ed.), 14—21.
Boretzky, Norbert
1984   "The Indo-Europeanist model of sound change and genetic affinity and change in exotic languages", *Diachronics* 1. 1: 1—51.
Bradley, David
1981   "Majority-minority linguistic inferfaces in Thailand", *Working Papers in Linguistics, Unviersity of Melbourne* 7: 79—86.
1987   "The Disappearance of the Ugong in Thailand", in: Nancy C. Dorian (ed.), *Investigating obsolescence: Studies in language contraction and death* (London: Cambridge University Press).
Brenneis, D. L.—F. R. Myers (eds.)
1984   *Dangerous words: language and politics in the Pacific* (New York: New York University Press).
Bürkle, Horst (ed.)
1978   *Theologische Beiträge aus Papua Neuguinea* (Erlangen: Ev.-Luth. Mission).
Carey, Peter
1986   Review of J. Ramos—Horta, *Funu, the unfinished saga of East Timor* (MS Oxford).
Clerk, Christian (ed.)
1984   *The effects of development on traditional Pacific island cultures* (London: Royal Commonwealth Society).
Crosby, Alfred W.
1986   *Ecological imperialism — the biological expansion of Europe 900—1900* (Cambridge: University Press).
Donaldson, Tamsin
1985   "From speaking Ngiyampaa to speaking English", *Aboriginal History* 9. 2: 126—145.
Douglas, Wilfred H.
1968   *The aboriginal languages of South-West Australia* (Canberra: Australian Institute of Aboriginal Studies).
Dyen, Isidore
1963   "Lexicostatistically determined borrowing and taboo", *Language* 39: 60—66.
Eades, Diana
1982   "You gotta know how to talk ...: information seeking in South-East Queensland Aboriginal Society", *Australian Journal of Linguistics* 2. 1: 61—82.
1983   *English as an aboriginal language in Southeast Queensland.* Ph. D. thesis, University of Queensland.
Evans, R.—K. Saunders—K. Cronin
1975   *Exclusion, exploitation and extermination* (Sydney: Australia and New Zealand Book Company).
Fischer, Harris
1962   "Einige linguistische Indizien des Kulturwandels in Nordost-Neuguinea", *Sociologus* 12. 1: 18—29.
Fischer, J. L.
1971   "Style contrasts in Pacific languages", in: Thomas A. Sebeok (ed.), *Current Trends in Linguistics* 8: 1129—1162.
Franklin, Karl
1977   "The Kewa Language in Culture and Society", in: Wurm (ed.), 5—18.
Gillian, Angela
1986   "Language, communication and power: some ethical considerations", Paper presented at the Waigani Seminar, University of Papua New Guinea.

Grace, George W.
1981   "Indirect inheritance and the aberrant Melanesian languages", in: J. Holly-
            man — A. Pawley (eds.), *Studies in Pacific languages and cultures*, 255 — 267
            (Auckland: Linguistic Society of New Zealand).
Hambruch, Paul
1914   *Nauru* (Hamburg: Friedrichsen).
Hockett, Charles F.
1950   "Age-grading and linguistic continuity", *Language* 26: 449 — 457.
Keenan, V. — V. Keenan
1971   "Becoming a competent speaker of Malagasy", in: Tim Shopen (ed.), *Lan-
            guages and their speakers.*
Krämer, Augustin
1919   *Palau* (Hamburg: Friedrichsen).
Lass, Roger
1980   *On explaining language change* (Cambridge: University Press).
Laycock, Donald C.
1975   "Observations on number systems and semantics", in: Wurm (ed.), 219 — 234.
1979   "Multilingualism: linguistic boundaries and unsolved problems in Papua New
            Guinea" in: Wurm (ed.), 81 — 100.
1981   "Melanesian linguistic diversity: a Melanesian choice?". Paper presented at
            Research School of Pacific Studies Seminar on Melanesia — Beyond Diver-
            sity, to appear in proceedings, Canberra.
Lee, J.
1983   *Tiwi today.* Ph. D. thesis, Australian National University.
Lee, Kee-Dong
1975   *Kusaian reference grammar* (Honolulu: Hawaii University Press).
Le Page, R. B. — A. Tabouret-Keller
1985   *Acts of identity* (Cambridge: University Press).
Lynch, John D.
1979   "Church, state and language in Melanesia". Inaugural lecture, Dept. of
            Languages, University of Papua New Guinea.
Malcolm, Ian G.
1982   "Speech use in aboriginal communities: a preliminary survey", *Anthropolog-
            ical Forum* V. 1: 54 — 104.
Malinowski, B.
1925   "The problem of meaning in primitive languages", in: C. K. Ogden — I. A.
            Richards (eds.), *The meaning of meaning*, 296 — 336 (London: Kegan Paul)
            (1946 ed.).
1937   *Coral gardens and their magic* (London: George Allen & Unwin).
McConvell, Patrick
1982   "Understanding language shift: a step towards language maintenance". MS,
            University of the Northern Territory (21 pp.).
McKay, Graham R.
1982   "Attitudes of Kunibidji speakers to literacy", *International Journal of the
            Sociology of Language* 36: 105 — 114.
Michaels, Eric
1986   *Aboriginal invention of television* (Canberra: Australian Institute of Aboriginal
            Studies).
Milner, George
1984   "The New Missionaries?: language, education and the Pacific way" in: C.
            Clark (ed.), 6 — 22.
Morgan, Frank
1986   "New visions: old echoes — radio and television training in South East Asia

and the Pacific". Paper read at the First Canberra Conference on International Communication.

Moorehead, Alan
  1966   *The fatal impact* (London: Penguin Books).
Mosel, Ulrike
  1980   "The influence of the church missions on the development of Tolai". Paper presented at the XXI Deutscher Orientalistentag, Berlin.
Mühlhäusler, Peter
  1987 a   "The politics of small languages in Australia and the Pacific", *Language and Communication* 7. 1: 1 — 24.
  1987 b   "Evolution des langues pidgin dans le Pacifique", *Diogène* 137: 49 — 68.
  1987 c   *Identifying and mapping the pidgins and creoles of the Pacific* (Duisburg: Linguistic Agency University Duisburg A — 179).
Nevermann, Hans
  1934   *Admiralitäts-Inseln* (Hamburg: Friedrichsen).
O'Barr, William M. — Jean F. O'Barr (eds.)
  1976   *Language and politics* (The Hague: Mouton).
Ong, Walter J.
  1982   *Orality and literacy* (London: Methuen).
Parsonson, G. S.
  1967   "The literate revolution in Polynesia", *Journal of Pacific History* 3. 2: 39 — 58.
Ray, Sidney H.
  1907   'The Jargon English of the Torres Straits', in: *Reports of the Cambridge Anthropological Expedition to Torres Straits*, 251 — 259 (Cambridge: University Press).
Renck, Günther
  1978   "Redend spricht sich Dasein aus", in: Bürkle (ed.), 222 — 255.
Romaine, Suzanne
  1987   "Pidgins, creoles, immigrant and dying languages — comment on Dorian *Investigating obsolescence*". MS Oxford University.
Rosaldo, Michelle
  1984   "Words that are moving: the social meanings of Ilongot verbal art", in: Brenneis — Myers (eds.), 131 — 160.
Sankoff, Gillian
  1976   "Political power and linguistic inequality in Papua New Guinea", in: O'Barr-O'Barr (eds.), 283 — 310.
Schmidt, Annette
  1985   *Young people's Dyirbal* (Cambridge: University Press).
Schütz, Albert J.
  1976   "Take *my* word for it: missionary influence on borrowings in Hawaiian", *Oceanic Linguistics* XV: 75 — 91.
Solenberger, Robert R.
  1962   "The social meaning of language choice in the Marianas", *Anthropological Linguistics* 4. 1: 59 — 64.
Thurston, William R.
  1982   *A comparative study in Anêm and Lusi* (Canberra: Pacific Linguistics B-83).
Voorhoeve, C. L.
  1977   "Ta-Poman: metaphorical use of words and poetic vocabulary in Asmat songs", in: Wurm (ed.), 19 — 38.
  1979   "Turning the talk: a case of chain interpreting in Papua New Guinea", in: Wurm (ed.), 177 — 208.
Wurm, Stephen A. (ed.)
  1975   *New Guinea area languages and language study* 1: *Papuan languages and the New Guinea linguistic scene* (Canberra: *Pacific Linguistics* C38).

1977   *Language, culture, society and the modern world* (New Guinea area languages and language study 3) (Canberra: *Pacific Linguistics* C40).
1979   *New Guinea and neighboring areas: a sociolinguistic laboratory* (The Hague: Mouton).

Sound change is drawn from a pool of synchronic variation

John J. Ohala

> "... [As for the stars] it is inconceivable that we should ever be able to study by any means whatsoever their chemical composition or mineralogical structure ..."
> Auguste Comte 1974: 74 [1830–1842].

1. Introduction

The Bible's story of the tower of Babel and similar myths in other cultures show that people have long puzzled over the causes of linguistic diversity. In addition to direct intervention by the gods, language change was also an early candidate answer to this question (see Plato's *Kratylos*) and, as is well known, is the principal cause of diversity entertained by modern researchers. I do not propose to review and evaluate the extensive literature which has accumulated over the past two millennia on the causes of language change but the title of the symposium at which this paper was given, "The causes of language change: Do we know them yet?", testifies to the fact that there has not yet been any consensus on what the causes are. In this paper I propose to give what I think is a currently acceptable answer to the question, focussing only on sound change. To give some nod to previous work on this question, I should admit that most of what I present here has been said before but perhaps not all as part of the same argument, perhaps not with the same evidential support, and perhaps coupled to other claims that I would dispute.

To give a direct answer to the question posed by this symposium: with qualifications, yes, we can identify some of the causes of sound change or at least locate the domain in which they lie. The ultimate proof of this is being able to duplicate sound change in the laboratory. Being able to study sound change in the lab is a breakthrough for historical linguistics comparable to that introduced in astronomy by Fraunhofer and Kirchhoff when they found that an analysis of light from stars could reveal their constituents in the same way that terrestrial substances could be analysed in the laboratory by their emitted or absorbed light (hence confounding Comte's prediction, the epigram offered in irony at the start of this paper). In my own work I impose a (for me) useful restriction: I study those sound changes attested in similar form in diverse languages. This helps to guarantee that they will owe something to universal and timeless physical or physiological factors — i. e., the things easily brought into the lab — and not to language- or culture-specific factors. This limitation tends to eliminate changes due to paradigm levelling, spelling pronunciations, and the like. I hasten to add, however, that there is no principled reason why these latter factors could not be studied in a controlled way — it just happens that, in general, they have not been (however, see Thumb and Marbe 1901; Bybee and Pardo 1981).

A further qualification is that we can identify only some of the causes of sound change and, perhaps, make improved speculation on some of the others. As we know from centuries of philosophical discussion, causation is a complicated matter. Consider, for example, a heart attack. Leaving aside the low-level mechanistic causes of the event (diminished oxygen supply to the heart muscles caused by a blockage of the flow of blood in the artery serving those muscles, etc.), one commonly attributes heart attacks to immediate causes or triggers such as a shock, physical exertion, and so on. But one can also identify pre-conditions which contributed to the event, e. g., the behaviour of the victim: his diet, whether he smoked, took exercise, lived a stressful life, etc. A public health official interested in improving the lot of the population as a whole would focus on the pre-condition causes since the other causes, sudden shocks, etc., are uncontrollable and can be expected to happen by chance no matter what measures might be taken. I propose to treat sound change the way public health workers treat heart attacks. By this I do not mean that I intend to try to prevent sound change — indeed, I do not think it is harmful at all and, in any case, there is little we could do to control it — but rather that I will try to identify those causes which are the pre-conditions for sound change. As for the immediate triggers of sound change in a particular language at a particular time, I will have little to say about them except to suggest that these things are bound to happen and that it is not so interesting to try to identify them. Opposed to this view, there are those who believe that unless a complete, nomological account can be given of the causes of sound change — that is, including why a particular sound change happened in a specific language at a specific time —, the whole enterprise is bankrupt (Dinnsen 1980; Lass 1980). I have answered these critics (Ohala 1987) by pointing out that completely nomological (exceptionless, lawful) accounts of natural phenomena do not exist in any scientific domain; all sciences resort ultimately to probabilistic explanations. That is, those causes they have under their control they deal with; those they do not, they handle in a probabilistic way. Like the public health worker, we may not be able to predict (or post-dict) everything, e. g., who will suffer a heart attack, but we can make probabilistic predictions useful enough for the larger population to make it worth the effort.

I will also have little to say beyond speculation about the spread or transmission of sound change, i. e., either how a changed pronunciation spreads through the lexicon, the segment inventory, or to other speakers of the language. I will try to show how a change in the pronunciation norm of a given word occurs in at least one speaker; what happens to this changed norm after that will involve different mechanisms and ones not properly part of the cause of change.

With these preliminaries out of the way, I now give in abbreviated form my conception of the mechanism of sound change.

2. The pre-condition cause of sound change: synchronic variation

There exists in any speech community at any point in time a great deal of hidden variation in the pronunciation of words. I say "hidden" variation because I am not referring to the obvious variation of the sort found in English *give me* vs. *gimme* or French *je ne sais pas* vs. [ʃepɑ]; such variation, in my view, is the consequence of sound changes that have already happened. Were I to include them in my account I would be, as it were, begging the question: assuming what I was required to demonstrate. By "hidden" I mean rather that speakers exhibit variations in their pronunciation which they and listeners usually do not recognize as variation. When pronunciation is transmitted, however, the existence of this variation can create ambiguity and lead to the listener's misapprehension of the intended pronunciation norm. A misapprehended pronunciation is a changed pronunciation, i. e., sound change. Analogues of the mechanism I have in mind may be found in scribal errors made by medieval manuscript copyists, in transcription errors between DNA and RNA, in the transmission errors of signals over telephone lines. In all of these cases as well as in normal speech transmission there is sufficient redundancy in the message to allow most such errors to be corrected, but the error correction is not perfect and so occasionally the signal is changed between the source and the destination.

3. Where does the variation come from?

3.1 One source of variation is the speaker

One of the most important discoveries of modern instrumental phonetics is the incredible amount of variation that exists in pronunciation, not only between speakers but also in the speech of a single speaker. This is what plagues those who are trying to accomplish automatic speech recognition. In fact, if synchronic variation is the stuff out of which sound change emerges, as I claim, the surprising thing is that sounds do not change more often. I have an answer for that, too, which I will give later but first I will give a taxonomy and examples of the sources of variation that can be traced to speech production. What is remarkable about synchronic variation in speech is the striking parallelism it exhibits with sound change manifested in dialect variation, morphophonemic alternation, and in cross-language tendencies in segment inventories, and phonotactics.

The vocal tract is a physical entity subject to physical constraints: anatomical, elasto-inertial, neuro-muscular, aerodynamic, acoustic. Whatever the intention of the speaker may be, the speech that emerges from the vocal tract is the product of that intention plus the effect of physical constraints. Though the speaker's intention may be the same from one utterance to another, the speech signal will vary if the effect of the physical constraints vary — as they will with rate and loudness of speech, etc. Some simple examples will illustrate this.

3.1.1 Aerodynamic constraints

Consider first some well-known aerodynamic constraints on voicing (Passy 1890; Chao 1936; Chomsky and Halle 1968: 301). Voicing requires a) the proper positioning of the vocal cords and b) air flow through the glottis. The rate of flow itself depends in part on there being greater air pressure below than above the glottis. During a voiced stop the air flowing through the glottis accumulates in the oral cavity and causes the oral pressure to rise. Normally within about 65 msec the oral pressure just about equals subglottal pressure, the air flow decreases, and voicing is extinguished (Ohala and Riordan 1979; Ohala 1983 a). Voicing can be extended beyond this interval but only if some active measures are taken to accommodate the glottal air flow, e. g., by actively expanding the vocal tract as in done in implosives (which is apparently the option taken by Sindhi; see Ohala 1983 a). The longer the stop closure or the further back the oral stop closure is made — such that there is less room for vocal tract expansion — the more likely devoicing of stops becomes.

These constraints on voicing have clearly shaped sound change in a number of languages. First, there is the purely statistical tendency that if languages have no voicing distinction in obstruents the series they do have is invariably voiceless. Second, there is the well-documented fact that if languages use the voicing contrast in stops but have gaps at certain places of articulation in the voiced series, including voiced implosives, these gaps are invariably in the back places of articulation (Chao 1936, Greenberg 1970, Gamkrelidze 1975, Sherman 1975, Pinkerton 1986, Maddieson 1984). Dutch, Thai, Czech, and many dialects of Modern Arabic show this. Third, Nubian shows morphophonemic variation that attests both to the tendency of long stop closures to devoice and for this to occur especially to back-articulated stops (Bell 1971, Ohala and Riordan 1979); see (1).

(1)   Morphophonemic variation in Nubian

Noun Stem	Stem + 'and'	
/fab/	/fab:ɔn/	'father'
/sɛgɛd/	/sɛgɛt:ɔn/	'scorpion'
/kadʒ/	/katʃ:ɔn/	'donkey'
/mɔg/	/mɔk:ɔn/	'dog'

Another example of an aerodynamic constraint is that governing the generation of turbulence or frication in air flow. Briefly, frication increases

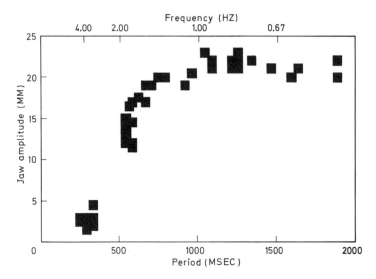

Figure 1. Amplitude (ordinate) vs. frequency (abscissa) of jaw movement during production of the sequence [sɑsɑsɑsɑsɑ ...] spoken at a gradually increasing rate by the author. Jaw movement transduced photoelectrically.

in intensity as a function of, first, the shape of the channel through which the air flows and, second, the velocity of the air. For a given quantity of air flow (volume velocity), the velocity increases as it is forced through a channel with a smaller diameter. This is the basis for the more fricated release of stops, especially apical stops, before high vowels and glides vis-à-vis their release before low vowels. Thus, a /t/ is more likely to have a noisy release before /j/ or /i/ than before /a/ and, as is well known, gives rise to (a) the English dialectal variants /tjun/ and /tʃun/, 'tune', (b) the morphophonemic alternation act ˜ actual ([ækt], [æktʃuəl]), and similar cases of spirantization in many other languages. To illustrate this phonetic effect figure 1 presents spectrographic and waveform displays of the syllables /ti/, /te/, /tɑ/ and reveals greater amplitude and duration of noise upon the release of the /t/ before /i/, less before /e/ and least before the low open vowel /ɑ/.

Other probable aerodynamic constraints which influence sound change have been reviewed in Ohala (1983 a).

Before going on to other types of constraints, let us consider the significance of the two just presented. What I am claiming is that the devoicing of voiced stops and the frication of stop releases can happen inadvertently or unintentionally. It is not so much that the spirit is willing but the flesh is weak but that the spirit is not constrained by aerodynamics but the flesh is. As a result, the speech heard by the listener contains "noise" — some extra details, some missing details, some distortions — which were not the intention of the speaker. Listeners, then, have the task of figuring out what aspects of the signal they hear is intended and what is noise. In general, they do fairly well at this but occasionally they mistake noise for signal and incorporate that into their lexical representations of words.

3.1.2 Elasto-inertial constraints

Figure 2 shows how the amplitude of jaw opening decreases when the frequency or rate of the gestures increases, i. e., when less time is allotted to it (data from a study done with Valerie Mamini; see Ohala 1981 a). The amplitude begins to show clear frequency-dependent attenuation at about 1.5 Hz ('frequency' here roughly corresponds to syllabic rate) and is subject to an absolute limit at about 4 Hz. Although more mobile articulators may be capable of faster movements, they, too, have their limits. This no doubt reflects elastic, inertial, and neuromuscular constraints (see also Nelson, Perkell, and Westbury 1984). In any case, it appears that if the rate of speaking is increased, as it is during unstressed syllables, or when a gesture has a target quite opposite from those of the segments before and after it, articulatory positions may not be achieved as well as when more time is devoted to the gesture. This is the well-known principle of "undershoot" (Lindblom 1963). I think this accounts for the frequently observed change of stops to fricatives in intervocalic position, as in Spanish, see (2a). This change, spirantization, typically affects voiced stops intervocalically more than voiceless stops, and this is true of Spanish, too; see (2b). I think this stems from the fact that voiceless stops are generally longer than voiced stops (Westbury 1979) which in turn is due in part to the aerodynamic constraint discussed earlier: voiced stops are kept short in order to avoid the constraint which imperils voicing. A further indication that it is the short time devoted to the gesture which leads to undershoot is the fact that in Spanish (and many other languages) this spirantization of voiced stops does not occur when preceded by homorganic nasals, as in (2c). In this case the stop gesture (if not all other articulatory gestures associated with the stop) is quite long: it is the duration of the closure for the nasal plus that for the

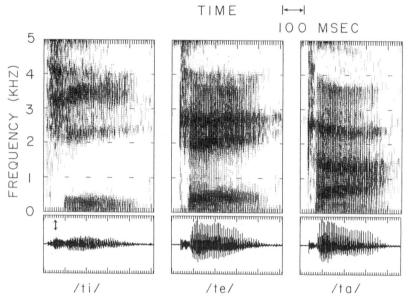

Figure 2. Spectrograms (top) and waveforms (bottom) of the syllables /ti/, /te/, and /tɑ/ spoken by the author. Arrows point to the greater-than-average noise at the release of the /t/ before the high close vowel /i/.

stop; as a consequence significant undershoot does not occur and the stop closure is realized as such.

(2a)   /goma/ [goma] 'gum' but /mago/ [maɣo] 'magician'
       /beso/ [beso] 'kiss' but /saber/ [saβeɾ] 'to know'
   b) /raton/ [raton] 'mouse'
       /tako/ [tako] 'wad'
   c) /mango/ [maŋgo] 'handle'
       /sombra/ [sombɾa] 'shadow'

Another case which probably involves elastic constraints is the perturbation of pitch (F0) after voiced and voiceless obstruents, specifically, the higher F0 found after voiceless segments as opposed to voiced. See figure 3 which shows the F0 curves on the vowels in the syllables /sɑ/ (solid line) and /zɑ/ (dashed line). This effect has been found in diverse languages (Ohala 1978 a). Its cause is not precisely known but there is good reason to suspect that like the other effects reviewed it has a physical cause — one hypothesis is that in implementing the voiced-voiceless

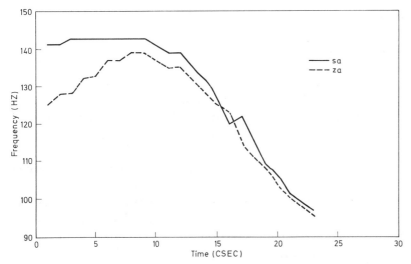

Figure 3. Fundamental frequency contours on the vowels in the syllables /sɑ/ (solid line) and /zɑ/ (dashed line), spoken by the author in the frame sentence 'Say _____'.

distinction some of the laryngeal tissues are tensed differentially in a way that affects F0 (Hombert, Ohala, and Ewan 1979, Ohala 1978 a). Quite plausibly this effect is behind the common pattern of distinctive tone developing on vowels that followed consonants that once manifested a voicing contrast (Edkins 1864: 54 ff.; Maspéro 1912: 112–114; Hombert et al. 1979; Ohala 1982); see (3, data from Svantesson 1983: 69).

(3)   *Southern Kammu*   *Northern Kammu*
         klaaŋ   kláaŋ   'eagle'
         glaaŋ   klàaŋ   'stone'

   Many more examples could be offered of sources of variation that can be traced to the various physical and physiological constraints applying during speech production (Ohala 1975, 1978 b, 1980, 1983 a, b) but perhaps the ones just reviewed are sufficient to document my claim of the pervasiveness of synchronic, inadvertent variation in pronunciation.
   I now turn to variation due to action of the listener.

3.2 Another source of variation is the listener

3.2.1 Confusion of similar sounds

The mapping between vocal tract shape and the output sound is a many-to-one mapping, i. e., the same or similar sound may result from two or more different vocal-tract configurations. When listeners repeat what they have heard they may use an articulation different from the original. Henry Sweet (1874: 15−16, 1900: 21−22) was among those who recognized this mechanism for sound change, exemplifying it with the variant forms of English 'through' as [θɹu] and [fɹu]. Modern acoustic analysis has revealed a great many other acoustic similarities between distinct articulations. These have been supplemented by confusion studies where listeners occasionally report they have heard a sound different from the one they were presented with. Crucially, those sounds shown to be similar by the acoustic analysis and/or the perceptual data are those which figure often in sound changes (Durand 1955; Winitz, Scheib, and Reeds 1972; Ohala and Lorentz 1977; Ohala 1975, 1978c, 1979, 1983c, 1985).

A literally classic example is the sound change of Indo-European labio-velar stops to labial stops (in certain vocalic environments) in Classical Greek, as in (4a, Meillet 1967). Other languages have similar sound changes as shown in (4b, Guthrie 1967−1970, Suarez 1973).

(4a)   *Proto-Indo-European*   *Classical Greek*
       *ekwos   hippos   'horse'
       *gwiwos   bios   'life'
 b)   *Proto-Bantu*   *West Teke*
       *-kumu   pfumu   'chief'
       Proto-Zapotec   *Matatlan Zapotec* *Isthmus Zapotec*
       *kkʷa-   kwan   pa   'interrogative
                                                           indefinite'

This impressed many linguists as a rather dramatic change, difficult to account for in articulatory terms, and so they attempted to construct some rather fantastic intermediate stages, including labial-velar stops [k͡p, g͡b] (Whatmough 1937). They were correct that it does not lend itself to an articulatory explanation but they might have saved themselves the trouble of inventing the implausible intermediate stages. Acoustic analysis reveals that these sounds are very close. Moreover, perceptual experiments show that they (or sounds similar to them) are often confused by listeners

(Winitz et al. 1972; Ohala and Lorentz 1977; Kawasaki 1982). (Moreover, in this case acoustic theory can derive or predict the similarity from first principles; Fant 1960.)

A similar case is that of palatalized labials and palatalized velars which change to apicals, as exemplified in several languages in (5, Bělič 1966, Li 1977, Malkiel 1963, Jaberg and Jud 1928 – 1940, Guthrie 1967 – 1970).

(5)   *Standard Czech   East Bohemian*
       mʲɛstɔ   nɛstɔ   'town'
       pʲɛt   tɛt   'five'
       Lungchow   T'ien-chow
       pjaa   tʃaa   'fish'
       Latin   Old Spanish   Spanish
       amplu > ampju   > antʃo   'large, spacious'
       Roman Italian   Genoese Italian
       pjeno   tʃena   'full'
       bjaŋko   dʒaŋku   'white'
       Proto-Bantu   Zulu
       pia   > -tʃha 'new'

Again, spectrograms reveal the closeness of, e. g., palatalized labials. Figures 4a and 4b demonstrate this. (Although since these are utterances produced by a native speaker of English, instead of a distinctively palatalized labial, we will have to content ourselves with the non-distinctive palatalization of labials that occurs before the palatal vowel /i/.) Figure 4a shows that /b/ and /d/ exhibit formant 2 and 3 patterns that are quite different before the vowel /ɑ/ — in fact formant 2 is rising in the former but falling in the latter —, whereas in Figure 4b, where the /b/ is phonetically palatalized, the two sounds have very similar patterns, showing only a slightly lower formant 2 and 3 in the case of /b/. What looks similar to the eye in these displays will sound similar to the ear and thus be subject to confusion.

These results are reinforced by listening tests: listeners are presented with spoken syllables or words (usually nonsense, i. e., eliminating higher-order redundancies) and are required to identify what they think they heard. The typical tabulation of the results, a confusion matrix, see Table 1 (from Winitz et al. 1972; spoken input sounds listed vertically, responses or output listed horizontally), reveals mistakes, at least some of which occur due to the auditory closeness of the target and the reported sounds. We see from this that the consonant in the syllable /pi/ is misheard

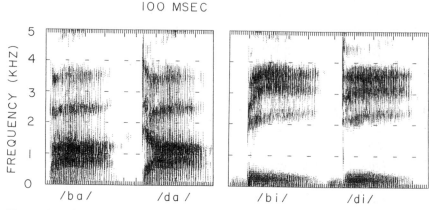

Figure 4. a. Spectrograms of the syllables /bɑ/, /dɑ/ spoken by the author. The transitions of formants 2 and 3 are quite different for the two stops. *b.* Spectrograms of the syllables /bi/, /di/ spoken by the author. Here the transitions of formants 2 and 3 are rather similar for the two stops.

as /t/ large percentage of time (38%), thus mirroring the sound change discussed earlier, where palatalized labials change to apicals. /k/ and /p/ also show a high degree of confusion before the vowel /u/, thus duplicating the sound change in (4). (This confusion matrix also shows an even higher percentage of confusions between /k/ and /t/ before the vowel /ɪ/, which helps to explain the very common change of "velar softening", e. g., English [tʃɪkən] 'chicken' from earlier *cicen* ([kiken]), cognate with 'cock'.)

When listeners confuse these sounds in listening tests they are, in effect, duplicating sound change in the laboratory. If they had spoken their responses out loud instead of marking them on paper, the parallel would be even more striking; this could easily be implemented by a trivial redesign of the typical confusion study.

3.2.2 Hypo-correction

Earlier I suggested that if there is so much variation in speech we should expect far more sound change than we actually find. Of course, part of the answer to this is that the listener who has to learn the pronunciation of words by hearing them from others has multiple sources of information concerning the pronunciation norm: other speakers' pronunciation, other listeners' reactions to his attempts at pronunciation, and, in certain literate

Table 1. Confusion matrix from Winitz et al. (1972). Spoken syllables consisted of stop bursts plus 100 msec of following transition and vowel; high-fidelity listening conditions.

	Heard:	/p/	/t/	/k/
Spoken:	/pi/	.46	.38	.17
	/pa/	.83	.07	.11
	/pu/	.68	.10	.23
	/ti/	.03	.88	.09
	/ta/	.15	.63	.22
	/tu/	.10	.80	.11
	/ki/	.15	.47	.38
	/ka/	.11	.20	.70
	/ku/	.24	.18	.58

cultures, the spelling. But there is another source of error correction: the listener's experience with speech. Confronted with a potential distortion, the listener can acquire sufficient experience to be able to factor it out. He knows that a slightly affricated release to a stop before a high front vowel or glide is to be expected and that it is not part of the speaker's intention. (I believe this phenomenon is related to that usually considered in psychology under perceptual constancy, e. g., the fact that when viewing objects illuminated by the setting sun we usually factor out the reddish tint imparted to all coloured objects by the sun's light and thereby achieve some colour constancy.)

We could represent this error correction using traditional phonological shorthand: the existence of the physical processes which give rise to spurious phonetic events, e. g., affrication of stops, may be represented as in (6).

(6)   t $--\rightarrow$ tʃ / _____ i   (physical phonetic process)

Such a process, I claim, gives rise in the mind of the listener to a rule (7) which undoes the process.

(7)   tʃ $--\rightarrow$ t / _____ i   (corrective rule counteracting (6))

Crucial to the implementation of rule (7) is the presence of the environment. If the environment were missing, however, that is, if the listener for some reason failed to detect it, the corrective rule would not be applied. Of course, the rule would also not be applied if the listener failed to construct the rule in the first place — as might be the case with an inexperienced listener. In either case, the physical phonetic process (6) would not be undone and would be taken by the listener at "face value" as the intended pronunciation. This is transparently the scenario of many familiar sound changes, as reviewed above, i.e., they constitute what Jakobson called phonologization of what were previously contextually conditioned phonetic events. What was "noise" in the signal gets incorporated in the signal. It is important to note that (6) is not a rule of grammar; it is a rule of physics, of the vocal tract. The listener has no access to the input of the rule, i.e., the intention of the speaker; he hears and copies at face value only the output.

Some implications of this conception of these sound changes should be emphasized. The change represented in (6) is a constant one and can be expected to occur, given the proper physical conditions, in the speech of every speaker of any language at any time. A sound change — a mini-sound change, if one prefers — occurs when a listener at some point in time takes the output of the rule as the pronunciation norm. We cannot predict when this misapprehension will occur but the probability of its occurrence must be relatively high.

From this we can conclude that when the development of distinctive vowel nasalization in French is described in the typical way as in (8),

(8)   bon — — → bõ

it is coded in a misleading way since it collapses two distinct processes. As given in (9) there is first a synchronic physical process of vowels being

(9)   bon — — → bõn
       bõn — — → bõ

nasalized before a nasal consonant, and second, there was the failure to detect the nasal consonant which therefore resulted in its omission. The first process is implemented by the speaker as an on-going condition. The second is implemented by the listener at a specific point in time. Again, neither constitutes a rule of grammar when the sound change first occurs. (It is, of course, possible that some other speakers/listeners, noticing alternate pronunciations of the same word, /bon/ ~ /bõ/, may formulate a rule in their grammars similar to (8), but such a rule or alternation, properly considered, is not part of the initiation of the sound change. It is, rather, part of the propagation of the already-initiated change.)

It is undoubtedly the case that when the vowel nasalization was taken to be distinctive by the listener it would have an exaggerated quality in his speech vis-à-vis the speech of the original speaker. Nevertheless, there is evidence that at its very inception the same degree of nasalization appears different to the listener depending on the interpretation given to it: Kawasaki (1986) showed that listeners judge the nasalization on the vowel in syllables like /mĩm/ to be greater when flanking nasal consonants have been spliced away than when they are retained.

Vowel nasalization also induces apparent changes in the quality of vowels, especially vowel height (Wright 1986). Beddor, Krakow, and Goldstein (1986) have shown that when syllables like [bẽnd] are produced, where the nasal consonant is preserved, this quality change is not noticed by listeners — presumably because they have implemented a corrective rule. But when the nasal — the segment which conditions the vowel nasalization — is deleted, the vowel quality change towards [æ] becomes readily apparent because in this case listeners cannot implement the correction.

This is a common and easily-demonstrated phenomenon using an interactive speech workstation that permits one to listen to selected parts of the speech signal: a speech sound "sounds" different depending on how much of the flanking sounds one includes. Without the flanking sounds, the stressed vowel in *welcome*, supposedly [ɛ], sounds more like [ɔ]; with the flanking sounds, the [ɛ] is readily heard. Such modified percepts mirror many common historical processes: the simultaneous change in the quality of a segment along with the loss of the environment which conditioned the change.

There are, of course, sound changes which have the character of being the phonologizations of phonetically motivated details in which the conditioning environment is not lost, e. g., vowel harmony (for its phonetic basis, see Öhman 1966). Either the corrective rules were not applied or were not created by some listeners. There is anecdotal evidence in support of the latter possibility: I interpret the vowel in *drink* as the same as that in *drip* /dɹɪp/ whereas other speakers equate it to the vowel in *dream* / dɹim/. (Similar disagreements exist about other vowels before /ŋ/ and also before /ɹ/.) Phonetically it is true that the vowel in *drink* is not identical with that in *drip* because — as I interpret it — the velar nasal has a long transition which could be taken as "tensing" the vowel. I apparently factor out this effect, attributing it to the consonant but other listeners attribute it to the vowel itself. (If the [ŋk] is spliced off, then I also hear this vowel as closer to that in *dream*.)

3.2.3 Hyper-correction

The existence of listeners' corrective rules sets the stage for another kind of variation leading to sound change: the inappropriate application of these corrective rules. The failure to implement the corrective rules was labelled 'hypo-correction'; implementing the rules when they are not called for, then, is 'hyper-correction'. This is familiar enough in other areas of grammar (e. g., the supposed Cockney [tʃɪkɪŋ] 'chicken', where the socially marked rule ɪŋ − − → ɪn which yields [stɛpɪn] instead of [stɛpɪŋ] 'stepping', is corrected; see, however, Sivertsen 1960: 129) and it may occur as well when listeners interpret the speech they hear. A few examples:

Darden (1970) describes a case in Slavic where the front vowel [a] becomes the back vowel [ɑ] in the environment of palatal or palatalized consonants; see (10).

(10)   mẽguk + ājisiji > mẽgučājsij > mẽgučājšiji 'softest'
        stoj + ā- > stojā 'stand'

This is, on the face of it, a rather unusual development since we expect back vowels to become front in the environment of front or palatalized segments. Well, apparently so did some of the listeners of this language. Accordingly, they applied their corrective rules and factored out what they thought was the overlaid frontness and reconstructed the back vowel [ɑ].

Shona, according to Mkanganwi (1972) shows a diachronic development where the labial velar glide [w] becomes the velar [ɣ] after labial consonants, as in (11).

(11) | *Proto-Bantu* | | *Pre-Shona* | | *Shona* | |
        |---|---|---|---|---|---|
        | *-bua | > | *-bwa | > | -bɣa | 'dog' |
        | *-mu- | > | kumwa | > | kumɣa | 'to drink' |

I interpret this as some listeners taking the labial part of the labial velar glide as a predictable offglide from the preceding labial consonant and therefore factoring it out, leaving just the velar component.

These are examples of dissimilation, of course, and constitute what may be characterized as auditory camouflage, i. e., the perceiver erroneously attributing a given detail to the surroundings rather than to the object it is actually a property of, e. g., attributing the whiteness of an arctic hare to the surrounding white snow and thus not recognizing it. I believe that the account just given for cases like these, so-called contact dissimilation, also applies to the better known dissimilation at a distance, e. g., Grassmann's Law in Sanskrit and Greek. (12) gives examples of Grassmann's Law and a few other cases. (Data from Grassmann 1863, Boyd-Bowman 1954, Karlgren 1923, Campbell 1973, Orr and Longacre 1968.)

(12)   Examples of dissimilation at a distance.

Languages involved		Example		
Indo-European >	Sanskrit	$*b^hend^h$ >	$band^h$-	'bind'
Pre-Classical	Classical			'hair'
Greek >	Greek	$*t^hrik^hos$ >	$trik^hos$	
Latin >	Italian	quīnque >	cinque	'five'
Ancient Chinese >	Cantonese	$*$pjam >	pin	'diminish'
Proto-Quichean >	Tzutujil	$*$k'aq >	$k^{'j}$aq	'flea'
Proto-Quechumaran >	Quechua	$*$t'ant'a >	t'anta	'bread'

As before, I claim that in these cases, given the same feature playing a distinctive role in two sites in a word, the listener interpreted its presence on one site as a predictable — and therefore detachable — spillover from the other site. Consistent with this — in fact predicted by it — is that dissimilation only involves features which phonetic studies have shown to be ones whose cues spread in time, e. g., aspiration, glottalization, retroflexion, labialization, palatalization, pharyngealization, etc., but should not involve features whose cues do not span long intervals, e. g., stop, affricate. For those features whose acoustic cues are well known through phonetic studies, this prediction is borne out (Ohala 1981 b, 1986).

There is additional evidence supporting this conception of dissimilation: As I discussed earlier, sound changes that come about due to hypocorrection, which is to say those where physically caused distortions get copied or phonologized, often involve loss of the conditioning environment along with the phonetically changed segment. In contrast, in cases of dissimilation, my account predicts that the conditioning environment may not be lost at the same time as the affected segment changes. That is, to consider a possible alternative version of Grassmann's Law in Sanskrit and the dissimilation of labialization in Latin, exemplified above, the kinds of sound changes in (13) should not happen.

(13) b^hend^h > ben   (where loss of the dissimilator is only found
        $k^wiŋk^we$ > kine   where it had caused dissimilation)

The conditioning environment may not be lost because it has to be there for the listener to assign the blame to for what he imagines to be the spread of one of its features elsewhere in the word. As far as I have been able to determine, this prediction is borne out — which amazes me since it could so easily have been falsified.

Furthermore, as pointed out to me by Paul Kiparsky, this account also explains what up to now remained a puzzle: sound changes due to hypo-correction often create new segments, e. g., the case mentioned above of the development of distinctive nasalization on vowels in French; but sound change due to dissimilation invariably results in segments already attested in the language's segment inventory, e. g., in Grassmann's Law the deaspiration of the voiced aspirates resulted in segments, the simple voiced stops, which were well established in the Sanskrit segment inventory. This would follow from the view of dissimilation as a normalizing or corrective process (even if inappropriately applied); the output of corrective rules must be a known entity.

Finally, there is experimental evidence. Beddor et al., cited above, have shown that their listeners who would compensate for the distorting effects of nasalization on vowel quality occasionally overcompensated and reacted as if the vowel they heard had a height in the direction opposite that caused by nasalization.

4. Discussion

I have given a relatively abbreviated account of what I believe to be some of the causes — the pre-conditions — of common sound changes attested in many unrelated languages. Although, as mentioned earlier, much of what I have presented has been said before by others, it is the combination of several points which differentiates this account from previous ones. Of these points, I would emphasize two.

4.1 Eschewing teleology

First, this account of sound change is entirely non-teleological. I have not said that sounds change in order to be easier to pronounce, to be easier to hear, to make phonological systems more symmetrical, to be easier to learn, or to achieve any other goal, however desirable it may seem, a priori, to linguists. In fact, I do not think sound change creates any significant improvement or defect in language. There is sufficient redundancy in language that the message which speech encodes gets through as well (or no worse) before and after sound change. The only teleology I need in my account − a very innocent one which does not contaminate its mechanistic purity − is that listeners do their best to imitate the pronunciations they hear (or think they hear) in others' speech and thus adhere to the pronunciation norm.

I exclude teleology not because it is impossible or even implausible that speakers choose, even unconsciously, to deviate from the established pronunciation norm, but rather because it is a sound research strategy. It is too easy to invoke teleology − purpose − without any real justification. Similarly, in explanations for phenomena in the physical world we eschew explanations of the sort "God wants it that way" etc., not because we are certain that God cannot influence things − in fact we cannot be sure of this − but rather because it is an extravagant assumption, too easily invoked, which deflects us from seeking more immediate causes.

In any case, there is a certain messiness connected with many teleological accounts of language change. For example, Lightner (1970) claims that distinctive vowel nasalization arises as in (8), above, in order to prevent merger and homophony between a form /bon/ which has lost its final /n/ and coexisting form /bo/. If so, one may legitimately ask why the lexical distinction is preserved so consistently with vowel nasalization and not some other feature which would serve as well, e. g., tone or creaky voice? Also, some homophony does result from such sound changes: in the history of French, *fin* 'end' > [fɛ̃]; *faim* 'hunger' > [fɛ̃]. Finally, if speakers had such control over their speech forms as to be able to compensate for the loss of the final nasal, one wonders why they deleted the final nasal in the first place. How can speakers be masters of pronunciation change in one area but helpless victims in other cases?

Teleology has occasionally been invoked for phenomena that, if properly investigated, might be amenable to a mechanistic account. Prague school phonologists and those influenced by them emphasize the role of overall phonological structure in determining sound change, e. g., the filling of a "hole" in the sound inventory of a language in order to make it more symmetrical or in the equilibrium (Jakobson 1978 [1931]; Martinet 1952). Symmetry undoubtedly pleases the aesthetic sense of the linguist but it is not clear what its value is for the native speaker for whom the sole function of the sound inventory is its capacity to carry signals, not to serve as an object of beauty. All human languages manifest asymmetry or disequilibrium in some part of their phonology but seem, nevertheless, to function adequately for communication. Still, "hole filling" sound changes and the fact that some sound changes seem to affect whole classes of sounds, e. g., Grimm's Law, suggest that somehow the phonological system of a language does play a role. I would speculate, though, that when, to pick an example discussed above, one vowel or a subset of vowels in a language becomes distinctively nasal, as happened to the French low vowels in the tenth century (Pope 1934: 169) listeners, by definition, learn to detect the acoustic differences between an oral and a nasal vowel. To the extent that the same acoustic cues would differentiate other oral/nasal vowel pairs[1], the listeners would be predisposed — auditorily sensitive, so to speak — to the presence of nasalization on other vowels, assuming these vowels were subject to the same conditions which led to the phonologization of the vowel nasalization in the first place. That is, the scenario for becoming distinctively nasalized would be essentially the same for all vowels as schematized in (9), but its initial occurrence on one vowel would set the stage for its occurrence on other vowels. There is no need to appeal to ill-defined notions such as "system pressure", "pattern symmetry", "equilibrium", and the like, nor to maintain that the language is any better or any more "fit" as a result of these sound changes. Indeed, after French took four centuries to create nasal counterparts for all of its vowels — achieving, one might imagine, a more nearly symmetrical vowel system, a series of mergers took place among the nasal vowels such that today only certain low vowels are distinctively nasal (Pope 1934: 169 ff.). It seems languages are never satisfied! More to the point, it seems that languages are not seeking the satisfaction of some "ideal" configuration.

It is somewhat ironic that whereas in generative phonology sound changes are taken as evidence that speakers have altered their grammars (King 1969), in the picture I present here it is the *lack of sound change* (in the face of the extensive phonetic variation in speech) which prompts the hypothesis that speakers create rules — corrective rules — in their grammars; sound change itself, in its initiation, is taken to be non-mentalistic.

4.2 Studying sound change in the laboratory

Second, and this is the most important aspect, I have tried to show how most details of this account can be studied in the laboratory. I can, in fact, give recipes for eliciting in the lab sound changes caused by the different mechanisms discussed: confusion of similar sounds, hypo-correction, and hyper-correction:

1. As discussed above, to duplicate in the laboratory sound changes due to the similarity of sounds one only needs to conduct a simple listening test in which one notes instances of listeners identifying one sound as another.
2. To demonstrate hypo-correction: record speech exhibiting the kind of physical phonetic effects discussed earlier, and then let subjects listen to these samples with the conditioning environment deleted or masked. Under these conditions, listeners are unable to engage the kind of error-correcting strategies discussed above and will tend to identify the sounds in their distorted form — more so than when they hear them with the conditioning environment intact.
3. To demonstrate hyper-correction: let listeners hear speech samples having a segment bearing a particular distinctive feature juxtaposed to a segment which might have contributed that feature spuriously. Listeners will report less of that feature than is objectively present by virtue of having factored it out. The experiments by Kawasaki (1986) and Beddor et al. (1986) cited above, as well as those by Mann and Repp (1980) and Ohala and Feder (1987), illustrate this.

Bringing the study of sound change into the laboratory obviously does not by itself immediately answer all the questions one might have about the details of its mechanisms but it does permit systematic work to be started on these questions. To cite one example: it seems that a great many sound changes are asymmetrical in their direction. An important example is velar softening, k — — → tʃ /i, mentioned above. Significantly, this asymmetry is manifested in the confusion studies, too; Table 1 shows that /k/ was confused with /t/ before /i/ 47% of the time but /t/ with /k/ in the same environment only 9%. It is possible to offer phonetically-based hypotheses for this phenomenon (Ohala 1983 b, c, 1985) which can ultimately be subjected to laboratory evaluation.

What is important about "laboratory evaluation" is the possibility of conducting controlled observations on sound change in order to carefully evaluate competing hypotheses concerning its mechanisms. In this sense "laboratory" should not be interpreted literally as "a space equipped with an elaborate array of instruments" but rather as a set of techniques or an arsenal of methods which can be used anywhere. Having recourse to such methods is the only way the study of sound change is going to progress beyond the Kiplingesque *Just-So* stories offered in the past.

Note

1. This is largely true. Vis-à-vis their oral counterparts, nasal vowels have greater bandwidth of formants, a lower ratio of the intensity of formant 1 to that of the higher formants, and, possibly, an extra nasal formant in the region around 500 Hz (see Ohala 1975 and references therein).

References

Beddor, Patrice S. — Rena A. Krakow — Louis M. Goldstein
   1986   "Perceptual constraints and phonological change: a study of nasal vowel height", *Phonology Yearbook* 3: 197 — 217.
Bělič, Jaromír
   1966   "K otázce zaniklého litomyšlského *t, d, n* za někdejší *p', b', m'.*" *Slavica Pragensia* 8, *Acta Univ. Carolinae Philologica*, 1 — 3.
Bell, H.
   1971   "The phonology of Nobiin Nubian." *African Language Review* 9: 115 — 159.
Boyd-Bowman, Peter
   1954   *From Latin to Romance in sound charts*. Washington, DC: Georgetown University Press.
Bybee, Joan L. — E. Pardo
   1981   "On lexical and morphological conditioning of alternations: a nonce-probe experiment with Spanish verbs", *Linguistics* 19: 937 — 968.
Campbell, Lyle
   1973   *Quichean linguistic prehistory*. [University of California Publications in Linguistics, No. 81.] Berkeley: University of California Press.

Chao, Yuen-Ren
1936   "Types of plosives in Chinese", *Proceedings of the 2nd International Congress of Phonetic Sciences*, 106 – 110 (Cambridge: Cambridge University Press).
Chomsky, Noam – Morris Halle
1968   *The sound pattern of English* (New York: Harper & Row).
Comte, Auguste
1974   *The essential Comte*. Selected from *Cours de philosophie positive*, edited by Stanislav Andreski, transl. by Margaret Clarke [first published 1830 – 1842] (London: Croom Helm).
Darden, Bill J.
1970   "The fronting of vowels after palatals in Slavic", *Proceedings of the Regional Meeting, Chicago Linguistic Society* 6: 459 – 470.
Dinnsen, Daniel A.
1980   "Phonological rules and phonetic explanation", *Journal of Linguistics* 16: 171 – 191.
Durand, Marguerite
1955   "Du rôle de l'auditeur dans la formation des sons du language", *Journal de Psychologie Normale et Pathologique* 52: 347 – 355.
Edkins, Joseph
1864   *A grammar of the Chinese colloquial language commonly called the Mandarin dialect* (Shanghai: Presbyterian Mission Press).
Fant, Gunnar
1960   *Acoustic theory of speech production* (The Hague: Mouton).
Gamkrelidze, Thomas V.
1975   "On the correlation of stops and fricatives in a phonological system", *Lingua* 35: 231 – 261.
Grassmann, Herman
1863   "Ueber die Aspiraten und ihr gleichzeitiges Vorhandensein im An- und Auslaute der Wurzels." *Z. f. v. Sprachforschung auf dem Gebiete des Deutschen, Griechischen und Lateinischen* 12: 2.81 – 138.
Greenberg, Joseph H.
1970   "Some generalizations concerning glottalic consonants, especially implosives", *International Journal of American Linguistics* 36: 123 – 145.
Guthrie, Malcolm
1967 – 1970   *Comparative Bantu*. 4 vols. (Gregg).
Hombert, Jean-Marie – John J. Ohala – William G. Ewan
1979   "Phonetic explanations for the development of tones", *Language* 55: 37 – 58.
Jaberg, Karl – Jakob Jud
1928 – 1940   *Sprach und Sachatlas Italiens und der Südschweiz*. Zurich.
Jakobson, Roman
1978   "Principles of historical phonology" [orig. published 1931, *Travaux du Cercle Linguistique de Prague* 4], in: *Readings in historical phonology*, edited by Philip Baldi – Ronald N. Werth, 103 – 120 (University Park, PA: Pennsylvania State University Press).
Karlgren, Bernhard
1923   *Analytic dictionary of Chinese and Sino-Japanese*. Paris: Librairie Orientaliste Paul Geuthner.
Kawasaki, Haruko
1986   "Phonetic explanation for phonological universals: the case of distinctive vowel nasalization", in: *Experimental phonology*, edited by John J. Ohala – Jeri J. Jaeger, 81 – 103 (Orlando, FL: Academic Press).
1982   *An acoustic basis for universal constraints on sound sequences*. Ph. D. dissertation, University of California, Berkeley.

King, Robert D.
1969   *Historical linguistics and generative grammar* (Englewood Cliffs, NJ: Prentice-Hall).
Lass, Roger
1980   *On explaining language change* (Cambridge: Cambridge University Press).
Li, Fang Kuei
1977   *A handbook of comparative Tai.* Univ. Press of Hawaii.
Lightner, Theodore M.
1970   "Why and how does vowel nasalization take place?", *Papers in Linguistics* 2: 179–226.
Lindblom, Björn
1963   "Spectrographic study of vowel reduction", *Journal of the Acoustical Society of America* 35: 1773–1781.
Maddieson, Ian
1984   *Patterns of sounds* (Cambridge: Cambridge University Press).
Malkiel, Yakov
1963   "The interlocking of narrow sound change, broad phonological pattern, level of transmission, areal configuration, sound symbolism." *Archivum Linguisticum* 15.2.144–173; 3.1–33.
Mann, Virginia A.–Bruno H. Repp
1980   "Influence of vocalic context on perception of the [š] vs [s] distinction", *Perception & Psychophysics* 28: 213–228.
Martinet, André
1952   "Function, structure, and sound change", *Word* 8: 1–32.
Maspéro, Henri
1912   "Études sur la phonétique historique de la langue annamite: Les initiales", *Bulletin de l'École Française d'Extrême Orient* 12.
Meillet, Antoine
1967   *The comparative method in historical linguistics.* Paris: Librairie Honore Champion, Editeur.
Mkangawi, K. G.
1972   "The relationships of coastal Ndau to the Shona dialects of the interior", *African Studies* 31: 111–137.
Nelson, Winston L.–Joseph S. Perkell–John R. Westbury
1984   "Mandible movements during increasingly rapid articulations of single syllables: preliminary observations", *Journal of the Acoustical Society of America* 75: 945–951.
Ohala, John J.
1975   "Phonetic explanations for nasal sound patterns", in: *Nasálfest: Papers from a symposium on nasal and nasalization,* edited by Charles A. Ferguson–Larry M. Hyman–John J. Ohala, 289–316 (Stanford: Language Universals Project).
1978a   "The production of tone", in: *Tone: a linguistic survey,* edited by Victoria A. Fromkin, 5–39 (New York: Academic Press).
1978b   "Phonological notations as models", in: *Proceedings, 12th International Congress of Linguists, Vienna, Aug. 28–Sept. 2, 1977,* edited by Wolfgang U. Dressler–Wolfgang Meid, 811–816 (Innsbruck: Innsbrucker Beiträge zur Sprachwissenschaft).
1978c   "Southern Bantu vs. the world: the case of palatalization of labials", *Berkeley Ling. Soc., Proc., Ann. Meeting* 4: 370–386.
1979   "The contribution of acoustic phonetics to phonology", in: *Frontiers of speech communication research,* edited by Björn Lindblom–Sven Öhman, 355–363 (London: Academic Press).

1980 "The application of phonological universals in speech pathology", in: *Speech and language: advances in basic research and practice* 3, edited by Norman J. Lass, 75–97 (New York: Academic Press).

1981 a "Articulatory constraints on the cognitive representation of speech", in: *The cognitive representation of speech*, edited by Terry Myers–John Laver–John Anderson, 111–122 (Amsterdam: North Holland).

1981 b "The listener as a source of sound change", in: *Papers from the Parasession on Language and Behavior*, edited by C. S. Masek–R. A. Hendrick–M. F. Miller, 178–203 (Chicago: Chicago Ling. Soc.).

1982 "Physiological mechanisms underlying tone and intonation", in: *Preprints, Working Group on Intonation, 13th Int. Cong. of Linguists, Tokyo, 29 Aug.– 4 Sept. 1982*, edited by Hiroya Fujisaki–Eva Garding, 1–12.

1983 a "The origin of sound patterns in vocal tract constraints", in: *The production of speech*, edited by Peter F. MacNeilage, 189–216 (New York: Springer-Verlag).

1983 b "The phonological end justifies any means", in: *Proc. of the XIIIth Int. Cong. of Linguists, Tokyo, 29 Aug.–4 Sept. 1982*, edited by Shirô Hattori–Kazuko Inoue, 232–243 (Tokyo: Sanseido Shoten).

1983 c "The direction of sound change", in: *Abstracts of the Tenth Int. Congr. of Phonetic Sciences*, edited by Antonie Cohen–Marcel P. R. v. d. Broecke, 253–258 (Dordrecht: Foris).

1985 "Linguistics and automatic speech processing", in: *New systems and architectures for automatic speech recognition and synthesis* [NATO ASI Series, Series F: Computer and System Sciences, Vol. 16], edited by Renato de Mori–Ching-Y. Suen, 447–475 (Berlin: Springer-Verlag).

1986 "Phonological evidence for top-down processing in speech perception", in: *Invariance and variability in speech processes*, edited by Joseph S. Perkell–Dennis H. Klatt, 386–397 (Hillsdale, NJ: Lawrence Erlbaum).

1987 "Explanation, evidence, and experiment in phonology", in: *Phonologica 1984*, edited by Wolfgang U. Dressler–Hans C. Luschützky–Oskar E. Pfeiffer–John R. Rennison, 215–225 (Cambridge University Press).

Ohala, John J.–Deborah Feder
1987 "Listeners' identification of speech sounds is influenced by adjacent 'restored' phonemes", in: *Proc. 11th International Congress of Phonetic Sciences, Tallinn, Estonia, USSR* 4, 120–123.

Ohala, John J.–James Lorentz
1977 "The story of [w]: an exercise in the phonetic explanation for sound patterns", *Berkeley Ling. Soc., Proc., Ann. Meeting* 3: 577–599.

Ohala, John J.–Carol J. Riordan
1979 "Passive vocal tract enlargement during voiced stops", in: *Speech communication papers*, edited by Jared J. Wolf–Dennis H. Klatt, 89–92 (New York: Acoustical Society of America).

Öhman, Sven E. G.
1966 "Coarticulation in VCV utterances: spectrographic measurements", *Journal of the Acoustical Society of America* 39: 151–168.

Orr, C.–Robert E. Longacre
1968 "Proto-Quechuamaran." *Language* 44: 528–555.

Passy, Paul
1890 *Étude sur les changements phonétiques* (Paris: Librairie Firmin-Didot).

Pinkerton, Sandra
1986 "Quichean (Mayan) glottalized and nonglottalized stops: a phonetic study with implications for phonological universals", *Experimental phonology*, ed-

ited by John J. Ohala—Jeri J. Jaeger, 125—139 (Orlando, FL: Academic Press).

Pope, M. K.
1934   *From Latin to Modern French with especial consideration of Anglo-Norman* (Manchester: Manchester University Press).

Sherman, Donald
1975   "Stop and fricative systems: a discussion of paradigmatic gaps and the question of language sampling", *Working Papers in Language Universals (Stanford)* 17: 1—31.

Sivertsen, Eva
1960   *Cockney phonology* (Oslo: Oslo University Press).

Suarez, J. A.
1973   "On Proto-Zapotec phonology." *International Journal of American Linguistics* 39: 236—249.

Svantesson, Jan-Olof
1983   *Kammu phonology and morphology.* [Travaux de l'institut de linguistique de Lund 18.] Lund: Gleerup.

Sweet, Henry
1874   *History of English sounds* (London: Trübner).
1900   *The history of language* (London: Dent).

Thumb, A.—K. Marbe
1901   *Experimentelle Untersuchungen über die psychologischen Grundlagen der sprachlichen Analogiebildung* (Leipzig: Wilhelm Engelmann).

Westbury, John R.
1979   *Aspects of the temporal control of voicing in consonant clusters in English.* Ph. D. Dissertation, Univ. of Texas, Austin.

Whatmough, Joshua
1937   "The development of the Indo-European labiovelars with special reference to the dialects of ancient Italy", *Acta Jutlandica* 9: 45—56.

Winitz, Harris—M. E. Scheib—James A. Reeds
1972   "Identification of stops and vowels for the burst portion of /p, t, k/ isolated from conversational speech", *Journal of the Acoustical Society of America* 51: 1309—1317.

Wright, James T.
1986   "The behavior of nasalized vowels in the perceptual vowel space", in: *Experimental phonology*, edited by John J. Ohala—Jeri J. Jaeger, 45—67 (Orlando, FL: Academic Press).

The role of children in linguistic change

Suzanne Romaine

0. Introduction

It should not be surprising to find some similarities between language change and a child's acquisition of language. Language "changes" as it is passed from one generation to another. To the extent that acquisition is a developmental process, which is ongoing in real time, looking at the stages which children go through in acquiring language is one way of observing change in progress. However, this is not the sense in which historical linguists usually talk about language change. They have in general taken a long-term view of change and compared groups of genetically related languages and successive stages within one language over many centuries. Much of the discussion of types of changes and explanations of how and why change takes place has been at a very abstract level. There has been correspondingly less attention paid to the changes which take place within the lifespan of an individual (i. e., age-grading), or within one generation of speakers in a speech community, and the relationship between changes at the individual and group level to long-term changes in the language system.

The main topic I will consider here is the role of children in the overall communicative structure of the speech community. I will establish whether there is evidence that variation in children's language use deviating from adult norms contributes to long-term restructuring of the language system. There are a number of different perspectives one could take on this question. One can take age-graded linguistic behaviour as a starting point. It is known that there are characteristic sociolinguistic patterns associated with different age groups (see Romaine 1984: 4.3). It is often the case that children use more non-standard variants than adults, but with increasing age, they more closely approximate the norms of adult speech as they become exposed to the standard language, particularly through formal education. There is also evidence to indicate that children may be more likely than adults to restructure certain aspects of their grammar in more far-reaching ways, particularly under the influence of their peers (cf. Romaine 1984: 6.3). This suggests that in the long run children may be the prime instigators of change, or that the process of acquisition involves certain natural processes which have been found to apply in language history. I will concentrate on these two dimensions of the problem, looking first, however, at the nature of the relationship between age-grading and long-term linguistic change.

1. Age-grading and language change: some early studies

One of the major aims of Labov's (1972) research on sociolinguistic patterns is to show how these are connected with certain types of language change.[1] One of the first empirical demonstrations of the importance of age-grading as a mechanism in the transmission of linguistic change, however, is in the work of Gauchat (1905) and Hermann (1929) in the Swiss village of Charmey. Gauchat found that there was variability in the realization of certain phonological variables related to age and sex. In one particular case he observed fluctuation amongst the middle generation (30 – 60 year olds) between the form used by the oldest generation (60 – 90 year olds) and the one used by the youngest generation (under 30 years). The pattern of age grading is shown in Table 1; the case in point is a change from [ʎ] to [j].

Table 1. Data from three generations of Charmey speakers (Gauchat 1905: 205)

Generation: I	II	III
90 – 60 years	60 – 30 years	under 30
ʎ	ʎ and j	j

In 1929 Hermann conducted a follow-up investigation to see if some of the variability observed by Gauchat had led to change. By looking at what had happened to the two younger generations of speakers and finding that the old form [ʎ] had been largely replaced by [j], he concluded that Gauchat had indeed obtained a record of sound change in progress. This finding was an important one from both a theoretical and methodological standpoint. Methodologically, it meant that sound change could be "observed" as it was taking place in a community by looking at the linguistic behaviour of different generations of speakers. In other words, there was a relationship between apparent time (i. e., age-grading) and real time (i. e., long-term) such that contemporary variation represented a stage in long-term change. This relationship may not always hold true, however. Differences in the behaviour of age groups at a single point in time may be only a manifestation of age-grading and tell us nothing about change in real time. The same "changes" may repeat themselves in each new generation as part of the developmental sequence of acquiring a language and contribute nothing in the long run to overall changes in the speech community. The only way to establish that patterns of age-grading represent a stage in real long-term change is by comparison of observation from two different points in time. In the case of Charmey, it was because Hermann could compare his own findings with those of Gauchat from thirty years earlier that he could conclude that the new variant [j] had become established in the community. Retrospectively then, there had been a change of the type $[\Lambda] \rightarrow [j]$.

From a theoretical perspective this case was significant in that it implicated variability in the process of change. The finding that change took place by means of variation between old and new norms, which eventually was resolved in favour of one of the competing variants challenged earlier views, which were based on the notion of a homogeneous system of rules which changed discretely from generation to generation. So strictly speaking then, the rule which I wrote above describes the beginning and end point of the change, but glosses over the process by which it came about. It can be amended as follows so as to show the intermediate stage: $[\Lambda] \rightarrow [\Lambda] \sim [j] \rightarrow [j]$. The introduction of a new variant into a speech community does not in itself constitute a change; it is only when others adopt it that it spreads and is transmitted from one generation to the next, and change takes place. This suggests that new innovations have to keep recurring within individuals until they are selected for some reason and transmitted. Labov's work has been particularly important in elucidating reasons why some changes eventually spread through a community. His study of a sound change on Martha's Vineyard (1963) is now taken to be a classic illustration of the social factors which fuel and give direction to variability. He found age-grading in the community with younger generations using the more centralized variants more frequently than older ones. By comparing his own observations with those made thirty years earlier by fieldworkers for the Linguistic Atlas of New England, Labov was able to determine that centralization was a new feature being introduced into the community.

2. Age-grading and language change: children vs. adults

I will next examine two cases of age-grading in terms of their implications for language change. As a first case, let us consider variation in the realization of post-vocalic *r* in the speech of Edinburgh school children, where age-grading is connected with sex differentiation. The children whose speech I studied used three variants of post-vocalic /r/: 1. [r] an alveolar tap or trill; 2. [ɹ] a voiced frictionless continuant; and 3. ø, lack of post-vocalic /r/. The first variant is the most frequent and is the one which is perhaps most widespread in varieties of Scottish English, as far as we can tell (cf., e. g., Grant 1914). The second most frequent realization is the voiced frictionless continuant; it is particularly associated with Scottish Standard English (and Highland English). It has also been identified as a marker of "polite speech" and has become a stereotype, especially of middle class female speech. The third variant is the most infrequent and there is no mention of it in the literature on Scots speech; the only record of it is a personal observation made by David Abercrombie, who identified it in a particular area of Edinburgh. It was partly for this reason that I chose this part of the city for my fieldwork. The choice among the three variants is phonetically conditioned by the following environment; namely, whether the word-final /r/ is followed by a word beginning with a consonant vowel or a pause. I will discuss those here (see Romaine 1978 for details), but will confine myself to the pattern of sex and age differentiation displayed by the variable.

Perhaps the most important social factor which affects the realization of the variable is the sex of the speaker. This can be seen in Table 2.

It is evident that there is sharp stratification of the variable: girls are almost always rhotic and most frequently use [ɹ], while boys are less frequently rhotic and tend to use [r] more frequently than girls. The findings lend empirical support to two earlier observations; firstly, that the use of [ɹ] is a marker of female speech; and secondly, that a "new"

Table 2. Sex differentiation in the realization of postvocalic /r/ in Edinburgh school children (Figures are %).

	Males	Females
Variant		
[r]	54	41
[ɹ]	24	51
ø	22	8

variant, *r*-lessness, is being systematically used. The question is whether this evidence is indicative of an ongoing change in the wider community.

There is no evidence from earlier records around the turn of the century of *r*-lessness in Scots speech or of [ɹ] as a feature of working-class speech in Edinburgh. However, since the latter variant has been part of the Lowland Scottish linguistic scene since at least the turn of the century, it is highly unlikely that the use of [ɹ] by these young children is a change which has been repeating itself in each new generation of working class speech. It is less easy to assert this conclusion for the use of *r*-lessness, since /r/ tends to be acquired late. Therefore, we cannot conclude much from the fact that it is a fairly frequently used form by the youngest children. However if the use of ø were purely a developmental phenomenon, we would expect it more or less to disappear with increasing age. As can be seen in Table 3, which shows the pattern of age-grading for the variable *r*, this is not the case. The ten-year olds use it, and if these scores are broken down for each sex, we can see that *r*-lessness is a well established male variant for the ten-year olds.

Table 3. Age-grading of post-vocalic /r/

Age	10	8	6
r variants			
[r]	50	44	46
[ɹ]	32	44	33
ø	18	12	21

Among the most important indicators of sound change in the adult population are irregularities in class and style variation or unusual patterns of age and sex differentiation (cf., e. g., Labov 1966 and Trudgill 1974). Trudgill (1972: 179) has emphasized the importance of sex differentiation as an agent in linguistic change. His claim is that patterns of sex differentiation deviating from the norm indicate that a linguistic change is taking place. From the indications we have so far, *r*-lessness and the use of [ɹ] would appear to be competing trends which exemplify two different types of linguistic change: change from above and change from below (Labov 1966: 328). Each of these is associated with social factors of a different nature. The pattern of sex differentiation for *r* is shown in Table 4.

Table 4. Age-grading and sex differentiation of post-vocalic /r/.

Age	10		8		6	
r variants	M	F	M	F	M	F
[r]	57	45	48	40	59	33
[ɹ]	15	54	37	54	16	50
ø	28	1	15	6	25	17

r-lessness seems to be an example of change from below. It manifests itself as a gradual shift in the behavior of successive generations well below the level of conscious awareness of the speaker. This kind of shift typically begins with a particular group in the social structure and becomes more generalized in the speech of other groups. Observations on the loss of post-vocalic /r/ in Edinburgh indicate that it is a new feature adopted by the younger generation of working-class speakers in a particular area of Edinburgh. Labov (1966) notes that change from below is usually accomplished without much public attention and will generally become subject to overt pressure from above at a later stage in its spread. It is not uncommon in sound changes of this type for social reaction to fasten on and force a reversal in whole or in part by pressure from upper groups in the social hierarchy. And, in this case, it is likely that this feature will arouse some attention since *r*-lessness belongs to prestigious speech in Britain, most notably RP.

The use of [ɹ], on the other hand, seems to be an example of a change from above, which is fairly well advanced. It is being spread by overt social pressure from the top of the hierarchy since [ɹ] has been associated with middle class, and particularly female speech in Scotland. Furthermore, it has been linked with Highland English, which is one of the few English accents native to Scotland, which has prestige in, and outside of, Scotland. In addition, [ɹ] has long been endorsed for teaching purposes in teacher-training colleges in Scotland (cf., e. g., MacAllister 1963). However, since attention was first drawn to its presence in the speech of teenage girls who attended the prestigious Edinburgh fee-paying schools, there has been no record of it in the speech of young working-class girls.

Thus, it seems that both males and females are innovating in this case and females are clearly the innovators in the prestige form. It is interesting that the males are innovating in a direction away from the local educated Scots prestige norm, but in adopting *r*-lessness their usage happens to coincide with a much larger national norm. This pattern of sex differentiation can be understood in connection with Trudgill's (1972) distinction between overt and covert prestige.

The introduction of *r*-lessness seems to be a separate development in Scots, which is not being adopted by conscious imitation of an overt prestige model such as RP.[2] If this had been the case, then we would have expected the females to initiate the shift of the norm in this direction. Females have tended to be the main innovators of overt prestige forms. The girls in this case, however, are more affected by the pressure exerted by local norms and assert their status within the Edinburgh social structure (cf. Romaine 1980 for a discussion of "local identity").

The somewhat irregular pattern of style differentiation obtained for the ten-year olds supports the idea that the male and female variants have roughly equal prestige, though of two different types. The fact that the boys use more [ɹ] forms in the reading passage suggests that there is overt prestige associated with the variant. However, the girls' increased use of ø in the same context could indicate that there is covert prestige attached to ø. Trudgill (1972: 10) has cited an instance in which it is not just the male speakers who attach covert prestige to certain linguistic features but also younger female speakers. And he has also reported a similarly complex change at work in Norwich in which overt and covert prestige coincide in the case of the variable *o* as in *top, dog* etc. In RP this vowel is realized as a rounded [ɒ], while the non-RP vowel, [a], is unrounded. The rounded vowel is being introduced into Norwich English by middle-class women as well as by working-class men in imitation of the local working-class speech in Suffolk. Thus, the target is objectively the same, but the subjective orientation of those who aim at it is quite different.

The Edinburgh case and many others demonstrate the importance of the social value of a variable, especially its association with a group in society who are perceived and evaluated by others in terms of their relative prestige or stigma, in tracking the spread of a change through society. Gauchat (1905: 230–2) for example, recognized that individuals were ultimately responsible for introducing new variants, but was at a loss to explain how it was that some were transmitted and accepted by others. He asks:

> comment s'explique le changement de l'articulation des débutants et comment faut-il que ces débutants soient faits pour devenir influents? Faut-il être un enfant de riche ou de maître de l'école pour jouer un rôle dans l'évolution linguistique?

Labov argues that we should approach the problem of why sound changes by looking for the social location of the originators, i. e., who is responsible for a change, how does influence spread in the community, and what are the social roles and relations of the innovators to others in the community? Labov's (1980) answer to these questions is that speakers who are most advanced in ongoing sound changes are those with the highest status in their local community (not necessarily the highest in the larger social hierarchy), and who have the highest number of contacts within and outside local networks and neighbourhoods. This social profile of innovators as individuals who are aware of and have contact with the next larger level of social communication receives support from research done in such diverse places as Belfast (Milroy 1980) and Mombasa (see also Russell 1982). Labov (1980: 262) argues that the functions of language reflected in these sound changes "cannot be limited to the communication of referential information". They have to do with "the emblematic function of phonetic differentiation: the identification of a particular way of speaking within the norms of a local community."

I will turn to another case of age-grading to see what implications it has for language change. The case in question, the variable *t* in Swedish, is quite a complex one in terms of its linguistic and social conditioning. It affects not only the realization of certain verb forms (e. g., the preterite and past participles) but also the inflected form of the definite article in the noun. The absence of final *t/d* has been well documented for a variety of urban and rural Swedish dialects since before the turn of the century. Wessén (1965) believes that to some extent the variation is correlated with the dichotomy between urban and rural speech; forms with *t* are modelled after the written language and are found more often in urban areas. This together with the influx of people to the towns from various parts of Sweden has tended to level out dialect differences. However, since the towns also exert their own linguistic pressure, forms retaining /t/ are to be found in the rural dialects too. Loss of /t/ is not due solely to the alleged conservatism of rural speech; it is widespread, for example, in dialects of Swedish spoken in Finland. Bergroth (1924: 16) observed that in Finnish Swedish the inflectional suffix /t/ was never pronounced in neuter singular nouns, (e. g. *huset*). Nyholm's research (1976) supports this report at least for the Swedish spoken in Helsinki. Table 5 compares his results (Nyholm 1976: 10) with those from some studies done in Stockholm (e. g., Raittila 1969). I have included in the table the results for Nordberg's survey of Eskilstuna speech and those of Widmark (1977: 252) for Uppsala. (The latter are based on self-reports of informants.) The results are shown for three social class groups, where I is the highest.

Table 5. Per cent of /t/ retained regional dialects of Swedish in relation to social class.

Class City	I	II	III	Average
Stockholm	88	94	76	86
Eskilstuna	84	62	35	60
Uppsala	54	45	26	42
Helsinki	7	8	2	6

We can see the effects of social class stratification and regional variation. The highest social group is closest to the standard and the lowest furthest from it. The geographical dimension shows the importance of Stockholm as the stronghold of standard speech; the further one goes from Stockholm, the less pervasive is the influence of the standard language. It is interesting that in Helsinki, which is most distant, the trend is still the same: those who are more educated are somewhat (although not much in real terms) closer to the standard.

The morphological consequences of loss of final *t/d* are quite far-reaching. If we look just at the verbal paradigm for instance, and compare the typical forms used in Helsinki with those of standard Swedish, we can see that only in two cases are the forms the same in the two varieties (i. e., the infinitive and imperative); otherwise, the two are different, with Helsinki Swedish making no distinction between the present, preterite and past participle, all of which are unsuffixed. (See Nyholm 1976: 22.)

Comparison of Helsinki and Standard Swedish verb paradigms[3]

	Helsinki Swedish	Standard Swedish
infinitive:	Det är svårt att kasta boll.	Det är svårt att kasta boll. 'It is difficult to play catch.'

present tense:	Hon kasta boll just nu.	Hon kastar boll just nu. 'She is playing catch now.'
preterite:	Hon kasta boll igår.	Hon kastade boll igår 'She played catch yester-day.'
past participle:	Hon ha kasta boll.	Hon har kastat boll. 'She has played catch.'
imperative:	Kasta boll!	Kasta boll! 'Play catch!'

There is evidence from the written language in addition to that from a number of regional dialects to support the existence of extensive absence of both /t/ and /d/ from the 16th century onwards. There is often a confusion between the two in spelling and hypercorrection, i. e., instances where /t/ and /d/ have been incorrectly added. In an examination of style differentiation in the comedies of Gyllenborg (an 18th-century play-wright), Widmark (1970 b: 11, 13) cites short forms such as *klappa* (*klappade* 'knocked'), *slute* (*slutet* 'the end' and *ha* (*hade*/*har* 'had'/'to have') as instances of colloquial 17th-century speech.

From the 18th century onwards, however, evidence for deletion in the written language declines. Under the influence of standardization of spelling and grammar, /t/ and /d/ were "re-"introduced. Vast morpho-logical syncretism was averted. Overall, the changes which are taking place in the morphology of Swedish are indicative of increasing stan-dardization. One of the most significant developments in the history of early modern Swedish (and for that matter, probably most of the standard languages of the major western industrialized nations) was the codifica-tion of grammar, norms of pronunciation, spread of universal education and literacy. This influence works its way "top down", that is, it affects the best educated first, and emanates from urban centres, like Stockholm, which are connected with the rise of the standard.[4]

The change towards the more standard realizations is most advanced in the noun and less so in the verbal paradigm; and in the latter, more standardization is evident in the past participle than in the preterite (cf. Nordberg 1972: 54 and Tingbrand 1973: 53). This can be seen in Tables 6 and 7.

Table 6 shows the results in Eskilstuna for the loss of *t*/*d* in preterite forms of first conjugation verbs (e. g. *kallade* 'called'). There is evidence of age differentiation, but little sex differentiation.

Table 6. Percentage of forms without *t/d* for preterite forms in Eskilstuna speech.

Class	I		II		III
	66		90		97
Sex		M		F	
		84		85	
Age					
Younger (16−45)	58		91		94
Older (61−75+)	73		91		98

Looking at the noun paradigm in Table 7 (i. e., loss of /t/ in forms like *huset*), we can see that the most important dimension is again age. In the two oldest age groups speakers use forms without /t/ at a rate of about 20% as compared to the youngest groups, who average 11%. There is also sex differentiation. The results here are for the lowest social group, III.

Table 7. Deletion of /t/ as a function of age and sex in Eskilstuna

Age		Younger (16−45)	Older (61−75+)	Total
Sex	M	17	29	21
	F	5	11	8
	Total	11	20	

Older men have the highest deletion scores and younger women the lowest. Although Leander and Synnemark (1970), who analysed the Eskilstuna results, do not comment on the implications of this pattern, it appears to be indicative of a change in progress towards the standard. Widmark's (1970 a) study of generational differences in Uppsala adds an important subjective dimension to this pattern of age-grading. She reports (1970 a: 7) that older informants more often than younger ones deny the use of /t/-less forms such as *regne* (where the standard should be *regnet*). This is, however, as Widmark suspects, probably an indication of the greater social pressure, which increases with age.

In general, then the Swedish results show a bipolarization of norms which reflects a dichotomy between the norms of standard written Swedish and the spoken language. The youngest informants of Class I show the least deletion and the oldest informants in Class III the greatest. And women tend to be ahead of men in adopting the standard.

We can also make some interesting observations about patterns of age-grading and their implication for long-term change in the case of the *t/d* variable in English. This variable, like its Swedish counterpart, is a well-developed sociolinguistic marker with patterns of social class and stylistic stratification, age-grading and sex differentiation. It affects the realization of final stops in consonant clusters in two main environments, one of which is strictly phonological, e. g., *mist*, and the second of which is grammatical, e. g., *missed*. Bimorphemic clusters arise through the suffixation of the preterite *t/d* to certain verb stems. Guy (1980) and others have found that there is great variability in the way in which some speakers treat so-called semi-regular verbs, e. g., *wept, kept*, etc. Some speakers delete the final /t/ here just as often or even more often than in monomorphemic clusters, while others have a low value for this conditioning factor, and delete *t/d* less often here than in monomorphemic clusters.

In terms of the English verb system, verbs like *weep* and *keep* are often referred to as semi-regular (Guy calls them ambiguous) because they form their preterites by vowel change and suffixation. There are thus two "marks" of the preterite. They fall into a category which is in a sense intermediate between the two major classes of verbs recognized by English grammarians: regular and irregular or strong and weak. The so-called irregular verbs are ordinarily divided into a number of sub-groups according to the way in which they form their past tense, i. e., with or without suffixation and/or different series of vowel changes. While the so-called irregular verbs today number less than 200 by some estimates (e. g., Bloch 1947), compared to the thousands of regular verbs, they are among the most frequently occurring verbs in the language. Although there has been a general tendency for verbs to move from the irregular to regular class, the number of strong verbs is now fewer than in earlier periods, and the remaining strong verbs have become subject to regularization, they nevertheless constitute an important core of English verb morphology. In a survey of modern English texts, Ellegård (1978) found that 42% of the verbs had irregular past tense forms (i. e., vowel change $\pm$ suffixation), but no less than ⅔ of these ended in *t/d*, e. g., *wrote*. The fact that 87% of all past tense forms (both regular and irregular) end in a stop is indicative of the strength of the *t/d* ending as a marker of the past tense. Of these, however, only a subset would provide sites for clusters which would count as input for the deletion rule, namely, those whose stems end in a consonant other than *t/d*.

So what then is the significance of Guy's (1980: 21 – 22) finding that the salience of the morpheme boundary for the class of semi-regular or ambiguous verbs varies considerably, both in relation to social class and pattern of acquisition? He found that there was a tendency for both working-class speakers and children to have high rates of deletion for this category of verbs. For these speakers apparently what has happened is that this class of verbs has been reinterpreted by analogy with the strong verbs which have no preterite suffix, only vowel change, e. g., *fed*. The high deletion rates may be an indication of what Pfaff (1980) calls relexification;[5] that is, the underlying forms for these verbs no longer have *t/d*. Thus, in the few cases where these speakers do use *t/d* we are dealing with addition rather than deletion. We may draw a parallel here between acquisition and the history of the preterite system in English. The class of preterites like *kept*, *slept*, etc., can be found without /t/ from the beginning of the Middle English period. The earliest cases I have been able to uncover come from the middle of the 12th century.

Seen from a synchronic perspective, these cases (e. g., *slep*) seemingly involve deletion. But are these unequivocal cases of deletion or sporadic failures to add /t/? According to Wright (1905), preterite forms like *kep*, which are widely diffused in the Midlands and also occur in northern dialects, have not lost a /t/, but are analogical formations. In other words, they do not represent cases of "true" deletion, which arise as the output of a deletion rule. A great many of these occur side by side with fully regular weak formations, e. g., *kepyd*, *tellyd* (*The Stonor Papers*). These and other forms like *cumit* (i. e., *came*, *The Scottish Correspondence of Mary of Lorraine*) result as an extension of a tendency to regularize the preterite system by using suffixation as the sole mark of pastness.[6] (See Romaine 1985 for further details of the history of this variable.)

Further support for relexification may be obtained from studies of the acquisition of past-tense forms by young English-speaking children and by creole speakers. (See, e. g., Bybee and Slobin 1982 b, Boyd and Guy 1979.) These indicate that the acquisition of the standard English past-tense forms may take place by gradual alteration of underlying forms. It is well known that children (and speakers of English-based creoles, e. g., the Guyanese creole discussed by Bickerton 1975) learn the past-tense forms of certain frequent irregular verb forms first, like *went*, *came*, etc. These seem to be learned as separate vocabulary items at an early age and are among the first past-tense forms to be learned — presumably because these verbs are so frequently heard by children. Only later do they learn the past tense of regular verb forms. As soon as children learn a few regular past-tense forms, e. g., *helped, stopped,* etc., they begin to replace their previously correct irregular verb forms with incorrect ones such as *goed* and *comed.* Even though the child knew the correct forms and used them for months, he seems to "forget" them, and the correct forms do not "reappear" until later. It is at the stage when the child regularizes the past-tense forms of the irregular verbs that he can be said to have acquired a productive rule of past-tense formation by suffixation. The rule is overgeneralized and overextended in its incipient stages. The tendency to regularize continues into primary school, which indicates that children's acquisition of certain aspects of English morphology is not complete by the time they enter school (cf. Berko 1958 for further details).

The child learns only later that there are some strong verb forms which take no suffix, e. g. *came.* In the overgeneralization phase a child may treat all verbs in this category alike (with the result that semi-regular verbs are treated like monomorphemic words with no special status attached to t/d). At an even later stage, the child may restructure some of the underlying forms while acquiring the morphological distinctions among the different classes of verbs. This process of learning the morphology of the verb system repeats itself in apparent time in each generation. Some speakers may never acquire fully the distinctions of the standard preterite system and control them systematically unless they have been exposed to them in prescriptive teaching in school.

I will draw two preliminary conclusions from the examples discussed so far:

1. The process of acquiring grammar involves internalizing the norms of the models one is exposed to. This involves a certain amount of restructuring and overgeneralization of rules. These can be seen as changes in apparent time.
2. In some cases there is a regular relationship between change in apparent time, i. e., age-grading, and change in real time, such that synchronic variability represents a stage in long-term change.

As far as the first conclusion is concerned, we have seen that there are many models available to children at different stages (and the same is true for adults). We are all exposed to different extents at different times to various influences, so it is misleading to think of the process of acquisition as if it were a single, unidirectional route leading to one particular target. Children evidently do take their peers as models, in addition of course to the adult models available to them. It is clear then that adults transmit norms to children and children to other children, but do children serve as models for adults? And do adults adopt the changes introduced by children?

3. Children as instigators of language change

Aitchison (1981: 183) concludes that children have little of importance to contribute to language change. She is right in thinking that very young children cannot be the main instigators of change — at least in the sense in which Labov speaks of the notion of an innovator as someone with local prestige, whose norms are adopted by others who wish to share the social value attached to a particular way of speaking. As Aitchison (1981: 180) points out: "Babies do not form influential social groups; changes begin within social groups, when group members unconsciously imitate those around them. Differences in the speech forms of parents and children probably begin at a time when the two generations identify with different social sets."

However, that is not all there is to say about the role of children in contributing to long-term change. Children's innovations could still lead to cumulative change, providing that they were maintained into adulthood, i. e., are not purely developmental. These innovations would then be passed on to children of the next generation. A number of schools of linguistic thought have ascribed to children a central role as instigators of linguistic change in this sense. Halle (1962) and other generativists have argued that only children were capable of implementing substantial changes, i. e., restructuring grammars. In Halle's view restructuring was to be seen largely as an ongoing process of simplification of the parents' output by the child. The idea that change takes place largely by dint of children's simplification is not, however, a new one. The Neogrammarians believed that the major cause of change was imperfect learning by children and that the locus of change lay in the discontinuity between one generation and the next. Passey (1891; quoted in King 1969: 78) claimed that: "All the major changes in pronunciation that we have been able to observe originate in child speech; if languages were learnt perfectly by the children of each generation, then language would not change."

To take a sociolinguistic example, let us suppose that a child grows up in an area of England where initial /h/ is generally deleted, e. g., in *heart*. On the basis of an input of largely *h*-deleted forms, the child will construct a hypothetical grammar in which underlying forms for words beginning with /h/ have no initial segments. Not until the child comes into contact with adults who do not delete /h/ or is exposed to the norms of written standard English will he know that some of the words in his lexical inventory "should" begin with /h/ and not with a vowel. At this stage he may add /h/ to some forms, especially in his more formal speech styles. This is essentially the scenario I outlined for *t/d* deletion. A generativist interpretation of these cases might argue that there had been rule inversion. In other words, the parents' grammar contains the full forms; a rule of deletion operates on some if not all of them and the child then takes the parent's deleted forms as input and these became his underlying forms. If we were to imagine further that there was no way for the child to "discover" which forms had /h/ and which did not in the parent's underlying grammar (say, for example, that English did not exist as a written language), the child might then never add a rule of /h/ insertion, but overgeneralize what for his parents was a variable rule of /h/ deletion. Future generations would then have eliminated initial /h/ entirely and the language would have "changed".

There are a number of difficulties with this kind of argument. For one thing, how do we find out whether children's grammars differ from those of their parents even when the output is the same? In other words, a surface ø may have two distinct underlying sources and therefore, identity of surface output is no guarantee for underlying equivalence. The situation is sketched out in Figure 1 for *t/d* deletion.

Time 1	Parent grammar	Time 2	Child grammar
Input:	underlying representation *grab* + past [græb + d]	Input:	underlying representation *grab* + past [græb + Ø]
Variable rule of *t/d* deletion:	t/d → Ø	Variable rule of *t/d* insertion:	Ø → t/d
Surface representation:	[græbd] or [græb]	Surface representation:	[græb] or [græbd]

Figure 1. Possible grammars

Since we have access only to the surface forms in our observations, we cannot really say whether the parents' and child's grammar are the same or different or whether the child has an interpretation or analysis of a structure which is unlike that of the parents. We can only make guesses at what these more abstract structures are like on the basis of what is produced. Sociolinguistic analysis gives us an idea of the relative frequency of two competing forms, and we can make some inferences from this. In cases where one variant appears relatively infrequently, such as *t/d* or /h/, then it makes more sense to talk about insertion rather than deletion.

Another problem with the type of argument we have been looking at is that it is often based on the implicit assumption that all varieties of a language have an underlying unity and that the standard language is to be taken as the point of reference in describing other varieties. Unfortunately, this is a practice which sociolinguists have fallen victim to. And historical linguists have generally taken it for granted that all the varieties of a language which are co-existent synchronically have evolved from the same parent. However, one cannot assume that all varieties of English have the same history; the linguistic details of the transmission of the language we call "English" are far more socially complex than the traditional histories of English would have us believe. It is misleading to describe non-standard varieties in terms of the extent to which they differ from the standard language. And if we were to use a frequency argument to justify the basis of our analysis, we should start out from the perspective of non-standard varieties, since standard English is in an important sense a minority language.[7] There is also some danger in taking the standard as the baseline because often the differences between standard and non-standard varieties involve ostensible simplification, at least from the perspective of the standard. Therefore the comparison can become invidious; that is, non-standard forms of speech are seen as impoverished and imperfect versions of a more elaborate standard. Notions such as deletion or addition of rules and grammar simplification or complication make certain assumptions about the starting point of the analysis.

Simplification, imperfect learning by children, and discontinuity between generations are not sufficient to provide a full account of language change. Adults introduce innovations too; and it is not clear that Halle (1962: 64) is right in thinking that "a wholesale restructuring of his grammar is beyond the capabilities of the average adult". Sankoff and Brown (1976) discuss a case in which the innovators in the introduction of a new syntactic construction, a relative-clause formation strategy, are adults rather than children. The idea that grammar remains relatively immutable after a certain period is based largely on the so-called "critical period of language acquisition" hypothesis. Those who have argued in favour of it claim that there are neurological and cognitive constraints which make language learning difficult after childhood. While there certainly are important qualitative differences between language acquisition in the child and adult (some of which must be due to the cognitive immaturity of the child's brain vis-à-vis the adult's), children are not necessarily more successful than adults in all areas of acquisition. The critical-period theory has recently come under re-evaluation (see Romaine 1988: 6.5).

Slobin (1977) has observed that children tend to use new forms to express old functions and old forms to express new functions. Both these tendencies can be observed in language change. Children also in the early stages tend to develop a one-to-one mapping of meaning and form; some historical changes also seem to follow this principle. Furthermore, processes such as dissimulation and metathesis are common in both historical change and child language. Children often produce forms like *foots* instead of *feet*. The method of plural formation illustrated by *feet* was once more widespread in English; the plural of Old English *boc* 'book' was *bec*, but the modern English plural is *books*, not **beek*. It may have been the case that the analogical formation *books* was introduced by children. Baron (1977) has claimed that it is possible to argue that children may have helped historically to initiate the development of some periphrastic causative constructions in English, e. g., *to make run*. Both diachronically and ontogenetically *make* emerges as the earliest periphrastic causative. Parallelisms of this type have led some to the very strong claim that ontogeny recapitulates phylogeny.

It may be that in a community of expanded-pidgin or dying-language speakers, the innovations of children have a better chance of catching on than in "normal" communities. Bavin (1989) found that children were introducing changes into the pronominal system of Warlpiri. It is interesting that she says that mothers were introducing some English animal names into Warlpiri baby-talk register since I found that one area in which there was increasing anglicization in young children's Tok Pisin was in the semantic domain of animal terms (see Romaine 1988: 4.4).

In normal communities the expectation is that adults act as brakes on the innovations produced by children so that analogical and other deviant forms like *foots* get corrected and do not persist. In the case of dying and pidgin languages it may be that children have greater scope to act as norm makers due to the fact that a great deal of variability exists among the adult community. Mougeon and Beniak (1989) cite evidence to support the developmental origin of some of the processes of simplification in Ontarian French. Simplified forms can persist in the speech of children in English-dominant homes presumably because there is little corrective pressure or model.

One of the changes which I have been documenting in young children's creolized Tok Pisin is the use of short forms as the result of the introduction of rules of morphophonemic condensation. Among the short forms in use are the following: *laus* [<*long haus* 'at home'], *disa/disla* [<*dispela* 'the/this'], and *blol* [<*bilong ol* 'theirs'] see Romaine and Wright 1987). The more basic a pidgin is, the more likely it is that its speakers will rely on strategies which maximize naturalness of encoding and decoding. It is only in a community of fluent second- and first-language speakers that rules which greatly enhance rate of production will have a chance of acceptance. While these rules simplify output at one level, and make it easier for the speaker to articulate at a faster rate and increase stylistic flexibility, they complicate the decoding process and increase the likelihood of comprehension difficulties. One effect of the introduction of allegro speech styles is an increase in depth of the phonological component, so that surface forms become derivable by rule from underlying form. It is also clear in the case of Tok Pisin that the speech of town children is seen as prestigious by children in rural areas. Innovations diffuse from urban centres like Lae and are eagerly imitated by rural children.

Hockett (1950) has discussed in detail the problem of inter-generational linguistic continuity. He hypothesized that sound change took place gradually, by infinitesimal steps, so that a change from an old form to a new one took place by means of a gradual shift in speaker production. In the case of a change involving, for example, a shift from /p/ to /f/. Hockett proposed that speakers aimed at a phonemic target /p/, but did not always achieve it. Realizations clustered around the target, but over time the frequency of realizations drifted more in the directions of /f/ by way of intermediate forms such as /p^f/. The notion of allophonic drift proposed by Hockett has been empirically demonstrated in Labov's studies of sound change (cf. especially, Labov, Yaeger, and Steiner 1972), where certain ongoing changes have been tracked in phonetic space. The increasing centralization of *ai* and *au* on Martha's Vineyard is an example of how realizations may be gradually readjusted in a certain direction by successive generations of speakers. Janson's work (1983) has shown that

there are significant differences in the production and perception boundaries of younger and older speakers (even within the same family with
respect to certain ongoing changes in Swedish). As production targets
shifted in the direction of new sounds, so did perception norms.

It is now known, however, that it is a mistake not to discriminate
between gradualness and sound changes which take place by infinitesimal
steps. The change observed by Gauchat and Hermann was gradual but
did not involve phonetically intermediate forms. Furthermore, the kinds
of processes involved in language acquisition are not just simplificatory
and imitative. Children play an active role in elaborating, constructing
and (re)-creating their language.

4. The role of natural processes in child language and language change

There is, however, still another line of argumentation one could take on
the question of the role of children vs. adults in language change. That
is whether the kinds of inherent natural processes which historical linguists
have identified as being responsible for change are present to the greatest
extent in children. In other words, do children engage in more of the
kinds of processes which have been seen to play a major role in change?
A number of researchers have drawn parallels between children's analogical innovations and the types of changes which can be observed in
language history. That is, the changes which take place in the acquisition
of a language recreate the stages through which the language has gone
through in its history. As Aitchison (1981: 173 – 174) points out, we do
not know enough about the early origins of language to say much about
this claim. Bickerton (1981) however has recently argued that there is a
connection between the original evolution of language, child language
acquisition, and the construction of a creole by the first generation of
creole speakers, but I will not consider this further here (see Romaine
1988: chapter 7).

Bybee and Slobin (1982 a and b) have tried to compare the innovations
of adults and children under experimental conditions in order to see to
what extent they paralleled certain types of historical change. They

compared three groups of speakers: university-age adults; pre-school children between the ages of 1 ½ − 5 years and school children between the ages of 8 ½ − 10. They looked at the innovations which these groups made in the production of English past-tense forms. In order to get the adult group to produce innovations, they asked them to respond as quickly as possible to a list of 180 verbs. Bybee and Slobin were able to establish a number of areas in which the innovations made by children and adults were similar.

Firstly, they found a relationship between frequency and regularization. It is well established that the lexical items most prone to analogical levelling or regularization are the least frequent items. This follows from the fact that items which have to be memorized as exceptions to more general rules will remain stable only if they are frequent enough to be reinforced. Bybee and Slobin (1982a: 30) found that all three groups regularized the least frequent verbs to a greater extent. This means that it is not due solely to young children's imperfect learning that some of these items have become regularized over time, but rather the general weakness of a low-frequency irregular form. Thus, in order for adults to maintain an irregular item without regularizing it, it must occur with a frequency above a certain threshold.

A second similarity found by Bybee and Slobin (1982a: 31) was in the regularization of verbs whose past tense forms involve a change from /d/ to /t/, e. g., *send*. This class of verbs is exceptional in that it is the only group which employs this process and does not involve also suffixation and/or vowel change. The tendency of all three groups to regularize this class reflects an ongoing historical trend to eliminate this class entirely. The number of verbs in this class has been undergoing attrition for some time now.

The third parallel between children's and adult's innovations has to do with "errors" made in vowel changes rather than with regularization. This concerns cases where children and adults produced innovative forms by making an analogy between two different verb classes, for example, the *sing/sang/sung* type class was treated as if it belonged to the *sting/stung* class. Bybee and Slobin (1982a: 33) say that this parallels a historical trend, which is tending to eliminate the distinction between the past-tense and past-participial form in favour of the past-participial form. This is how the *sting/stung* class arose originally. They claim that the non-standard forms that adults use under the pressure of having to respond quickly are the same as the non-standard forms the younger children do. I have already indicated that it may be incorrect to talk of the use of a paradigm like *sing/sung* as an "error" in the development of some children's speech. The children, for example, are probably just internalizing the norms of the adults around them, who also use these forms. They are of course not the norms which are prescribed for use in the standard language, and since the tendency began to eliminate these distinctions, prescriptive grammarians have been trying to maintain them artificially, i.e., against the forces which are operating in the spoken language.[8]

For those who have grown up using the non-standard forms, it is the standard forms which are no doubt unstable and "imperfectly learned". In producing what Bybee and Slobin refer to as non-standard forms, the adults (and children) may be reproducing the forms they habitually use in their everyday casual speech. So strictly speaking, they are not entitled to claim that these are innovations. Again, it is a question of what forms we have assumed speakers to have internalized.

Bybee and Slobin (1982 a: 37) conclude that the strategies used by the youngest, pre-school children differed from those used by the older children and adults. The pre-school children were not yet influenced by the language-specific constraints of speaking English and therefore the strategies they employed in producing past tense forms reflected more closely universal operating principles for dealing with morphophonemics. The strategy used by the youngest children is based on "affix-checking" rather than on a notion of a rule of suffixation. According to this hypothesis children have an idea, or schema, of what the end product must be like, even though they have not yet formulated a process to arrive at it. In this case then children know that past tense verbs end in a stop. When they hear forms like *hit* and *cut*, they count the final /t/ as the suffix. Berko (1958), who gave children nonce forms to test their knowledge of morphological processes in English, found that children tended not to add a past tense suffix to verbs ending in *t/d*. Likewise they added no plural suffixes to nouns which already ended in a sibilant.

The older children and adults seemed to have a more English-based strategy. They operated with a principle which adds a past-tense *t/d* to a base. They tended to make errors in adding *-ed* to a base which should not have changed. As far as the history of English is concerned, there are some parallels to be drawn between the schema- and rule-based strategies. When verbs borrowed from French and Latin into Middle English became nativized, they began to take the same endings as English regular verbs. However, when foreign loanwords ending in /t/ were first introduced, they often appeared without any further ending. The earliest of these forms are found in *Ancrene Riwle* (1225). Chaucer was responsible for introducing a number of them, e. g., *creat*, but he almost never adds -*ed* to them.[9]

In a careful study of texts from the 13th to 16th century Reuter (1934) established that the assimilation of these words proceeded gradually, possibly by lexical diffusion. Higden, for example, who was one of the most prolific borrowers, introduced hundreds of these forms, many of which are first recorded in his translation of the *Polychronicon*, a compendium of world history dating from the 15th century. Some forms appear with and without -*ed* as in the examples in (1)

(1)   Mappa mundi is purtrayed and i-*paynt* (LI, CIII, 12)
        þe worlde is i-*paynted* (LI, III, 13)

The process of assimilation was largely complete by the end of the 16th century: after 1550 the instances of forms lacking -*ed* are in the minority. While some of these verbs are no longer in use, Reuter (1934: 107) estimates that about 56% of them have survived in modern English.

These facts can be interpreted in such a way as to add support to both the schema-orientated and rule-based strategies. Those who first borrowed this class of verbs into English were highly literate men like Chaucer, who were conscious of the innovations they introduced. They were aware of the fact that the verbs they borrowed were taken over into English from the past-participle form and that the /t/ ending indicated pastness already — at least in French and Latin, the donor languages. Thus, the English schema happened to coincide with the foreign schema. The fact that these foreign forms ending in /t/ were late to take the native English -*ed* ending indicates that the final /t/ was taken to be a sufficient mark of past-tenseness. Further support can be derived from the fact that verbs whose stems did not end in /t/ all appear with the -*ed* added. Another factor in favour of the existence of a past-tense schema is that there were back formations; that is, cases where present tense forms were created by dropping the final /t/, e. g., *compack, corrupe, redemp*. This indicates the pervasiveness of /t/ as a mark of past-tenseness but at the same time supports the view that speakers use rule-based strategies. In other words, removing the ending to form the present tense presupposes knowledge of it as a sign of the past tense.

Bybee and Slobin (1982 a: 36—37) conclude from their experiments that "there is nothing particularly special about the relation between small children's innovative forms and morphophonemic change. The innovations of older children and adults, though perhaps rarer, where they can be elicited, may also serve as predictors of change." One reason why some of the innovations produced by children in the course of language acquisition do not persist is that children are not free to impose universal tendencies where these conflict with adult norms and pressures. Children past a certain age who continue to produce "incorrect" past-tense forms will be corrected. The existence of a highly codified standard language and a high rate of literacy in a society will act as brakes on linguistic change (cf., e. g., Zengel 1968). That is not to say that these influences stop change, but merely that they exert considerable pressure which will limit the extent to which spoken and written language can differ. Despite the fact that *who*, for example, has practically ousted *whom* in most spoken varieties of English, there is a great deal of resistance to the use of *who* in print in cases where prescriptive grammar dictates the use of *whom*. Much more research needs to be done on the relationship between language acquisition by children and historical change to see why certain changes in apparent time eventually get converted into changes in real time and why others do not.

Notes

1. A good summary of the implications of patterns of social class stratification, style shifting, sex differentiation, and age-grading can be found in Chambers and Trudgill (1980: Chapter 5 and 6).
2. There are of course working-class accents of English which are non-rhotic, e. g., Cockney, and it could be that there is some influence from a model of this type. John Wells has in fact suggested this to me (and cf. Wells 1982: 2/5.2), but in the absence of any evidence which would suggest such a connection, I am sceptical.
3. This is a comparison of a first-conjugation weak verb.
4. There is also evidence of lexical diffusion (cf., e. g., Leander and Synnemark 1970: 79 − 80 and Janson 1966).
5. She uses the term in a way which is different from its common use in creole studies.
6. In Scots the preterite ending is usually *-it*.
7. This can be argued demographically, but in social terms it is the most important variety of English.
8. Wright (1905: 344), for example, remarks that "there is not a single New English verb which has preserved what would have been the regularly developed parts." He is speaking here of Class II verbs, but I suspect that the average educated speaker of English today who knows little of the history of the language and has had little contact with non-standard varieties would be surprised at the great variability in past-tense formation.
9. He uses the form *corrected* twice however (Reuter 1934: 36 − 37). We also see variability in the realization of the reflex of the Old English *ge-* past participle prefix.

References

Aitchison, J.
1981   *Language change: progress or decay?* (London: Fontana).
Baron, N.
1977   *Language acquisition and historical change* (Amsterdam: North Holland).
Bavin, E.
1989   "Some lexical and morphological changes in Warlpiri", in Dorian (ed.).
Bergroth, H.
1924   *Svensk uttalslära* (Helsingfors).
Berko, J.
1958   "The child's learning of English morphology", *Word* 14: 150–177.
Bickerton, D.
1975   *Dynamics of a creole system* (Cambridge: Cambridge University Press).
Bloch, B.
1947   "English verb inflection", *Language* 23: 399–418.
Boyd, S.–G. Guy
1979   "The acquisition of a morphological category", Paper presented at the winter meeting of the LSA, Los Angeles.
Bybee, J.–D. Slobin
1982 a   "Why small children cannot change language on their own", in: A. Ahlquist (ed.), *Papers from the 5th International Conference on Historical Linguistics* 29–38 (Amsterdam: John Benjamins).
1982 b   "Rules and schemas in the development and use of the English past", *Language* 58: 265–290.
Chambers, J.–P. Trudgill
1980   *Dialectology* (Cambridge: Cambridge University Press).
Dorian, N. C. (ed.)
1989   *Investigating obsolescence: studies in language contraction and death* (Cambridge: Cambridge University Press).
Ellegård, A.
1978   *The syntactic structure of English texts* (Gothenburg Studies in English 43) (University of Gothenburg, Sweden).
Gauchat, L.
1905   "L'unité phonétique dans le patois d'une commune", in: *Aus romanischen Sprachen und Literaturen; Festschrift Heinrich Morf*, 175–232 (Halle: Max Niemeyer).
Grant, W.
1914   *The pronunciation of English in Scotland* (Cambridge: Cambridge University Press).
Guy, G.
1980   "Variation in the group and individual: the case of final stop deletion", in: W. Labov (ed.), *Locating language in time and space*, 1–35 (New York: Academic Press).
Halle, M.
1962   "Phonology in a generative grammar", *Word* 18: 54–72.
Hermann, E.
1929   "Lautveränderungen in den Individualsprachen einer Mundart", *Nachrichten der Gesellschaft der Wissenschaften zu Göttingen, Philosophisch-Historische Klasse* II: 195–214.
Hockett, C.
1950   "Age-grading and linguistic continuity", *Language* 26: 449–457.

Janson, T.
1977 "Reverse lexical diffusion and lexical split: loss of -D in Stockholm", in: W. S-Y. Wang (ed.), *The lexicon in phonological change*, 252–265 (The Hague: Mouton).
1983 "Sound change in perception and production", *Language* 59: 18–34.
King, R. D.
1969 *Historical linguistics and generative grammar* (Englewood Cliffs, N. J.: Prentice-Hall).
Labov, W.
1963 "The social motivation of a sound change", *Word* 19: 273–309.
1966 *The social stratification of English in New York City* (Washington, DC: Center for Applied Linguistics).
1972 *Sociolinguistic patterns* (Philadelphia: University of Pennsylvania Press).
1980 "The social origins of sound change", in: W. Labov (ed.), *Locating language in time and space*, 251–264 (New York: Academic Press).
Labov, W. – M. Yaeger – R. Steiner
1972 *A quantitative study of sound change in progress* 1–2 (Philadelphia: US Regional Survey).
Leander, M. – M. Synnemark
1970 "Ändelsevariation i neutrum bestämd form hos några grupper Eskilstunabor" (*FUMS Rapport* No. 9) (Uppsala).
MacAllister, A.
1963 *A year's course in speech training* 9 (London: University of London Press).
Milroy, L.
1980 *Language and social networks* (Oxford: Blackwell).
Mougeon, R. – E. Beniak
1989 "Language contraction and linguistic change: the case of Welland French", in: Dorian (ed.).
Nordberg, B.
1972 "Morfologiska variationsmönster i ett centralt svenskt stadsspråk", in: B. Loman (ed.), *Språk och samhalle*, 14–44 (Gleerups: Lund).
Nyholm, L.
1976 "Formväxling i Helsingforssvenskan – En studie i intervjuspråk" (*FUMS Rapport* No. 44) (Uppsala).
Passey, P.
1891 *Étude sur les changements phonétiques et leurs caractères généraux* (Paris: Firmin-Didot).
Pfaff, C.
1980 "Lexicalization in Black English", in R. Day (ed.), *Issues in English creoles*, 163–181 (Heidelberg: Julius Gross).
Raittila, M.
1969 "Variation i preteritum av svaga verb i Stockholms språket". Unpublished manuscript.
Reuter, O.
1934 *On the development of English verbs from Latin and French past participles* (Societas Scientiarum Fennica, Commentationes Humanarum Litterarum 6) (Helsinki).
Romaine, S.
1978 "Post-vocalic /r/ in Scottish English: sound change in progress?", in: P. Trudgill (ed.), *Sociolinguistic patterns in British English*, 144–158 (London: Edward Arnold).
1980 "Stylistic variation and evaluation reactions to speech", *Language and Speech* 23: 213–232.

1984   *The language of children and adolescents: the acquisition of communicative competence* (Oxford: Blackwell).
1985   "The sociolinguistic history of *t/d* deletion", *Folia Linguistica Historica* 2: 25—59.
1988   *Pidgin and creole languages* (London: Longman).
Romaine, S. — F. Wright
1987   "Short forms in Tok Pisin", *Journal of Pidgin and Creole Languages* 2: 63—67.
Russell, J.
1982   "Networks and sociolinguistic variation in an African urban setting", in: S. Romaine (ed.), *Sociolinguistic variation in speech communities*, 125—141 (London: Edward Arnold).
Sankoff, G. — P. Brown
1976   "The origins of syntax in discourse: the case of Tok Pisin relatives", *Language* 52: 631—666.
Slobin, D.
1977   "Language change in childhood and history", in: C. Ferguson — D. Slobin (eds.), *Studies of child language development*, 175—208 (New York: Holt, Rinehart & Winston).
Tingbrand, B.
1973   "Norge ha vi förresten *vart* ganska mycke i å *åke, tittat*. Om verbböjning i Eskilstunaspråket" (*FUMS Report* No. 29) (Uppsala).
Trudgill, P.
1972   "Sex, covert prestige and linguistic change in the urban British English of Norwich", *Language in Society* 1: 179—196.
1974   *The social differentiation of English in Norwich* (Cambridge: Cambridge University Press).
Wells, J. C.
1982   *Accents of English*, 1—3 (Cambridge: Cambridge University Press).
Wessén, E.
1965   *Svensk språkhistoria* (Stockholm: Almqvist & Wiksell International).
Widmark, G.
1970 a   "Generationsskillnaderna i språket", *Språkvård* 2: 3—10.
1970 b   "Stildifferentiering i Gyllenborgs Komedi Swenska Sprätthöken", *Nysvenska Studier* 49: 5—77.
1977   "Lokalt och riksspråkligt: en undersökning av Uppsalaspråk", in: C. Elert, S. Eliasson, S. Fries, S. Ureland (eds.), *Dialectology and sociolinguistics: essays in honor of Karl-Hampus Dahlstedt*, 246—262 (Umeå).
Wright, J.
1905   *The English dialect grammar* (London: Henry Frowde).
Zengel, M.
1968   "Literacy as a factor in language change", in: J. Fishman (ed.), *Readings in the sociology of language*, 296—305 (The Hague: Mouton).

Contact and isolation in linguistic change

Peter Trudgill

This paper examines the relationship between linguistic change and social context and concentrates on the role of contact in linguistic change. The paper considers the extent to which changes that take place in contexts of high degree of contact between language varieties will be significantly different from those which occur in low-contact contexts. I recognize, of course, that varieties do not actually simply fall into the two categories of high contact and low contact. The reality is a continuum from high to low contact, with the further complications that degree of contact may change through time, and that contact can be of many different types. Nevertheless, for the purposes of this short paper, I shall continue to talk, for convenience, of high- and low-contact varieties.

The paper accepts the distinctions made by scholars, notably C. J. Bailey, between concepts such as "unmarked", "simple", "natural", and "normal" in human language, but it concentrates on what is normal in language change, where "normal" is essentially a statistical concept which has to do with what happens most often. The paper stresses, however, that it is important to recognize, to a greater extent than is sometimes done, that what is normal in some social contexts, such as high-contact situations, is not normal in others, such as low-contact situations and vice versa. Moreover, since "normal" really therefore means "normal in certain social contexts", we must be very careful not to regard some social contexts as being more important than others for the study of language change. In particular, we should not regard high-contact situations as being in some way more important than low-contact situations simply because they may happen to be more usual in the modern world.

I will begin my discussion by comparing high-contact dialects with low-contact dialects. I will then move on to the comparison of high-contact and low-contact languages. In each case I will examine first of all the role of contact in influencing speed of change, and then its role in producing particular types of change.

Of course, at the level of dialects of a particular language, it is well known that degree of contact is an important influence on rate of change. It is a principle very familiar to dialectologists and geographical linguists that geographically-peripheral areas tend to be less innovating as compared to varieties spoken in more central areas. For example, the English dialects of the south-east of England are in most, although not all respects, considerably more innovating than those of northeastern England where, for example, monophthongal forms such as *oot* and *hoose* can still be heard, although they disappeared from the south several centuries ago. Similarly, the most conservative dialects of Norwegian are by general consent those found in remote inland valleys, while the most innovating are those in the well-trafficked southern coastal areas. The latter have, for example, lost the marking of the dative case on nouns, while the former have retained it. And very many other examples could be given.

The conservatism of these peripheral or isolated varieties surprises no one, but we should note that it is actually not a simple matter to produce detailed or analytical explanations for why contact does mean change in this way. Explanations, however, have been advanced. In a sociolinguistically very sophisticated paper called "Linguistic change, social network and speaker innovation", James and Lesley Milroy (1985) have pointed out that "linguistic change is *slow* to the extent that the relevant populations are well-established and bound by *strong* [network] ties, whereas it is *rapid* to the extent that *weak* ties exist in populations".

However, I want now to go on to argue that dialect contact plays a role not only in affecting rate of change but also in affecting type of change. This is obviously not particularly controversial. Everyone would accept, I assume, that borrowing, for instance, takes place only in contact situations. It is, however, possible to take this issue somewhat further. In my recent book *Dialects in contact* (1986), I examined developments which typically occur in situations of high contact between mutually-intelligible varieties, concentrating on dialect-mixture and new-dialect formation. Dialect contact, it appears, leads most usually to what we can call "simplification", as has been observed by a number of scholars. Jakobson long ago, for instance, noted that dialects which serve a relatively wide socio-spatial function tend to have simpler systems than dialects with a more restricted function. And Labov has pointed out that, in contact situations, phonological mergers spread at the expense of contrasts. In dialect contact generally, it seems that we most often encounter a process of koinéization, in which levelling and simplification both play a role. By levelling we mean the loss of minority, marked, or complex variants present in the dialect-mixture in favour of majority, unmarked, or simpler forms also present. By simplification is meant in this case especially the growth of new or interdialect forms (see Trudgill, 1986) that were not actually present in the initial mixture but developed out of interaction between forms that were present, where these interdialect forms are more regular than their predecessors.

– Explanations for why koinéization takes exactly the form it does are again not necessarily straightforward, but it seems likely that the greater learnability of regular forms is an important factor. Andersen (1988) stresses the role of child-language acquisition in imposing order on contact situations which are characterized by "blurred norms". We can imagine children, for example, playing an important role in the levelling process by selecting the most common variants. And we can imagine them aiding the simplification process by selecting simpler forms already present in the mixture in preference to more complex forms. But notice that it is most likely to be post-adolescents who provide new simpler alternatives in the form of interdialect variants not originally present in the mixture.

Interestingly, koinéization also seems to be a process that is on the increase in many parts of the world, with increasing urbanization, in particular, leading to a growth in the number of new, mixed, and therefore levelled and simplified, dialects.

In any case, we can say that the changes we have labelled koinéization are those which are normal in high dialect-contact situations. But what of changes that take place in other contexts? What can we expect to happen in low-contact situations? It emerges, in fact, that much less is actually known — unless I am wrong — about the sorts of developments that typically occur in dialects in relative isolation. In low-contact situations we know that the speed of linguistic change will typically be slow. But it is not entirely clear what types of linguistic change we can expect to be normal in these contexts. However, there now seems to be the beginnings of an interesting consensus that many of the changes that take place in this sort of situation are of a type that move in the opposite direction to those that occur as a result of simplification. Not only is the social context the opposite: low dialect contact versus high dialect contact; the linguistic consequences are in a sense the opposite also: complication as opposed to simplification.

Evidence for this hypothesis is advanced, for example, by Andersen (1988). Andersen suggests that his Slavic-language data do indeed point to the reverse of Jakobson's observation that koinés develop simpler systems. Andersen claims in fact that "dialects that serve predominantly local functions are more prone to elaborate phonetic detail rules than dialects with a wider sphere of use." Andersen argues that "there is a connection between the limited socio-spatial function of a dialect, its relative closedness [in a network sense], and its ability to sustain exorbitant phonetic developments". (Note the obvious relevance of the Milroys' work at this point.) Andersen also points out that such dialects will "preserve morphological irregularity with relatively great faithfulness". A detailed example that Andersen employs to make the point about phonetic elaboration is the following. He points out that in a number of widely dispersed geographically isolated areas of Europe, the same type of unusual phonetic norm elaboration has occurred. The areas are: the upper reaches of several Romansch-speaking Alpine valleys; the upper reaches of a number of Provençal-speaking Alpine valleys; the most peripheral part of Flanders; the sparsely-populated Eifel plateau of Luxembourg; the heart of the Hessian hills in Germany; and the most isolated parts of the Jutland peninsula in Denmark. The unusual phonetic development is the development of parasitic consonants out of diphthongs. Thus, in Waldeck in Hesse, parasitic k has developed after i and u (with η instead of k before m and n). Thus *Eis* 'ice' $= iks$; *aus* 'out' $= uks$; *neun* 'nine' $= ni\eta ne$; and so on. Andersen claims that it is not a coincidence that this relatively strange phonetic change has occurred in these isolated areas, and not in areas of high contact.

Note, however, that there is a caveat I feel we should introduce here. I agree entirely with Andersen's argument, but I also have to say that I feel just a little uncomfortable about terminology such as "exorbitant phonetic developments". The fact is that those of us who ourselves live in high-contact situations and therefore speak koinés have to guard against making the too easy assumption that these koinés are more "normal" in some absolute sense rather than simply normal in a particular social context with which we happen to be most familiar. Andersen's numerous examples make it plain that the development of parasitic consonants is perfectly normal in isolated social contexts.

Note, too, that there may be a tendency, because of the levelling element of koinéization, to regard isolated varieties as somewhat bizarre just because they are unusual from the point of view of a particular language. Many scholars of English, for instance, regard the peripheral and conservative dialects of north-east Scotland as somewhat strange because one of the changes they have experienced is that of *hw* becoming *f*, as in *what* = *fit*, *where* = *faur*. Now this is odd. But it is only odd amongst dialects of English. A change from *hw* to *f* is not at all strange from a phonetic point of view, or from the point of view of, say, the Polynesian languages. We shall return to this point later.

I now want to turn to draw some parallels between what we know about differences between high- and low-contact dialects and differences between high- and low-contact languages. Here, too, it is widely agreed that, other things being equal, languages whose speakers have frequent contact with speakers of other varieties change faster than varieties whose speakers have infrequent external contacts. We can note that, for example, Danish is in most respects considerably more innovating than the more conservative Faroese. That is to say that Danish and Faroese, having descended from a common ancestor, Old Norse, today differ considerably one from the other. This is because of linguistic changes which have taken place in the last 1,000 years or so — but, crucially, far more of these changes have taken place in Danish than in Faroese. And we can surely agree that the Faroes have for the last 1,000 years been a more isolated linguistic community than Denmark.

If we now turn to the question of how high and low contact situations affect the nature of change, it is again clear that changes which take place in some high-contact situations have been relatively well studied. Our investigations of lingua francas, pidgins, creoles, and other high-contact language varieties involving adult second-language learning have led us in fact to expect, in these situations, developments such as the following: change from analytic to synthetic structure, reduction in redundancy, and increase in regularity. Now notice that many of these changes were originally thought of by some older historical linguists as being normal in all contexts, and of course we cannot rule out the possibility altogether that these changes might sometimes be evolutive. But we also have to consider the strong possibility that the widespread feeling that these changes are "normal" may have stemmed from the fact that many examples occur in the languages with which the earlier European historical linguists were most familiar — and that this familiarity may have been misleading. As is very well known indeed, changes of this type are attested in the histories of the Indo-European languages of Western Europe, as well as in the Semitic languages and elsewhere. In comparing continental Scandinavian with Old Norse, English with Old English, German with Old High German, French with Latin, we find features such as reduction in overt case-marking and an increase in prepositional usage; reduction in conjugations, declensions and inflections; loss of the dual number; increase in periphrastic verb forms; more restrictions on word order; and so on.

It is, however, much more satisfactory to advance explanations for these phenomena in terms of contact than in terms of internal motivation. All changes of this type can again be described by the technical term of simplification. Given the language-learning abilities of small children, moreover, simplification must refer especially or even only to simplification for the post-adolescent non-native learner. It is not, *pace* Jespersen, simplification for the native speaker. Any acquisition of a language variety by adults is liable to lead to the favouring of simple over complex forms. It is quite possible, therefore, that changes of this type, far from being normal in all contexts, will be normal mainly — or even only — in high-contact situations. It should be made clear at this point, however, that this can only be true of certain high-contact situations, namely those where it is principally post-adolescent second-variety acquisition that is involved. High-contact situations come in many different forms, and we will not necessarily expect to find simplification in those (very many) contact situations where childhood bilingualism and second-variety acquisition are the norm. In these situations, on the contrary, we are liable, although not certain, to find intensive borrowing and interpenetration of linguistic systems, with possible resulting complication. It is precisely the imperfect language-learning abilities of the adult which, we postulate, is the chief mechanism behind simplification.

At the International Historical Linguistics Conference at Stanford in 1979, I gave a paper which was entitled "On the rise of the creoloid". In that paper, I used the term "creoloid" to refer to language varieties which, relative to some earlier stage or to some parent variety, have undergone considerable pidginization, but without ever passing through the stage of actually being a pidgin. That is, they have undergone the processes of admixture and simplification, but have not experienced the process of reduction, because they have maintained a continuous tradition of native speakers. They are usually, moreover, still mutually intelligible with the source language, if this survives. A good candidate for the label of creoloid, then, is Afrikaans, which looks like a decreolized Dutch-based creole, but really is not. Relative to Dutch, it demonstrates admixture and simplification, but it is clearly not a Dutch-based creole in the same sense that, say, Sranan is an English-based creole. The paper then went on to argue, as we just have above, that relative simplification, of the type that we see in pidgins, creoles, and creoloids, crucially represents simplification for the adult non-native learner, and that adult language acquisition, as we have just noted, occurs more often in high-contact situations than in low-contact situations. Now, given the changes that have taken place, in the last several centuries, in communications, transportation, and perhaps especially in demography, we can probably suggest that high-contact linguistic situations have become much more common in recent times. It will therefore not be surprising if more languages than in earlier ages have undergone greater simplification and ended up looking like creoloids. There may well be, that is, an evolutionary trend in human languages, but this is due to demography rather than anything else. There are simply many more people around now than there were 1,000 years ago, and like koinés, creoloids may be on the increase. It may therefore be increasingly likely that our views as linguists of what is normal in linguistic change will be skewed towards what happens in high-contact situations, unless we are careful.

In my 1979 paper, I also suggested that those forms of linguistic change that are found in creoloids and other high-contact varieties could be referred to as being "non-natural", in the sense that they take place mainly as a result of contact between varieties. They are, that is, not entirely due to the inherent nature of linguistic systems themselves, but to learning processes that take place in particular sociolinguistic contexts. I now believe that the term "non-natural" is not particularly helpful, and I therefore note that these types of change are approximately what C. J. Bailey refers to, in his 1982 book, as abnatural developments. According to Bailey, abnatural changes are developments which occur "as a result of contact with other systems". This term has the advantage of being compatible with the notion that these changes are actually perfectly normal in certain social contexts.

If we now turn our attention to low-contact languages, we have to note once again that rather less is known of the sorts of changes these varieties undergo. Andersen's observations about isolated dialects, however, give us a certain amount of confidence in predicting that the same sort of relationship will obtain between changes which occur in high- and low-contact situations at this level also. It seems quite possible, that is, that we are likely to find in low-contact languages changes that are the converse of abnatural developments. In my 1979 paper, I labelled these changes "natural" changes, but they are roughly the same sorts of changes that C. J. Bailey (1982) refers to as connatural developments. According to Bailey, connatural developments "are those that take place when languages are left alone i.e. when they have no contact with other systems." We should add too that connatural changes will also occur in high-contact varieties, but that they will be most common, and most readily apparent, in low-contact situations.

One problem with this is that, unlike the considerable amounts of information that we have on koinés, creoloids, and other high-contact varieties, we have very few studies of low-contact varieties as such. That is, few studies have attempted to explain the characteristics of low-contact varieties precisely in terms of low contact. However, although we are obviously on much less sure ground here than we are with the well-studied creoles and koinés, I want to suggest, with some support from Bailey, that changes typical of low-contact social contexts would include phenomena such as movement from analytic to synthetic structure, and a general increase in redundancy, such as development of complex forms of grammatical agreement. We might also expect the development of case-endings or verbal-person inflections out of independent lexical items, through cliticization and morphologization processes. And, recalling that Andersen argues that low-contact dialects are more likely to preserve morphological irregularity, we might even go one stage further and predict an increase in such languages in morphological irregularity. In phonology, we might again look for the reverse of the observations made by scholars such as Jakobson and Labov; that is, we might expect a growth in the number of phonological contrasts. This latter speculation is supported by Bailey who, citing also a personal communication from Eric Hamp, points out that connatural developments lead to phenomena in low-contact varieties such as the proliferation of clicks in the Khoisan languages; and the proliferation of other "unusual" consonantal articulations in isolated languages such as Scots Gaelic, Amerindian languages of the Pacific Northwest of the USA, and languages of the Caucasus. Note that, of course, the Pacific Northwest and the Caucasus are, or were, highly multilingual areas with considerable possibilities for contact. These situations, however, were stable situations involving therefore good opportunities for the development of child bilingualism, for borrowing, and for lingua francas, with correspondingly low levels of adult language learning. It is also likely that in certain relatively small language communities, it is the tight social networks and the absence of dialect contact which are the most significant factors not only in producing slow rates of change but also in producing connatural changes. Even in the case of, say, Danish versus Faroese, it may well be that the factor of high versus low dialect contact is as important, if not more so, than the factor of high versus low language contact. That is, one of the most important factors about isolated language varieties may be not just that they are isolated but that they are demographically small.

However, this now leads us once again into an area where there may be less consensus. Bailey, for example, has argued that connatural developments may, while being perfectly normal in themselves, lead to results or states, in languages such as the Caucasian and the Khoisan, which "no one would wish to call natural." He also writes of, for instance, "incredible consonant clusters" in certain languages and suggests that too many connatural changes in a language can lead to states that are "intolerable". He also indicates that languages need a balance between connatural and abnatural developments to keep them "healthy". I feel uneasy about this in the same way that I do about the "exorbitant" phonetic developments.

I would like to suggest that, whatever we want to claim about naturalness, it is surely important to stress that both the changes in isolated languages which lead to these states and the states themselves can be regarded as being (at least) entirely normal. To suggest that there is something unusual about certain Caucasian consonant systems is obviously correct, but only if one ignores the context of contact. It is fairly clear that these systems are genuinely more marked and/or less simple than other systems. We have to be very careful not to fall into the Eurocentric trap of regarding our high-contact world as producing language varieties that are in general more normal or interesting than others. We saw above that it is easy to fall into the trap of supposing that there is something bizarre about north-east Scottish dialects of English just because these are the only dialects which have the change of *hw* to *f*. There is a parallel here with the tendency to regard some languages as more bizarre than others.

Many of us may regard, say, Khoisan clicks as being a little bizarre. We should remember, however, that Khoisan languages, up to perhaps a couple of thousand years ago, were probably spoken over the whole southern third of the African continent, an area rather larger than Western Europe. I submit than if the whole of Western Europe, at the time of the development of linguistic science, had spoken languages containing clicks — or if linguistic science had been developed in southern Africa at that time — we might have regarded clicks as considerably more normal than we do now, perhaps even placing them nearer the top than the bottom of our phonetic alphabet charts. If we argue that what is usual in a high-contact situation is simply not the same as what is usual in an isolated situation, and if certain changes are more normal in high-contact and others in low-contact situations then it follows that the states that result from these changes will also be less or more normal, depending on degree of contact. We must not be misled by the fact that, as we have already noted, high-contact situations have, in the last few centuries, become much more common than low-contact situations — we must not be misled into thinking that they are more important. It may be that it is not really that Caucasian consonant systems are genuinely linguistically abnormal, but rather that, these days, low-contact situations are unusual.

Of course, we have to acknowledge that there was probably never any such thing as a truly isolated language. But it is surely true that isolated languages — and therefore low-contact type changes — were more common formerly than they are today. Isolated varieties are presumably getting harder to find every year. By way of illustration, a few years ago I was planning to begin some work on the English of the Falkland Islands, only to find that suddenly this variety had become very non-isolated. And even my current work on the English of Tristan da Cunha indicates some influence, by the 1960s, from South African English. This, of course, is simply the other side of the coin of the rise of the creoloids and the koinés. Nevertheless, I want to argue for the importance of the study of low-contact varieties. For one thing, even though there will be fewer changes to study in these languages because of their lower rate of change, they will be of the greatest interest for any scholar adopting in historical linguistics the "use of the present to explain the past" approach. When it comes to contact, the present is not like the past, and it is by investigating isolated languages that we are most likely to gain insights into the sorts of linguistic changes that occurred in the remote past.

A further reason is the following. Bickerton has argued for the importance of the study of the development, by children, of creole languages in high-contact situations, as a window into the nature of linguistic competence. I want to suggest, in a kind of mirror-image of his argument, that if we are keen to learn more about the inherent nature of linguistic systems and of their propensity to change, we can also usefully turn our attention to linguistic changes of the type that occur in low-contact varieties. And of course this will be easiest to do by researching the most isolated language varieties that it is possible to find. Even if isolated languages and dialects do have, to those of us of a European-language background, and to those of us who speak standard koinés, "amazingly" large consonantal inventories or "peculiar" phonetic features, they are of interest precisely because they represent, to the clearest extent, the limits to which languages can go when, as Bailey says, they are "left alone".

The relevant high-contact varieties are the result, at least in part, of relatively high involvement of imperfect learning by adults, and of *ad hoc* second-language and second-dialect acquisition strategies. Their characteristics are thus relatively easy to explain. Conversely, it is possible that isolated varieties may result from situations where the language faculty of the child has played a relatively greater role. In any case, developments in isolated languages are more likely to have been system-internal, and thus perhaps more likely to have been due to the inherent nature of linguistic systems as such. They may also, perhaps, be less easy, for that reason, to explicate. If we are interested in the potentialities of language systems, I do not see that there is any contradiction in arguing that linguistic developments in languages like the Caucasian languages, or dialects like Hessian, which mainstream Europeans and North Americans find "exorbitant" or "incredible", may nevertheless be not only perfectly normal in their social context, but also among the most revealing developments of all for the student of linguistic change.

Acknowledgements

Other versions of this paper were given at the Conference on Social Context and Linguistic Change, Stanford University, California, August 1987, and the Conference on Variation in Second Language Learning, University of Michigan, Ann Arbor, October 1987. I am grateful to participants at all three conferences for their helpful comments. I am also especially grateful to Donna Christian, Ralph Fasold and Jean Hannah for their comments on earlier versions of the paper.

References

Andersen, H.
  1988   "Center and periphery: adoption, diffusion and spread", in: J. Fisiak (ed.),
            Historical dialectology, 39–83 (Berlin: Mouton de Gruyter).
Bailey, C. J.
  1982   *On the yin and yang nature of language*. (Ann Arbor: Karoma).
Jakobson, R.
  1929   "Remarques sur l'évolution phonologique du russe comparée à celle des autres
            langues slaves", in: *Selected writings* 1: 7–116 (The Hague: Mouton).
Milroy, J. – L. Milroy
  1985   "Linguistic change, social network, and speaker innovation", *Journal of
            Linguistics* 21: 339–384.
Trudgill, P.
  1983   "On the rise of the creoloid", in: P. Trudgill (ed.), *On dialect*, 102–107
            (Oxford: Blackwell).
  1986   *Dialects in contact*. (Oxford: Blackwell).

Some contact structures in Scandinavian, Dutch, and Raeto-Romansh: inner-linguistic and/or contact causes of language change

P. Sture Ureland

Introduction

The topic of the present conference — language change and its causes — is not a new topic in the history of language research. It belongs to one of the oldest problems in the history of linguistics. Ever since the Renaissance there have been grammarians and philosophers of language who have tried to explain the rise and development of Romance languages from Latin to the modern varieties of Romance (e. g. Dante and Biondo in Italy and Lucena and Nebrija in Spain). The search for the causes underlying linguistic change has been coupled with the question of the genesis of new languages and has fascinated scholars for a long time, not only in the era of modern linguistics. This search for underlying causes was present in Western thinking already in the late Middle Ages and was characterized by an ambivalent attitude to the causes of linguistic change from the very beginning: Do inner-linguistic evolutionary and/or extra-linguistic socio-ethnic factors cause language change?

In his *De Vulgari Eloquentia* Dante stresses the first cause, the so-called evolutionary principle: "since man is on the whole an extremely instable and changeable creature, it (language) cannot remain the same or unchangeable, but must change like everything else in us, namely like customs and habits, according to differences in space and time" (translation of Kontzi 1978: 3). The general change of everything human in space and time was consequently the first explanation of the varying development of Romance languages. This evolutionary principle has until today remained the most widely spread and accepted explanation.

The second attempt to explain linguistic change and glottogenesis during the Middle Ages is the ethnic and language-contact hypothesis, which occurs almost contemporaneously with the evolutionary hypothesis. Both in Italy and in Spain there were sufficient remainders and documentation of ancient military conquests, cultural accomplishments, and ethnic changes to give rise to speculations about ethnic origin and language change through contacts between Vulgar Latin and Romance-speaking populations on the one hand and, on the other, foreign invaders of Celtic, Germanic (Goths, Vandals, Langobards, Burgundians), and Semitic (Carthaginians and Arabs) origin. A combination of the two causes of language change, the inner-evolutionary and the ethnolinguistic is therefore found as early as Machiavelli, who claims that some change occurs "in the course of time ... during hundreds of years", and secondly "when it comes about, that a new population settles down in a province. In this case it gives rise to change in the course of a generation" (translation of Kontzi 1978: 3). During the Renaissance this combined view was the prevailing view of language change and glottogenesis in Spain, Portugal, Italy, and France. This view enabled proponents of rising new national states to use ethnic arguments of the past to motivate and explain growth and colonial expansion. In Spain it was the Basque and Visigothic influence, in France the Celtic, and in Italy the Etruscan and Langobardian influence which was believed to have caused the specific ethnic and linguistic characteristics. Later on, in the 19th and 20th centuries, geological metaphors such as substratum (Ascoli 1881–82), superstratum (Wartburg 1932) and adstratum (Valkoff 1932) were coined to describe the effects of language contact in all European languages, not just in Romance.

Furthermore, in medieval language speculation there is also a social and stylistic distinction between levels of speech and writing. Kontzi 1978 draws attention to the fact that medieval scholars were very much aware of the wide gap between Classical Latin as spoken and written by an intellectual elite (in the court, at church, in the monasteries, in science etc.) and Vulgar Latin (*sermo quotidianus*) as spoken by the uneducated majority of the population. The various social and stylistic varieties of Latin and Romance were looked upon as natural products in the cultural development since the fall of the Roman Empire. Modern sociolinguistic research has now provided us with a valuable social view of language change which is amply and rightly represented in the contributions to this volume. However, there is no denying the fact that early Renaissance scholars had made correct and pertinent observations of language change and thereby drawn surprisingly adequate conclusions from empirical facts then available to them in the formulation of the three principles of language change mentioned above: 1) the inner-evolutionary, 2) the ethnic, and 3) the social-stylistic. Many mistakes, exaggerations, and unnecessary polemics in the past and the present could have been avoided had linguists read early works on language change more attentively.

It is thanks to Romance linguists such as Kontzi (1978, 1982) and Schmitt (1982) that such evidence of early insights into language change has been put into an adequate historiographical framework. I think that for our purposes also this information is valuable for further discussions. In the history of linguistics so much loss of important insights into the nature and history of language is common. What is presented as a breakthrough in the theory of language change often turns out to have been said or written ages ago.

Before I go into some concrete examples of how language contact may give rise to new structures in Scandinavian, Dutch, and Raeto-Romansh (cf. section 3), a short orientation on the position of the second principle of language change as formulated by medieval language philosophers is called for, that is, how language contact is taken into consideration in the descriptions of language change in some representative publications of recent date.

1. A short historiography of language change research in the 1960s and 1970s

1.1 In America

There are two major publications in the 1960s and 1970s which come to mind and which I would like to dwell upon at some length here, quite simply because they are typical examples of the state of historical linguistics in America: the two volumes *Directions in historical linguistics* edited by Lehmann and Malkiel (1968) and *Linguistic change and generative theory* edited by Stockwell and Macaulay (1972). Both volumes were a result of conferences held in 1966 and 1969 in Texas and California respectively in the heyday of the generative paradigm, but each from a completely different premise. Whereas the volume published by Lehmann and Malkiel is to be seen as a plea for the importance of historical linguistics in the days of synchronic generative grammar, the articles in the volume by Stockwell and Macaulay are to be seen as exercises in applying generative principles and generative formalism to historical topics. In the latter volume the whole perspective is completely monolingual and all the contributors are preoccupied with inner-linguistic factors of language change: internal reconstruction (Bailey), internal evolution of rules (Labov), language drift (R. Lakoff), markedness and sound change (Vennemann) and so forth. There is a total lack of macrolinguistic perspectives such as socio-historical events, bilingualism, diglossia, loan and interference processes. For an exhaustive description of language change and not only of phonetic change these macrolinguistic factors must be considered, in particular in dealing with lexical and syntactic change. In sharp contrast to the high expectations with which the reader opens this volume a series of trivial statements are made already in the introduction, which summarizes the results of the 1969 conference: "The use of naturalness as a criterion demands that our knowledge of the phonetic facts be as accurate as possible" (ix); "there is great need for more accurate information on dialect variation" (ix); "assimilative processes may be largely due to the physiological properties of the articulatory mechanism..." (xvi). When in the same introduction the contact perspective is occasionally mentioned, as is the case in Bailey's paper, it is mostly under the term "borrowing" and it is then seen as a "possible cause of linguistic change" (xii). Even in the articles by R. Lakoff on "drift" and by Vennemann on "Sound change and markedness theory" there are few if any perspectives of language contact which may cause language change. Although the importance of borrowing between languages and dialects must have been known to all the participants of the 1969 conference, hardly any mention of borrowing occurs in the contributions. The overall perspective is excessively monolingual and only inner-linguistic evolutionary processes are stressed, as if no contacts existed. It is a monolingual world without bilingual or bilectal speakers, in which each language or dialect functions completely independently of all other languages and language varieties. What we experience here is the paradigm of systemic linguistics with its postulates of complete homogeneity and the code-character of language. It rules the entire approach and thinking of the authors. Such a theoretical stand may be motivated for synchronic descriptions but not for accounting for historical change, which requires a totally different approach, allowing variation, borrowing, and language contact to be included. Vennemann (1972: 268, fn. 32) for instance is even astonished at the fact that well known scholars like the German dialectologist Adolf Bach include possible strata influences from non-

Germanic languages to explain some of the perplexing High German consonant shifts.[1] The regrettable effect is a loss of the contact perspective in the articles of the Stockwell and Macaulay volume and this loss leads to a neglect of the most important function of language: the communicative one. Language functions in time, space, and the social dimension and changes according to its communicative roles.

By concentrating on historical and dialectological phonology — seven articles out of nine deal with phonological change —, and by leaving out the lexicon completely, the editors are able to give a lopsided view of language change, which in their view is regular or orderly and mostly phonological. The conscious exclusion of data on lexical and syntactic change is obvious for anyone who has studied change in these two components of language. Such data are not explainable in a monolingual generative framework, as the foreign influences are too numerous to be swept under the carpet of systematism. The articles on syntax by Bever and Langendoen and Robin Lakoff deal with specific problems of perceptual strategies for identifying syntactic structures and language drift, which are also problems which need no contact perspectives. Also Labov's article on the "Internal evolution of linguistic rules" is overly formal and contributes a synchronic sociolinguistic technique to describe variation in American English dialects, but hardly an approach to the study of variation in historical texts.

In Lehmann and Malkiel's volume the perspective of historical linguistics is different in that both Lehmann and Malkiel are concerned with reintroducing historical linguistics in its own terms without enforcing a theoretical frame work. The most important article in this volume is the one by Weinreich, Labov, and Herzog, "A theory of language change". This is a programmatic stand on the results of sociolinguistic research and how these should be integrated into historical linguistics with the useful distinction between categorial and variable rules, the social stratification of rules, and the heterogeneous character of language on the whole. The authors do not purport to present a "fully worked-out theory of linguistic change", as this would be "too ambitious a goal for the present time" (102). There is in the article also no agreement between Weinreich, Labov and Herzog concerning the causes of linguistic change. Unfortunately, Weinreich fell ill during the drafting of the article and died before it was finished. He contributed only to sections 1 through 2.4 and the overall impression of his efforts is that the other two co-writers must have dominated the final version of the article, as there is no mention of the contact perspective in the sections up to 2.4. This fact seems strange to anyone who has studied Weinreich's works. He was deeply and passionately involved with bilingual and multilingual research (cf. Weinreich 1953) and an omission of borrowing and interference for describing language change cannot be a reflection of his view.

1.2 In Europe

1.2.1 Systemic and contact linguistics

Research in America on language change and as represented by the two volumes just discussed stands in sharp contrast to the development in Europe during the same period. The overall concern with theory-construction and the preoccupation with systemic linguistics along the lines of American structuralism and generative grammar during the 1960s and 1970s did not affect all European linguists and philologists to the exclusion of other necessary and valuable perspectives of language such as the sociolinguistic and ethnopolitical variables underlying language change. By giving exaggerated attention to the systemic character of phonological and morphological structures and thus alienating historical linguistics from sociohistorical factors in the formal discussion of an abstract rule calculus of generative nature, most generative treatments of historical problems suffered from empty formalism — a mortal sin in the eyes of every true linguist who works in the framework of the dimensions of time, space, and the sociopolitical variables. It is true that American scholars like Weinreich, Haugen, Fishman, Greenberg, and even Labov maintained an ethnolinguistic approach to language in the tradition of Boas, Sapir, and other Amerindian linguists. Their contribution to the systemic theory formation is nil, but their impact on European studies in minorities and lesser used languages has been considerable. However, the tradition of cultural morphology and language contact studies along the lines of Vossler and Schuchardt was to have a significant influence on the development towards European minority studies and the ethnopolitics of language (e. g. Kloss 1952 (1978) and 1969).

For obvious reasons the ethnic and political situation in many multilingual societies in Europe required a deeper political and social engagement on the part of linguists. This was the case under the Austro-Hungarian Monarchy in the 19th century, when Schuchardt wrote his dissertation on *Slawo-Deutsches und Slawo-Italienisches* (1884), in which he stressed the language contact aspects in the development of German, Slavic, and Italian in the multilingual state where he lived. Since Schuchardt it has again become a respectable topic among European linguists, although not without a long intervening period of silence. Thanks to outstanding research on language contact carried out by others, the leading neogrammarian theoretician, Hermann Paul, was forced to include a new chapter on "Sprachmischung" (Chapter 22) in the second edition of his *Prinzipien der Sprachgeschichte* (1886), just two years after the publication of Schuchardt's dissertation. This chapter was lacking in the first edition of 1880. By drawing upon Schuchardt's research in the multilingual areas of the Austro-Hungarian monarchy and the research of Whitney, Lundell, Windisch, and Jespersen, Paul emphasizes the contact perspective and admits by quoting Schuchardt that "unter allen Fragen mit denen die heutige Sprachwissenschaft zu tun hat, keine von grösserer Wichtigkeit ist als die Sprachmischung" (Paul 1886 [1970]: 390).

However, neither the Leipzig school, nor any of the major schools of structuralism were to integrate language contact as one of the major causes of linguistic change into the theoretical apparatus, quite simply because the systemic conception of language change (neogrammarianism) or the systemic conception of phonology and morphology (structuralism: Saussure, Trubetzkoy, American phonemics, Danish glossematics etc.) prevailed. The place for contact perspectives in theoretical linguistics for describing language change was even more constrained during the dominance of the generative school in the 1960s and 1970s, which delimited the scope of linguistic research to a monolingual and monolectal speaker, who was not conceived of as mastering more than one language and one dialect and whose competence therefore was only describable in terms of monolingual and monolectal rules. The goal of such studies was mostly standardized varieties of the major national languages (English, German, French, Japanese etc.). It was a period in which the interest centred on synchronic rule formulation, economy of formalism, and generalization of known observations to universals at the expense of historical, areal, social, and multilingual variation. The scientific paradigm which developed after 1960 can be defined as a one-sided concern with monolingual descriptions and with synchronic systematism, to such a degree that nowadays, for instance, empty chairs of theoretical linguistics at German universities are being advertised as implying synchronic-systemic, but not diachronic, areal, or social linguistics as well. The term "general linguistics" has thus become a synonym for "synchronic-systemic linguistics" for proponents of the new paradigm.

Fortunately, this development has not been the only trend in European linguistics. The role of the geographical dimension for language change was discovered in the past century by the early dialectologists (Wenker, Wrede, Gilleron, Ascoli etc.). Likewise the role of socio-historical events in promoting linguistic change was also included in the descriptions of the European national languages (migrations, conquests, Christianization, feudalism, Reformation, Enlightenment etc.). In all grammars which tried to describe not only phonological and morphological change but also semantic, syntactic, and lexical change, the need of the contact perspective manifested itself in most handbooks under such terms as borrowing and loan translation. It was as if a given language lived a double life: on the one hand the systemic nature of phonological and morphological structures was stressed, whereas on the other hand the lexicon was seen as a dumping ground for all sorts of exceptions.

1.2.2 Language contact studies and language change

Studies of the loan processes in the European vocabularies and syntax have given impetus to a different approach to language change. If by language change we also mean lexical and syntactic change, the development of a theory of linguistic change in Europe must be described as that of language contact research. Far away from the desks of systemic linguists dialectologists, historical linguists, and contact linguists working in the field of language contact and lesser used languages (minority languages) have described the enormous impact of foreign borrowings on the lexicon and syntax of each European language in the past and present. Betz was one of the first theoreticians to draw the consequences of the significance of lexical borrowing between Latin and German (cf. Betz 1949) since Christianization. He saw contacts between European languages as one of the more important factors for linguistic change and as a channel of cultural exchange between the European nations and civilizations (cf. Betz 1944). Lately Fehling (1979), drawing upon Nygaard (1906, 1896), Havers (1933), Blatt (1957), and Nykrog (1957), has suggested a similar dependency of European syntax upon classical syntax (Latin, Greek, and even Hebrew) for the codification and standardization of Medieval vernaculars. As far as the lexicon is concerned Betz' goal was to describe cultural exchange due to language contact on a more general European level (*Sprach- und Kulturausgleich*), whereas some years later Weinreich (1951) made a case study of the consequences of a specific language contact within Swiss German speaking communities in the Grisons who also spoke the local Raeto-Romanic variety (Sutselvian). Weinreich put the emphasis on linguistic change within the individual and was able to show with his contrastive structural approach how language contact processes (interference, transference, integration, borrowing etc.) give rise to fundamental restructuring in all the components of grammar, from phonology to syntax, from lexical items to semantic structures. The felicitous combination of a formal linguistic and socio-ethnic approach in this dissertation was to inspire modern language contact studies, which encompasses in his tradition both macro- and microlinguistic aspects of language change.

2. Paradigm change towards contact linguistics

2.1 In handbooks and conference proceedings

In the past few years in Europe a change of scientific paradigm has been noticeable from an overly formalistic type of theoretical linguistics — what is called mainstream linguistics — to a more down-to-earth occupation with language in space, time, and the social dimension. Especially geographical, social, and stylistic variation have caught the interest of scholars. Such variation is caused by contacts between different dialects, sociolects, and idiolects of one and the same language. The pattern of variation increases considerably when the effects of contract between several languages in a multilingual area are focused upon. Interest in such inter- and intralinguistic variation has increased so much that a whole number of research centres and projects (in Bale, Brussels, Bayreuth, Graz, Hamburg, Kiel, Mannheim, Stockholm etc.) have been created; new journals have been started (e. g. *Journal of Multilingual and Multicultural Development, Multilingua, The Reports of the Minority Rights Group* (London) etc.) in order to meet the growing need for publication outlets for language contact studies and the problems of linguistic minorities in Europe ("Gastarbeiterdeutsch", city language projects, border minorities and so on). In May 1982 the European Bureau for Lesser Used Languages came into being at a colloquium held in Brussels; its aim is "to preserve and promote the lesser used autochthonous languages of the member states of the European Communities, together with their associated cultures." Its newsletter, *Contact Bulletin*, appears three times a year. Such a change of direction in linguistics and minority research is also clearly visible in recent philological handbooks dealing with historical linguistics and dialectology, in which perspectives of language contact now play a considerable role. I am referring here to two voluminous handbooks of Germanic studies: *Sprachgeschichte* edited by Besch, Reichmann, and Sonderegger (1984 – 1985) and *Dialektologie* edited by Besch, Knoop, Putschke, and Wiegand (1982 – 1983). In Low German Studies also language contact aspects can now be found, as in the *Handbuch zur Niederdeutschen Sprach- und Literaturwissenschaft* edited by Cordes and Möhn (1983). In Romance studies too the necessity of including language contact for an explanatory description of the development of Romance languages has been acknowledged (see for instance the *Lexikon der Romanistischen Linguistik*, edited by Holtus, Metzeltin and Schmitt (1987 – 1989) which is dedicated to problems of language contact, migrating languages, and creole languages). In this context of diachronic contact studies I would also like to mention the last five volumes of the Linguistic Circle of Mannheim, which deal with historical language contacts: strata-linguistic aspects (1982), glottogenetic aspects (1985), general aspects of diachronic language contacts (1986), and language contacts within a given geographical area (Scandinavia) (1984) or within a given historical framework (the Hanseatic League) (1987) (cf. Ureland 1982, 1985, 1987, Ureland and Clarkson 1984, and Nelde, Ureland, and Clarkson 1986). In each of these handbooks and conference volumes contact linguistics plays a considerable role, be it in the form of the older type of stratum research, lexical borrowing or the modern type of interference research. It can be asserted, on the basis of all the publications mentioned here, that contact linguistics is here to stay as a valuable complement to systemic linguistics of a neogrammarian or structuralist-generative orientation. It can also be predicted that contact linguistics will function as a catalyst for a new linguistic orientation in the 1990s and have great importance for the study of language change.

Before I give examples of some contact-induced structures in European languages (cf. section 3), I would like to discuss some models of language change and present a figure containing the major macrolinguistic factors for glottogenesis as worked out during the 1984 conference of the Linguistic Circle of Mannheim (cf. Ureland 1985: 9).

2.2 Models of language change

In the course of the history of linguistics the development of the European languages has been explained within various descriptive models: the historical-comparative model (Rask, Grimm, and Bopp); the biological-evolutionary model (Schleicher); the wave model of Schmidt; the geological strata model in the spirit of Ascoli, Wartburg, and Valkoff; the social ethnic variation model of Hymes, Fishman, and Labov; the roofing model of Kloss and Goossens, and finally the cosmological planetary model of Goossens. The adequacy of these models was discussed in detail at the sixth symposium on glotto- and ethnogenesis in Mannheim (cf. in particular Oeser 1985: 5). The causes of glotto- and ethnogenesis have thus been described in terms of such metaphors as laws of change, pedigrees of family relationships between languages, geological layers and so forth. Research on linguistic change has tended to borrow concepts and metaphors from a number of sciences which have happened to enjoy a certain popularity at various times since 1800: from archaeology, biology, geology, mechanical physics, sociology, and astronomy. In structural and generative linguistics, metaphors from economics have dominated: the principle of least effort, economy of features (the simplicity measure), and universal statements. For a description of phonetic change such concepts and metaphors have proved useful. At the 1984 glottogenetic symposium in Mannheim the interest of most speakers was focused on the macrolinguistic variables of language change; change in syntax and the lexicon was dealt with more than inner-linguistic factors of systemic restructuring in phonology and morphology, which are otherwise the main concern of historical linguists.

2.2.1 Macrolinguistic factors of language change

In my introductory article to the glottogenetic volume just mentioned (Ureland 1985) I enumerate eleven factors underlying glottogenesis in Europe, arrived at during the Mannheim symposium. In Figure 1 these factors are presented and briefly discussed. Two kinds of factors are contained in the figure which will be discussed here: those of inherent change and those caused by language contact.

Figure 1 gives a comprehensive picture of the eleven types of factors underlying language change which may lead to the rise of a new language,

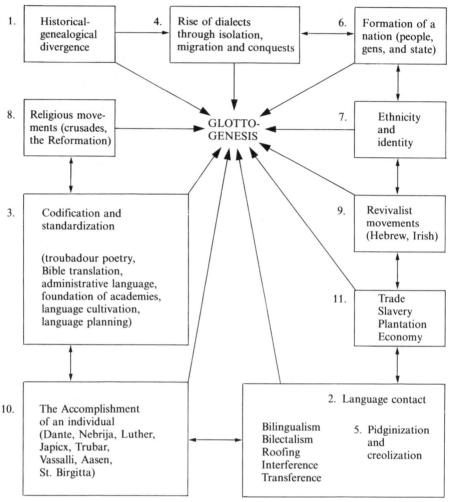

Figure 1. Factors giving rise to glottogenesis in Europe

but not necessarily so in each individual case, since the result of a change must somehow be socially and politically accepted in the codification and standardization process. To what extent it is accepted is not possible to predict. The interdependency of the eleven factors is therefore expressed by the contrapunctual arrows. By linking inherently motivated factors such as 1 (historical-genealogical divergence) and 4 (dialectological splitting-up) with factor 3 (codification and standardization) via such major socio-historical factors as 6 (formation of nations), 7 (ethnicity and identity), 8 (religious movements), 9 (revivalist movements), 10 (the accomplishment of an individual), and 11 (trade contacts) in an intricate pattern of genesis the accidental character of language change in each genesis process is indicated. The factor trade is mentioned last, but not because it is the least significant cause of change. It is often a precondition for linguistic contact, not only in the rise of pidgins and creoles but also for the development of the European languages. There is a random ordering of factors in Figure 1 which allows a variable sequence of processes for genesis. The main point in Figure 1 is to connect the inner-linguistic factors of 1 and 4 to the macro-linguistic or sociolinguistic ones in the other numbers. Figure 1 is also an attempt to present a typology of language change and glottogenesis, which was one of the aims of the genesis symposium in Mannheim. Despite the scepticism on the part of the historians participating the linguists felt that such a typology is worth working out. Linguists use other methods and approaches than historians, who regard each historical event, including that of glotto- and ethnogenesis, as so unique and non-repeatable that no generalization on the causes and preconditions of the rise of a given language or a given nation can be in agreement with the principles and working methods of the science of history. As a linguist I must disagree with the historians on this point. Even if each change of language and thus the possible rise of a new language implies a chain of unique historical processes in a given socio-historical situation, there are nevertheless a certain number of common characteristics underlying the genesis of European languages: Christianization, the introduction of the Latin or Greek alphabet, codification of laws, standardization of an administrative language, book printing, Bible translations, the Reformation, the creation of modern technical vocabularies plus a number of other factors. All these historical events are more or less common to all European languages, even if they are activated and influential under varying social conditions at different historical periods in different geographical areas of Europe. To enhance the explanatory adequacy of linguistics such common processes of genesis and language change should be described and united in a typological representation of linguistic change. By subsuming linguistic change under the general framework of social and political change we can avoid empty formalism and scientific isolation from other disciplines. In the framework of such a common genesis schema the question of the rise of European languages can be effectively tackled. A language does not arise in isolation; a linguistic change does not come about without social and political causes. A new language or a new language variety arises in a continuous interaction through contacts with other languages, language varieties, and different cultures. This complex view of European glottogenesis and language change is not represented in the standard philological hand-books, or if so only indirectly. Other evolutional schemata dominate the picture of the rise of the European languages and the causes of language change. The main goal of the Mannheim symposium was to break the dominance of the historical-biological view of the rise of the European languages and to introduce a historical contact perspective along the lines sketched in Figure 1. By doing so we have not rejected the value of the historical-comparative or historical-genealogical approaches to language change.

3. Some contact-induced structures

3.1 Scandinavian SOV structure

Throughout this article the importance of ethnopolitical processes for the rise of literary languages in Europe has been stressed. Several theories and hypotheses have been launched to come to grips with the difficult problem of linguistic change and linguistic genesis. As far as the Scandinavian languages are concerned, the process of change and genesis cannot be studied with focus on Scandinavia alone, as the cultural and historical situation in northern Europe between 500—1200 A. D. — the period of the glottogenesis of North Germanic — was characterized by migrations both to and from Scandinavia and by the resulting ethnic, linguistic, and cultural fusion in Scandinavia and the surrounding areas. From 800 until about 1200 we also have to consider the impact which the language of the new Christian religion and the integration of Mediterranean life style and technology had on the developing languages of the north. Medieval Latin was the vehicle for propagating the new faith and establishing the ecclesiastical institutions (churches, monasteries, and bishoprics) or for writing (gospels, church laws, chronicles, charters, treaties, letters etc.). Therefore Latin became the international language all over northern Europe, roofing all cultural activity as it had already done in western Europe since the days of the Roman Empire and Christianization. The ancient Scandinavian languages were exposed to Latin in all linguistic domains and as they were developing languages the influence of Latin for the literary standard and codification was enormous. The *Ausbau* to fully-fledged standard languages was a slow process which took many centuries of standardization and was not completed until the 18th century. The codification of the laws in the 13th and 14th until implied a great deal of language planning and standardization on the part of the editorial boards and chanceries, which took account of international practice with Latin as a prototype for the literary and stylistic development. There existed of course a marginal runic tradition, particularly in Denmark, Norway, and Sweden, which could be drawn upon, but without the Latin texts in jurisprudence, religion, and documentation as prototypes the comparatively swift development of Old Norse, Old Danish, and Old Swedish to effective and useful instruments of written communication would not have been possible.

The best-known illustration of the impact of foreign influence (Latin or Continental Germanic) on Old Scandinavian languages is, besides the lexicon, the syntax: the emergence of verb-final (SOV) order in *subordinate clauses*. Very few such verb-final structures occur in the main clauses of the approximately 2,000 runic inscriptions written in the younger futhark after 800 A. D., whose word order was investigated by Larsson 1931.[2] They do, however, occur in the inscriptions of the older futhark in Krause's edition of the Proto-Scandinavian inscriptions (cf. Krause 1971),[3] e. g.

(1)   (EK) GO DAGASTIR RUNO FAIHDO
        'I (Name) the rune made' (Einang, Norway, 350–400 A. D.:
        Krause 1971: 145)

But the verb-second order (SVO) has been shown to be more frequent in the older runic inscriptions: between 61% and 66% according to Ureland (1978: 120) and Braunmüller (1982: 141). It occurs in such inscriptions as the following:

(2)   H. H. WARAIT RUNAR ÞAIAR
        'H. H. (Name) carved runes these' (Istaby, Sweden, 7th century
        A. D.: Krause 1971: 150)

There is no question about the double SVO and SOV character of the Proto-Scandinavian runic material. The claim that Proto-Germanic must have been SOV because of the "higher proportion of SOV order to SVO in the earlier runic inscriptions" (cf. Yoshida 1982: 341 who repeats Lehmann 1971, 1974 and Stockwell 1977) has thus been shown to be false. The claim that Proto-Germanic was predominantly SOV is not based on Germanic material alone but on comparative Indo-European evidence as well, primarily on Sanskrit and Hittite, which are SOV. As the Proto-Scandinavian runic inscriptions are the oldest documents of Germanic besides the *Codex Argenteus*, which is not representative for syntax because of the transfer effect from the Greek original, it is likely that Proto-Germanic also was vacillating between an SVO and an SOV type. The Delbrück-Lehmann Hypothesis that Proto-Indo-European was SOV has also been challenged by Friedrich 1975, who finds the selection of examples for the SOV hypothesis too one-sided. For the reconstruction of Proto-Indo-European word-order such important languages as Homeric Greek and Old Irish which were rather VO languages have not been considered to the same extent as Vedic Sanskrit, New Hittite, and Germanic (cf. Friedrich 1975: 5). Therefore as far as Proto-Scandinavian is concerned there is every reason to posit both structures: SVO and SOV.

In Figure 2 an inner development of Germanic syntax is sketched, which describes how in Proto-Germanic both orders of elements occur in varying ways and in different historical periods. The development in this figure is represented as being parallel without major influence from surrounding languages. In the oldest stages down to 800 A.D. (in Old English, Old High German, and Proto-Scandinavian) both structures are preserved, whereas about 1200 it is primarily in Middle High German that the SOV structure in subordinate clauses is well preserved. In the runic material of 800 − 1200 the SVO structure dominates (up to 99%) (cf. note 3) and later in English the SOV structure also disappears (the parallel loss of SOV order in Scandinavian and English may be a result of historical contacts, which will be our concern below). The dominance of SVO structures is also the case in the next stage of development down to 1250, when the oldest documents of Old Icelandic, Old Norwegian, Old Danish, and Old Swedish show predominantly verb-second order (see in particular Figure 4). In the framework of the parallel inner development as presented in Figure 2 the amazing fact is that in Old Swedish and Old Danish (and to a certain extent also in Old Norwegian and Old Icelandic charters of the 15th century) SOV structures in subordinate clauses start to occur after 1250 and remain in written documents into Early Modern Swedish, Danish, and Norwegian. In Modern Swedish they disappear after the 18th century. From the viewpoint of an inner developmental scheme, it is as if the SOV structures have "surfaced" from

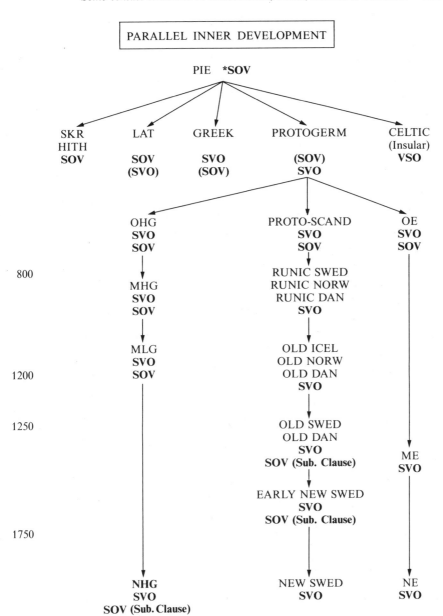

Figure 2. Parallel inner development of the Germanic verb phrase

the past, that is, from Proto-Scandinavian or even Proto-Germanic.[4] In discussing the inner developmental hypothesis of the disappearance and re-emergence of North Germanic SOV I have here intentionally ignored the possible language contact effects.[5] This is mostly the state of affairs in traditional treatments of syntax in the Old Scandinavian laws, which are supposed to reflect "purely Germanic" development, untouched by disturbances from Latin (cf. Schlyter 1835, Wessén 1968: 22, and Ståhle 1976).[6] However, this national romantic view of syntactic development in North Germanic has been criticized lately as being completely unrealistic and does not reflect what we know about the Old Scandinavian laws and the role of Latin and Continental Germanic during the enormously international period of Christianization and codification (cf. Utterström 1975, 1978, 1983, 1987, Sjöholm 1976, Ehrhardt 1977, and Ureland 1986). Instead of the one-dimensional biological-genealogical model sketched in Figure 2 I will propose another line of development which implies contact with SOV structures in Latin and Continental Germanic (Middle Low German and possibly Middle Dutch) during periods of natural bilingualism (in the Hanseatic Period) and through indirect exposure to Medieval Latin syntax (through learned bilingualism). Thus Figure 3 contains information about contacts with surrounding languages which is lacking in the genealogical representation of Figure 2. The significance of loan syntax (transference), which is caused by the roofing effect of Latin and Continental Germanic during the centuries in which the Scandinavian languages were being codified and standardized, is built into Figure 3.

The effect of Latin SOV structures is visible as early as the Danish and Swedish runic inscriptions before 1200 and are of the following type:

(3)   MARTIN MIK GIARÞI   (DR 320, 322, 326, 327, 332: Sahl-
       'Martin me made'   berger 1980: 9)

(4)   UIFIN ÞITTA FAÞI   (Oklunda Stone, 11th century: Sahlberger
       'Vifinn this made'   1980: 9)

Both Larsson 1931: 26 and Sahlberger 1980: 9 agree on the non-nativeness of these inscriptions which show a foreign continental word-order calqued on the Latin prototype: *X me fecit*. Although the verb-last structure only occurs in an tiny minority of runic inscriptions in churches (on baptismal fonts) or on rune stones close to churches from the period 1000 – 1200 A. D., it is invariably a sign of syntactic transfer from Continental SOV

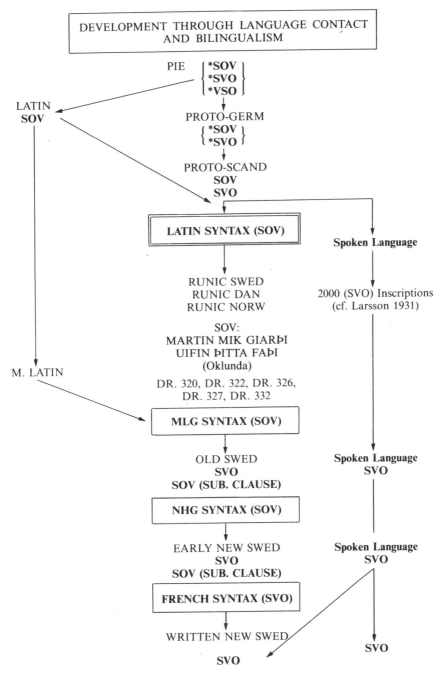

Figure 3. Development of the Germanic verb phrase through language contact and bilingualism

proto-types.[7] However, in Figure 3 a special column is set for the development in spoken language and in this column no Continental Germanic SOV influence is indicated, as it is known from the 2,000 runic inscriptions investigated by Larsson 1931 that the SVO order is practically the only one on stones raised outside the perimeter of the churches and that this order reflects true North Germanic SVO syntax. It is this order which remains unchanged in modern spoken Danish, Norwegian, and Swedish.[8] For the creation of literary languages the significance of SOV calques exemplified here must not be underestimated, as the church and its language formed the centre of religious and intellectual life after Christianization. The SOV influence from Latin or Middle Low German during this period is also visible in the following subordinate clauses excerpted from two laws (that of Skåne (SkL) 1202−1216 and Uppland (UpL) (1296)):

Old Danish

(5)   hin aer wapn af hanum *tok*   (SkL: Schlyter 1859: 95,3)
      'the one who his weapon took'

Old Swedish

(6)   þa han lik *iorþaer*   (UpL: Schlyter 1834: 35,1)
      'when he a corpse buries'

By placing the Middle Low German SOV roof above Old Danish and Old Swedish and connecting it with the Latin SOV structures we can account for the transfer of such SOV structures as given in (5) and (6). This does not mean that the SOV structures are obligatory here, since SVO structures also occur in subordinate clauses and are actually in a majority in most literary genres, e. g.

Old Swedish

(7)   at han *gaf* half mark   (VgL I: Collin−Schlyter 1827: 19,17)
      'that he gave half a mark'

However, there is no doubt about the foreign SOV order in the subordinate clause of (6) and this order remains long into the Early Modern Swedish period, e. g. in the court records of Stockholm (StTb) from the 15th century:

(8)   piganess fader som slagen *bleff*   (StTb 1487: Nov. 26: Carls-
           'the maid's father who killed was'   son 1924: 237)

The SOV order also occurs in the 17th century, e. g. in Gustav Adolph's letters to Ebba Brahe in 1613:

(9)   varefter jag ock stor längtan *hafver*   (Thörnqvist 1977: 134)
           'after which I also long very much'

The SOV structure in subordinate clauses is also represented in the Swedish Bible translation of 1541:

(10)   the thetta *sadhe*   (Luke 24,24)
           'who said this'

It is not until the 18th century that the foreign (German) SOV order in subordinate clauses disappears from formal written Swedish. Figure 3 has a further roof to reflect the new influence of French SVO on written Swedish around 1700. This is to be seen as a result of a new type of bilingualism (Swedish — French) among the educated classes during the 18th century in Sweden.

This change back to SVO order also in the subordinate clauses was supported by three facts; first, the SVO order had always been the order of the main clause since the early runic inscriptions; second, it had also been the more frequent order in written subordinate clauses; third, it had remained the natural order in spoken language. This was of immediate importance for the standardization during the 18th century, when the Swedish writer Dalin argued for a more natural written language to correspond to spoken syntax.[9]

As has been demonstrated here with the help of the SOV order in subordinate clauses in Old Swedish and Early Modern Swedish, it is the interaction of factor 2 (language contact with Continental Germanic and/ or Latin plus French), factor 3 (codification and standardization), and factor 10 (the influence of an individual) which brought about the emergence and later disappearance of the SOV order in modern written Swedish (the same applies to written Danish and Norwegian). Figure 4 illustrates the degree of Germanization and Latinization in Old Scandinavian. The percentages of SOV structures are a good indication of the depth of contact and are based on Larsson (1931: 125—127), who, in his painstaking investigation, has covered the most important sources of

Scandinavian from 1200 to 1500. The Middle Low German or Medieval Latin influence has been indicated in Figure 4 by a roof and has been drawn thinner to the right in order to symbolize the waning continental SOV influence in the western Scandinavian sources as opposed to the eastern ones. There are also less SOV structures in the early documents (before 1250) and especially in the Old Norse and western Swedish sources. Therefore another roof has been drawn — the West Scandinavian SVO roof — which is probably a result of less Continental (Latin and German) influence and a different history of missionary activity, i. e. that coming from the British Isles and not from northern Germany (Hamburg—Bremen). This is how the lack of SOV structures in the Old Icelandic classics is to be explained. Also remarkable is the low percentage of SOV structures in the early Danish laws before 1250: in Valdemar's Law (VSjL) (0%), the Law of Skåne (SkL) (1%) Erik's Sealand Law (ESjL) (1%) and the Law of Jutland (JL) (4%) which all have very few SOV structures. Chronology seems to play a decisive role for the importation of SOV structures; the caesura seems to be around 1250. The early Swedish laws show a higher SOV percentage than the Danish laws because they occur later: the older Law of Västergötland (VgL I) and Östergötland (ÖgL) have 6% and then, in an increasing pattern, the SOV structures begin to penetrate the texts: in the central and northern Swedish laws: 16% (HL, Hälsingland), 29% (UpL, Uppland), 36% (SdmL, Södermanland) and 38% (MES, King Magnus' City Law).

The charters of the 14th century in Norway and Iceland show between 11% and 13% SOV structures; the degree of SOV in subordinate clauses in the Danish Fishing Rights (13th—14th centuries) is 28%, the Visby Sea Laws (13th—14th centuries) 22%—42% and the Danish charters of the 15th century 41%. An even higher percentage of SOV is to be found in the charters of Stockholm and Central Sweden in the 14th century: 27%—60%. In the famous Stockholm Court Records (StTb) Helmik, the scribe of German origin, has 44%, whereas Ingvald, the scribe of Swedish origin, has only 17%.

In the Vadstena Monastery literature (1451) the percentage of SOV structures is 20, whereas in St. Birgitta's texts there are from 4% to 44% SOV structures, depending on the literary genre of the texts.

Considerable geographical differences are also visible in Figure 4: around Lake Mälar the influence of Middle Low German and Medieval Latin SOV was the greatest, but in the west the SVO structures prevailed (in Iceland, Norway, and in western Sweden). The real increase of SOV structures seems to have occurred after 1250. Thanks to Larsson 1931

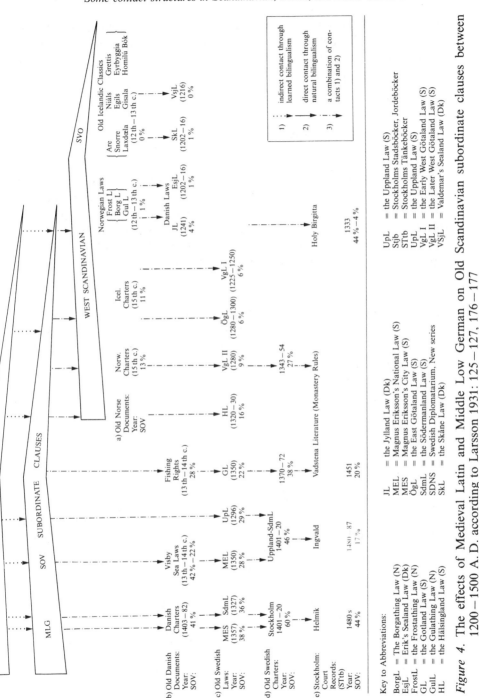

Figure 4. The effects of Medieval Latin and Middle Low German on Old Scandinavian subordinate clauses between 1200−1500 A.D. according to Larsson 1931: 125−127, 176−177

Key to Abbreviations:

BorgL = The Borgathing Law (N)
EsjL = Erik's Sealand Law (Dk)
FrostL = the Frostathing Law (N)
GL = the Gotland Law (S)
GulL = the Gulathing Law (N)
HL = the Hälsingland Law (S)

JL = the Jylland Law (Dk)
MEL = Magnus Eriksson's National Law (S)
MES = Magnus Eriksson's City Law (S)
ÖgL = the East Götaland Law (S)
SdmL = the Södermanland Law (S)
SDNS = Swedish Diplomatarium, New series
SkL = the Skåne Law (Dk)

UpL = the Uppland Law (S)
Stjb = Stockholms Stadsböcker, Jordeböcker
STtb = Stockholms Tänkeböcker
UpL = the Uppland Law (S)
VgL I = the Early West Götaland Law (S)
VgL II = the Later West Götaland Law (S)
VsjL = Valdemar's Sealand Law (Dk)

we can reconstruct the degree and chronology of continental syntactic penetration, of which the borrowing of the SOV structure in subordinate clauses is the clearest case (see Ureland 1986: 46—53 and Wollin 1987 for more details).

3.2 Dutch and Frisian reflexive structures

The second example of contact-induced structures in European language change is from Dutch and West Frisian dialects. In a number of publications I have discussed the historical, geographical, and social parameters for the penetration of Middle High German *sich* as a core-ference marker in Dutch and Frisian (cf. Ureland 1978 b: 631—636, 1979 a: 91—98, 1979 b: 250—263 and 1980: 53—65). For the present discussion of language change caused by contact it will suffice to study Map 1 which shows the geographical distribution of reflexive structures in Dutch and Frisian and which has been drawn on the basis of data excerpted from Amsterdam (1934) and Louvain (1937) questionnaires. As far as the number of linguistic structures are concerned there are three major classes in a fairly clear geographical concentration: a) object forms of the personal pronoun (3rd sg masc): *him, hem, höm, hum, hom* (symbol |) or the variant with a deleted initial consonant in atonal positions (symbol ⌐): *im, em, öm, um, om* or with an epenthetic nasal initial consonant: *nem, nöm, num* (symbol ∟); b) the reflexive pronoun *zich*, which occurs in the dialects in a number of forms: *zich, zech, zoch, zuch,* and *zi* (symbol S) or, with a non-shifted final consonant *zik, zök* and *zuk* (symbol $); c) the possessive pronoun plus the lexical form *eigen*: *zijn eigen* (symbol ●) which occurs in a great number of phonetic forms of which *zijn, sien,* and *zun* (symbol −) are the more interesting variants. Besides these three major classes there are also four smaller classes which are either mergers of the three or are other innovative structures: d) *em eige* (symbol x) and *zich eigen* (symbol ∧), which are analogical forms coined on the pattern of *zijn eigen* and which are found only in those areas where the map shows the heaviest concentration of *zijn eigen*-forms (e. g. Area E with every third form as *zijn eigen*); e) *himsalle(m)* and *himsels* (symbol ▲), which is found primarily in West Friesland and which is reminiscent of the English *himself*; *zich self* (symbol △) *zezölere* (symbol v) and *zezölven* (symbol f) are also a combination of two patterns (*zich* and a redundant addition of *zelf*). Finally, there are some dialects,

Key to symbols:

| = him, hem, høm, hum, hom
⌐ = im, em, øm, um, om
L = nem (H 63), nøm (H 84),
    num (N 21)
S = zich, zi, zech, zuch, zoch
$ = zik, zok, zuk
▲ = himsalle(m) (B 4), himsels (B 81)
    (B 98)
● = zijn eigen
− = zijn (I 141a), sien (L 119), zun
    (L 185)
X = em eige (E 187)
△ = zich zelf (E 77)
V = zezölere (K 349a)
F = zezölven (K 307)
■ = zijn baard afdoen (L 355)
    (H 113)
∧ = zich eigen (D 4)
    (D 5)

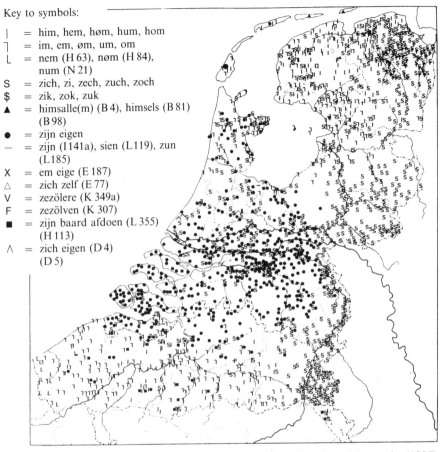

Map 1. Reflexive structures retrieved in Amsterdam (1934) and Louvain (1937) questionaires: *hij heeft zich gewassen* and *hij moet zich nog scheren* (3rd Sg. Masc.)

especially in southern Dutch areas, where no reflexive structure was selected but a normal intransitive construction as in g) *zijn baard afdoen* (symbol ■).

Of these seven classes of coreference structures in Dutch and Frisian only the *zich*-form and its variants will concern us here, as it is known to be a classic example of a borrowed morphosyntactic item from Middle High German into Dutch and Frisian (cf. e. g. Frings and Vandenheuvel 1921, Frings 1957, Zelissen 1969). The borrowing of such an important function word as a reflexive pronoun was due to inherent forces, i. e. to avoid homonomy between the true object personal pronoun *hem* and the use of *hem* as a coreference marker in reflexive constructions, e. g. West Flemish *De man wast'em* (Ostend, H 16) 'The man washes (himself)' and West Frisian *De mon wasket him* (Oudkerk, B 28) 'The man washes (himself)'. Although the function of *hem* and *him* as a coreference marker may be clear after the verb for washing, there are many other verb constructions in which the coreference function is not transparent to the listener and which may thus cause confusion. A second explanation of the borrowing of Middle High German *sich* into Dutch and Frisian has been the language contact effect during periods of bilingualism in the history of the Dutch and Frisian languages. As the marking of coreference belongs to the basic functions in morphosyntax the importation of new means to express coreference is a language change of great magnitude and has therefore been chosen here as a good example.

The Standard Dutch form for expressing coreference is now *zich*, e. g. *hij heeft zich gewassen* 'He has washed (himself)' and *hij moet zich noch scheren* 'He has to get a shave'. Map 1 shows three interesting patterns of geographical distribution which indicate the role of the influence of neighbouring areas in the east, where the Dutch and Frisian *zich* and *zik* forms originated: in Middle Franconian (Köln) and Low Saxon areas in the north east. Along the rivers Maas (Limburg), the Rhine (Veluwe), and the Ijssel (Gelderland) the areal advance of *zich* is clearly visible. A similar compact spread of *zik* can be seen in the north-eastern corner of the province of Groningen. Besides this specific spread of *zich* and *zik* in the eastern parts there is a general sprinkling of *zich*-forms all over the central and northern parts of the area, which is due to the influence of the Dutch standard (Algemeen Beschaafde Nederlands), which has incorprated *zich* as the normal coreference marker. The real exception to the general sprinkling effect of the Dutch standard is to be found in the southern Dutch dialects (Areas H, N, O and P), where 0% or, in some parts, less than 10% of the reflexive forms are *zich*-forms (see in particular Zeeland and West Flanders in areas H and N, where no such *zich*-forms have so far been observed in fieldwork or in dialect questionnaires).

The numerical distribution of forms of reflexive structures is shown in Diagram 1, which indicates an increasing pattern of the *zich*-forms from west to east in relation to other types of coreference markers (*him/im*, *himsels*, *zijn eigen*): area A (Texel, Vlieland, West Terschelling) and area B (East Terschelling, Ameland, Schiermonnikoog, Northern and Central West Friesland) have 12% *zich*-forms, but area C (Groningen and Northern Drente) has 72% *zich/zik*-forms. The same pattern of distribution of *zich/zik*-forms from west to east can be seen in Diagram 2 for areas D

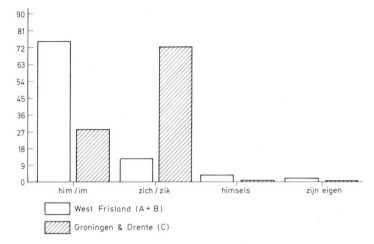

Diagram 1. Distribution of reflexive forms in West Frisland (A + B) and Dutch dialects (C) as retrieved in Amsterdam (1934) and Louvain Questionnaires.
3rd Singular Masculine

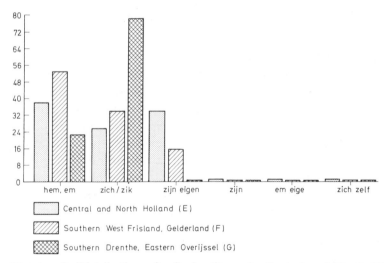

Diagram 2. Distribution of reflexive forms in Central and North Holland (E), Southern West Frisland, Gelderland, Western Overijssel, and Veluwe (F), Southern Drenthe, Eastern Overijssel, and Twente (G)

Note: only four forms retrieved in area D: 'zich' 1 ×, 'zijn eigen' 1 ×, 'zich eigen' 2 ×

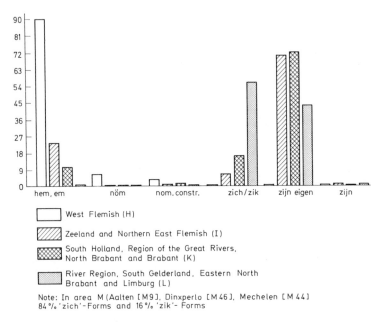

90
81
72
63
54
45
36
27
18
9
0

hem, em   nöm   nom. constr.   zich / zik   zijn eigen   zijn

☐ West Flemish (H)

▨ Zeeland and Northern East Flemish (I)

▨ South Holland, Region of the Great Rivers,
   North Brabant and Brabant (K)

▨ River Region, South Gelderland, Eastern North
   Brabant and Limburg (L)

Note: In area M (Aalten [M9], Dinxperlo [M46], Mechelen [M44]
84 °/₀ 'zich'-Forms and 16 °/₀ 'zik'- Forms

Diagram 3. Distribution of reflexive forms in West Flemish (H), Zeeland, and
Northern East Flemish (I), South Holland, Region of the Great
Rivers, North Brabant and Brabant (K), the River Region, South
Gelderland, Eastern North Brabant, and Limburg (L)

and E (Central and North Holland), which have 25%, area F (Southern
West Friesland, Gelderland, Western Overijssel, and Veluwe) with 33%
zich-forms and area G (Southern Drenthe, Eastern Overijssel, and
Twente) with 78% *zich/zik*-forms; this decrease of *zich*-forms from west
to east is also visible in Diagram 3: area H (West Flemish) has 0% *zich*-
forms, area I (Zeeland and Northern East Flemish) 6%, area K (South
Holland, Region of the Great Rivers, North Brabant, and Brabant) 16%,
and area L (River Region, South Gelderland, Eastern North Brabant,
and Limburg) 55%, while area M (Aalten, Dinxperlo, and Mechelen,
border areas close to Arnhem and Nijmegen) has 100% *zich/zik*-forms;
Diagram 4 shows for the southernmost areas of the Dutch dialects an
abrupt increase from area N (West Flemish) with 0% *zich*-forms and
areas O (Southern East Flemish and South Western Brabant) and P
(South Brabant with Brussels and Louvain) with 7% *zich*-forms to area
Q (South Limburg) with 93% *zich*-forms

Space does not allow a lengthy discussion here of all the details of
geographical and numerical distribution. The historical change from a

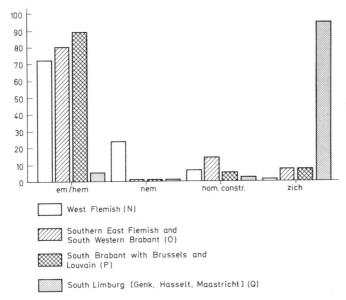

West Flemish (N)

Southern East Flemish and
South Western Brabant (O)

South Brabant with Brussels and
Louvain (P)

South Limburg [Genk, Hasselt, Maastricht] (Q)

Diagram 4. Distribution of reflexive forms in West Flemish (N), Southern East
Flemish, and South Western Brabant (O), South Brabant with Brussels and Louvain (P) and South Limburg (Q)

North Sea Germanic type of coreference marker (ambiguous personal object pronouns: *hem, haar, hulle*), which are still found in West Frisian, North Dutch (Noord Hollands), and North-Eastern Dutch dialects (Veluws, Gelders, and Drents, and to some extent Gronings), and in all the southern Dutch dialects in Belgium except Limburgs, to the clear coreference forms of *zich* and *zik* is also demonstrated in Map 1 and Diagrams 1 — 4. It is the historical contact between the Middle Franconian German dialect speakers during the expansive period of the City of Cologne in the 13th and 14th centuries (cf. Zelissen 1969) on the one hand and the Dutch dialect speakers on the other (in Limburg, East North Brabant, Veluwe, Gelderland, Overijssel, and Twente) that has brought about the clearly decreasing east-west pattern of the *zich*-forms described above. Furthermore, there was another cultural movement which also changed the map: that of Middle Low Saxon (the language of the Hanseatic League) which brought *zik*-forms into north-eastern Dutch dialects in Twente and Groningen during the period of the Hanseatic League, the 13th and 15th centuries, after the Middle High German *sich* had been adapted to *sik* (cf. Frings and Vandenheuvel 1921, Frings and van Ginneken 1919: 105 — 108 and Frings 1944 on the two types of expansion —

that of Cologne and Westfalia — which caused an interesting contact pattern between various German and Dutch dialects). Map 1 and Diagrams 1−4 summarize the results of the final penetration of the two forms caused by these two different socio-historical events.

The third significant source of change towards *zich* as a general coreference marker is the Standard Dutch variety (ABN) into which the *zich*-form was incorporated and made into the non-ambiguous marker for coreference linkage during the 16th and 17th centuries in the Bible and the language of administration. The occurrence of *zich* instead of native personal object pronouns in the more westerly dialects of West Friesland, North, Central, and South Holland (Areas A, B, D, and E) as well as the region of the Great Rivers is due to the influence of (written) Standard Dutch: cultural borrowing and transference. It is in particular the standardization effect of the *Staaten Bijbel* and the language of the Reformation literature which brought about the change in the choice of coreference markers from ambiguous object personal pronouns to *zich* during the 16th and 17th centuries (van Loey 1980 (1959): 143).

3.3 Raeto-Romanic structures in texts written in German in the Engadine, Switzerland

After giving two examples of historically introduced contact structures from Scandinavian and Dutch, we turn to a third language area for some examples of contact structures which we can observe ourselves: the Engadine in the Swiss Canton Grisons. Synchronic studies of interference, transference, and integration of syntactic and morphosyntactic structures can yield factual evidence of the nature of disturbances which arise when two languages are in contact with each other. Weinreich (1952 and 1953) points out the great amount of interference which affects all the components of a language in contact with another language. The contact is also of such a nature that the interference effect is contrapuntal: language X ↔ language Y. Mostly only one direction of the contact is studied and focused upon by linguists, but this is just because their interest is limited. A true contact investigation should be contrapuntal.

Before discussing some of the contact structures in the Engadine material, it is necessary to stress the difference between a language change which occurs in the course of one or more generations and affects the entire community (change in *langue*) and a change which seems to be a result of the conflict of two languages within a bilingual person (change in *parole*). Whereas the former linguistic change is a socio-political event in that a given innovation must be accepted by a greater number of speakers or be somehow codified as a new norm, the latter change within a bilingual individual or caused by a bilingual individual can be seen as a random phenomenon which belongs to a specific communicative act. However, it is precisely in the microscopic speech acts that we can study the embryo of a change towards a new structure. In the light of this insight gained from bilingual studies we will exemplify some interferences in the syntax, semantics, and phraseology from pupils' compositions in the 6th form in the Engadine, Switzerland.[10]

3.3.1 Transfer of Raeto-Romanic syntax

In a number of compositions the Romansh accusative plus prepositional object order is copied into German as in the following composition (Zernez (Zer), Engadine):

(11)   Da gab sie *das Wasser den Armen Mann* (Zer 6:8:11)

Qua det ella *l'aua al hom pover* (Eng Rom)
Da gab sie dem armen Mann das Wasser (St Germ)
'Then she gave the water to the poor man'

The Standard German order of the dative plus the accusative object is violated in (11) and changed to the order accusative plus another accusative object but without the insertion of a preposition. However, such copying of the prepositional object from Romansh is also found as in the following example excerpted from a composition written in Samedan (Sam), also 6th form:

(12)   Gibte sie das Wasser am Vater (Sam 6:12:24)

Gab sie dem Vater das Wasser (St Germ)
Hät sie s'Wasser am Vater ge (Swiss Germ)

It is impossible to decide, whether the Romansh prepositional construction has triggered the *am Vater* construction in (12) or whether the Swiss German construction was the triggering factor. It is of course also possible that both languages interfered.

3.3.2 Change of syntactic verb category

An example from the compositions which illustrates well the semantic change caused by Romansh is the following sentence from a 6th form pupil from Sta Maria (Sta) in the Münster Valley:

(13)   Als der alte Mann trinkt, kam er jünger (Sta 6:3:34)

Chur cha l'hom vegl ha bavü, *gnit* el plü giuven (Eng Rom)
Als der alte Mann trank, wurde er jünger (St Germ)
'When the old man drank, he got younger'

The use of *kam* as an auxiliary is here a direct copying of the corresponding structure in Romansh, where the verb *gnir* 'come' also can be used as an inchoative auxiliary and mean 'become' especially together with an adjective as in (13). Another striking example of syntactic-semantic transfer between Romansh as the source language and German as the goal language is in the following sentence written by an Engadine pupil in Scuol (Scu):

(14)   und lebten darin froh und fröhlich *für ihren ganzen leben* (Scu 6:14:34)

e vivettan cuntaints *per tuot lur vita* (Eng Rom)
und lebten froh und glücklich darin ihr ganzes Leben lang (St Germ)
'and lived happily in it (the house) all their lives'

In Standard German a construction with a time adverb (*lang*) is necessary here. However, the pupil prefers to construct a prepositional phrase with *für*, which is a direct copy or transfer of the Romansh temporal phrase: *per tuot lur vita*.

3.3.3 Transfer of phraseology

In this list of contact structures excerpted from compositions written by bilingual pupils in the Engadine I would like to finish with some examples from phraseology:

(15)   Er wusste nicht mehr *was machen* (Scu 6:4:7)

         El nu savet plu *che far* (Eng Rom)
         Er wusste nicht mehr, was er machen sollte (St Germ)
         'He did not know what to do'

The *che-far*-construction is simply translated here into the German replica construction: *was machen* (cf. also a similar transfer in English *what to do*, possibly from a parallel French construction: *il ne savait pas quoi faire*.

(16)   Und geht mit seiner Frau *für Mais* (Scu 6:9:5)

         E va cun sia duonna *per furmantun* (Eng Rom)
         und geht mit seiner Frau, um Mais zu ernten (St Germ)
         'and leaves with his wife to pick corn'

(17)   (Er spielte) *die Rolle als Dummer* (Scu 9:5:16)

         la rolla sco pluffer (Eng Rom)
         die Rolle des Dummen (St Germ)
         'the role of the stupid man'

In (16) and (17) more Romansh structures have entered the German sentences by transference and translation, whereby a violation of Standard German is the result: A verb with a German prepositional phrase (*gehen für Mais*) instead of an infinitival construction (*gehen um Mais zu ernten*). The prepositional construction Romansh *ir per X* has thus been copied (transferred) into the the German replica sentence. In (17) the adverb *als* has been literally translated and used according to the Romansh model phrase *sco pluffer* 'as the stupid man' instead of a Standard German construction with a genitival phrase: *des Dummen* (10).

Notes

1. Vennemann's former negative attitude towards contact-induced structures has now been modified to the extent that he (as co-author with Oskar Schmidt) accepts the hypothesis that the contact between two languages (Upper Saxonian and Low German) may lead to a new phonological system, that of High German based on a Low German substratum: "Zugleich verstehen wir unsere Untersuchung als eine Fallstudie zur Theorie des Sprachkontakts, nämlich zur Frage der Entlehnung systematischer lautlicher Eigenschaften aus einem sprachlichen Substrat" (Schmidt and Vennemann 1985: 2).

2. In Ureland 1978 I list the following older runic inscriptions as having SOV order according to Krause 1971): Einang 63 (4th century), Gallehus 43 (ca. 400), Järsberg 70 (6th century), Björketorp 97 (ca. 670) (sub. clause), Stentoften 96 (650) (also sub. clause), Kragehul 27 (ca. 600), Lindholm 29 (6th century), Kalleby 61 (ca. 400), Tune 72 (ca. 400), Åsum 131, Roes 102 (ca. 750), and Stentoften 96 (ca. 650).

3. In Ureland 1978 I present the structures of two of the few verb-final clauses found in the younger runic inscriptions according to Janson 1963: 36: Subj + Modal Adverb + V on the Rök Stone (9th century): HVAR HAESTR SE GUNNAR ETU VETT-VANGI AN KUNUNGAR TVAIR TIGIR SVAÐ A LIGGIA 'where Gunn's horse (= the wolf) sees food on the battle field twenty kings are buried' and the second SOV example is the following: NU'K MINNI MEÐR ALLU SAGI (Rök Stone: Janson 1963: 36) 'Now I may tell you the memories completely' with the structure Time Adverb + Subject + Object + Modal Prep. Phrase + V.

4. See note 3.

5. Such neglect of contacts in dealing with syntactic change is also characteristic of the approach of Yoshida, who rejects Lehmann's suggestion of including the contact perspective to explain the development of western Indo-European languages to an SVO type through influences from indigenous languages of Old Europe (cf. Lehmann 1973).

6. The view that the SOV order in older Germanic subordinate clauses is a remnant from Proto-Germanic is to be found in Yoshida 1982: 328−329.

7. I depart from the assumption that the SOV order in subordinate clauses also is non-native in Old Scandinavian texts (Old Danish, Old Swedish etc.) in contrast to Yoshida (1982: 32). He gives an example of a Latin imperative epitaph with VSO order and compares it to a runic inscription (that from Ström, ca. 450) without drawing the conclusion that there may be a connection between the syntax of Latin epitaphs and that of the older runic inscriptions. We know from the younger runic inscriptions that Latin prototypes like *X me fecit* were transferred into the texts of baptismal fonts. Why should a similar transfer copying Latin SOV order not have been possible in the older runic inscription as well. How independent were the old rune inscribers of Latin epitaph culture?

8. Notice, however, that in some locutions and phrases transferred from earlier literary models spoken Swedish and Norwegian have preserved the SOV order: Mod. Sw. *vara vem det vara vill* 'whoever it may be' and dialectal Norwegian *kva som komma kan* 'whatever may happen' and *det som gjort er* 'what has been done' (Iversen 1929: 432).

9. In his investigation of 17th and 18th century Swedish syntax Platzack (1983) ignores the impact of Dalin's language planning influence. Instead a grammar-internal explanation along the lines of Lightfoot 1979 is suggested as an explanation of the loss of SOV in subordinate clauses and the loss of the order complement plus infinite verb, which is supposed to have occurred contemporaneously with the introduction of the HAVA-Deletion Rule introduced according to Platzack through German influence.

10. A more detailed report on the sociolinguistic and ethnopolitical situation of German in contact with Romansh varieties is given in Ureland (1988).

References

Ascoli, G. J.
1881−82   "Lettere glottologiche", [transl. into German in Kontzi (ed.) 1982: 29−53], *Rivista di Filologia e d'istruzione classica* 10: Torino.
Betz, Werner
1944   "Lehnbildungen und der abendländische Sprachausgleich", *PBB* 67: 275−302.

1949   *Deutsch und Lateinisch — die Lehnbildungen der althochdeutschen Benedikti-nerregel* (Bonn: Bouvier).

Besch, Werner — Ulrich Knoop — Wolfgang Putschke — Herbert Wiegand (eds.)
1983   *Dialektologie — ein Handbuch zur deutschen und allgemeinen Dialektforschung*
          1 — 2 (Berlin: de Gruyter).

Besch, Werner — Oscar Reichmann — Stephan Sonderegger (eds.)
1984 — 85 *Sprachgeschichte* 1 — 2 (Berlin: de Gruyter).

Bever, T. G. — D. T. Langendoen
1968   "The interaction of speech perception and grammatical structure in the
          evolution of language", in: Stockwell — Macaulay (eds.), 32 — 95.

Blatt, Franz
1957   "Latin influence on European syntax", *Travaux de Cercle Linguistique de
          Copenhague* 11: 33 — 69.

Braunmüller, Kurt
1982   *Syntaxtypologische Studien zum Germanischen* (Tübingen: Narr).

Carlsson, Gottfrid (ed.)
1924   *Stockholms stads tänkeböcker* 2: *1483 — 92* (Stockholm: Häggström).

Collin, H. S. — C. J. Schlyter (eds.)
1827   *Samling af Sveriges gamla lagar. Äldre västgötalagen* (Stockholm).

Cordes, Gerhard — Dieter Möhn (eds.)
1983   *Handbuch zur niederdeutschen Sprach- und Literaturwissenschaft* (Berlin:
          Schmidt).

Ehrhardt, Harald
1977   *Der Stabreim in altnordischen Rechtstexten* (Heidelberg: Winter).

Fehling, Detlev
1980   "The origins of European syntax", *Folia Linguistica Historica* 1: 353 — 387.

Friedrich, Paul
1975   *Proto-Indo-European syntax: the order of meaningful elements* (Journal of
          Indo-European Studies, Monograph No. 1).

Frings, Theodor
1944   *Die Stellung der Niederlande im Aufbau des Germanischen* (Halle: Niemeyer).
1957   *Grundlegung einer Geschichte der deutschen Sprache* (Halle: Niemeyer).

Frings, Theodor — Jan van Ginneken
1919   "Zur Geschichte des Niederfränkischen in Limburg", *Zeitschrift für deutsche
          Mundarten* 14: 97 — 219.

Frings, Theodor — J. Vandenheuvel
1921   *Die südniederländischen Mundarten* 1: *Texte* (Marburg: Elwert).

Havers, Wilhelm
1931   *Handbuch der erklärenden Syntax* (Heidelberg: Winter).

Holtus, Günter — Michael Metzeltin — Christian Schmitt (eds.)
1987 — 1989 *Lexikon der Romanistischen Linguistik* Vols. 1 — 8 (Tübingen: Niemeyer).

Iversen, Ragnvald
1929   "Om slutt-stilling av verbet i norsk folkemål", *ANF*, Supplementary volume
          to volume 40. Studies dedicated to Axel Koch, 431 — 440.

Kloss, Heinz
1969   *Grundfragen der Ethnopolitik im 20. Jahrhundert. Die Sprachgemeinschaften
          zwischen Recht und Gewalt* (Wien: Braumüller).
1978   Die Entwicklung neuer germanischer Kultursprachen seit 1800[2] (Düsseldorf:
          Schwann) [[1]1952].

Kontzi, Reinhold (ed.)
1978   *Zur Entstehung der romanischen Sprachen* (Wege der Forschung 162) (Darm-
          stadt: Wissenschaftliche Buchgesellschaft).

1982   *Substrate und Superstrate in den romanischen Sprachen* (Wege der Forschung 475) (Darmstadt: Wissenschaftliche Buchgesellschaft).

Krause, Wolfgang
1971   *Die Sprache der urnordischen Runeninschriften* (Heidelberg: Winter).

Labov, William
1968   "The internal evolution of linguistic rules", in: Stockwell—Macaulay (eds.), 101—171.

Lakoff, Robin
1968   "Another look at drift", in: Stockwell—Macaulay (eds.), 172—198.

Larsson, Carl
1931   *Ordföljdsstudier över det finita verbet i de nordiska fornspråken* I (Uppsala: Lundequistska bokhandeln).

Lehmann, Winfred P.
1968   "Saussure's dichotomy between descriptive and historical linguistics", in: Lehmann—Malkiel (eds.), 5—20.
1971   "On the rise of SOV patterns in New High German", in: *Festschrift für Alfred Hoppe*, ed. by K. G. Schweisthal, 14—24 (Bonn: Dümmler).
1973   "A structural principle of language and its implications", *Language* 49: 47—66.
1974   *Proto-Indo-European syntax* (Austin: University of Texas Press).

Lehmann, Winfred P.—Yakov Malkiel (eds.)
1968   *Directions in historical linguistics* (Austin, Texas: University of Texas Press).

Loey, Adolf van
1980   *Schönfeldts Historische Grammatika van het Nederlands* (Zutphen: Thieme) [¹1955].

Nelde, Peter—P. Sture Ureland—Iain Clarkson (eds.)
1986   *Language contact in Europe*. Proceedings of the Working Groups 12 and 13 at the XIIIth International Congress of Linguists, August 29—September 4, 1982, Tokyo (Tübingen: Niemeyer).

Nygaard, Marius
1896   "Den lærde stil i den norrøne prosa", in: *Sproglig-historiske studier tilegnede C. R. Unger* (Kristiania).
1906   *Norrøn syntax* (Kristiania: Aschehoug).

Nykrog, Per
1957   "L'influence latine savante sur la syntaxe du français", *Travaux du Cercle Linguistique de Copenhague* 11: 88—114.

Oeser, Erhard
1985   "Methodologische Bemerkungen zur interdisziplinären Problematik der Ethno- und Glottogenese", in: Ureland (ed.), 1—6.

Paul, Hermann
1886   Prinzipien der Sprachgeschichte[2] (Tübingen: Niemeyer).

Platzack, Christer
1983   "Three syntactic changes in the grammar of written standard Swedish around 1700", in: *Festschrift till Bengt Loman, 7. 8. 1983*, 43—63 (Åbo: Åbo akademi).

Schlyter, Carl Johan
1835   *Om Sveriges äldsta indelning i landskap och landskapslagarnas uppkomst* (Uppsala).

Schlyter, Carl Johan (ed.)
1834   *Uplands-lagen* (Stockholm: Norstedt).
1859   *Skånelagen* (Lund: Berlingska).

Schmidt, Oskar—Theo Vennemann
1985   "Die niederdeutschen Grundlagen des standarddeutschen Lautsystem", *PBB* 107: 1—20.

Schmitt, Christian
1982   "Die Ausbildung der romanischen Sprachen — Zur Bedeutung von Varietät und Stratum für die Sprachgenese", in: Ureland (ed.), 39–61.

Schuchardt, Hugo
1884   *Slawo-deutsches und Slawo-italienisches* (Graz).

Sjöholm, Elsa
1976   *Gesetze als Quellen mittelalterlicher Geschichte des Nordens* (Stockholm).

Ståhle, Carl Ivar
1976   "Om Dalalagens ålderdomlighet och ålder — och Kopparbergsprivilegiernas oförbätterliga 'sik biwiþar'", in: *Nordiska studier i filologi och lingvistik tillägnade Gösta Holm*, 392–402 (Lund).

Stockwell, Robert P.
1977   "Motivations for exbraciation in Old English", in: C. N. Li (ed.), *Mechanisms of syntactic change*, 291–314 (Austin: University of Texas Press).

Stockwell, Robert P. – Ronald K. S. Macaulay (eds.)
1972   *Linguistic change and generative theory.* Essays from the UCLA Conference on Historical Linguistics in the Perspective of Transformational Theory. February 1969 (Bloomington and London: Indiana University Press).

Törnqvist, Nils
1977   *Das niederdeutsche und niederländische Lehngut im schwedischen Wortschatz* (Neumünster: Wacholtz).

Ureland, P. Sture
1978 a   "Typological, diachronic and areal linguistic perspectives of North Germanic syntax", in: John Weinstock (ed.). *The Nordic languages and modern linguistics* 3, 116–141 (Austin: University of Texas at Austin).
1978 b   "Reflexive structures in the North Sea language area — A stratalinguistic approach", in: W. U. Dressler – W. Meid (eds.), *Proceedings of the Twelfth International Congress of Linguists Vienna, August 28–September 2, 1977*, 631–636 (Innsbruck: Innsbrucker Beiträge zur Sprachwissenschaft).
1979 a   "Reflexive structures in North Sea Germanic — an areal linguistic approach", in: *Handelingen van Het Vijf en dertigste Nederlands Filologencongres, gehouden te Leiden op Dinsdag 28 en Woensdag 29 Maart 1978*, 91–98 (Amsterdam: Holland Universiteits Pers).
1986   "Some contact-linguistic structures in Scandinavian languages", in: Nelde–Ureland–Clarkson (eds.), 31–79.
1988   "Language contact in the Alps — penetration of Standard German in bilingual areas of the Engadine, Switzerland", *Folia Linguistica*, XII: 103–122.

Ureland, P. Sture (ed.)
1982   *Die Leistung der Strataforschung und Kreolistik. Typologische Aspekte der Sprachkontakte* (Akten des 5. Symposions über Sprachkontakt in Europa) (Tübingen: Niemeyer).
1985   *Entstehung von Sprachen und Völkern. Glotto- und ethnogenetische Aspekte europäischer Sprachen* (Akten des 6. Symposions über Sprachkontakt in Europa) (Tübingen: Niemeyer).
1987   *Sprachkontakt in der Hanse. Aspekte des Sprachausgleichs im Ostsee- und Nordseeraum* (Akten des 7. Symposions über Sprachkontakt in Europa) (Tübingen: Niemeyer).

Ureland, P. Sture – Iain Clarkson (eds.)
1984   *Scandinavian language contacts* (Cambridge: University Press).

Utterström, Gudrun
1975   "Die mittelalterliche Rechtssprache Schwedens. Einige quellenkritische und sprachliche Beobachtungen", in: Dahlstedt (ed.), *The Nordic languages and modern linguistics* 2, 734–755 (Stockholm: Almqvist and Wiksell).

1978   "Ålderdomlighet utan ålder? En replik om Dalalagen", *Arkiv för nordisk filologi* 93: 199−204.

1983   "Konstruktioner kring Dalalagen", *Arkiv för nordisk filologi* 98: 194−201.

1987   "Schwedische Provinzrechte − Ideologie und Interpretation", in: Ureland (ed.), 232−241 (Tübingen: Niemeyer).

Valkhoff, Marius

1932   *Latijn, Romaans, Roemeens* (Amersfoort).

Vennemann, Theo

1972   "Sound change and markedness theory: on the history of the German consonant system", in: Stockwell−Macaulay (eds.), 230−274.

Wartburg, Walter von

1932   "Die Ursache des Auseinanderfallens der Galloromania in zwei Sprachgebiete: Französisch und Provenzalisch", *Forschungen und Fortschritte* 8, 21: 268−361.

Weinreich, Uriel

1952   *Research problems in bilingualism, with special reference to Switzerland* (Diss., Columbia University) (Ann Arbor: University Microfilms).

1953   *Languages in contact* (The Hague: Mouton).

Weinreich, Uriel−William Labov−Marvin I. Herzog

1968   "A theory of language change", in: Lehmann−Malkiel (eds.), 97−195.

Wessén, Elias

1968   *Svenskt lagspråk* (Lund: Gleerup).

Wollin, Lars

1987   "Birgitta, Erasmus und Luther. Lateinisch-deutsch-schwedischer Sprachkontakt im Spätmittelalter", in: Ureland (ed.), 203−229.

Yoshida, Kazuhiko

1982   "Towards word order and word order change in the older Germanic languages", *JIES* 10: 313−345.

Zelissen, P. G.

1969   *Untersuchungen zu den Pronomina im Rheinisch-Maasländischen bis 1300. Ein Beitrag zu einer mittelripuarischen Grammatik* (Helmond: Drukkerij Helmond).

Index

Jadranka Gvozdanović
Language System and Its Change
On Theory and Testability

1985. 14.8 x 22.8 cm. X, 221 pages. Cloth.
ISBN 3 11 010477 6 (Trends in Linguistics. Studies and Monographs, 30)

This study investigates possibilities of transforming linguistic theory into testable hypotheses, and methods of testing these hypotheses.

This work formulates a theory about principles of organization, of phonological systems, grammatical systems and the lexicon, deduces hypotheses about possible variation given a certain type of organization, and relates these hypotheses to data on language variation. It also shows, in a section on language typology, that grammar provides a classificatory basis even in cases in which phonology and the lexicon fail to do so.

The language data originate from publications as well as unpublished materials.

Edgar C. Polomé
Research Guide on Language Change

1990. 15.5 x 23.0 cm. Approx. 470 pages. Cloth.
ISBN 3 11 012046 1 (Trends in Linguistics. Studies and Monographs)

This collection of 33 invited papers presents a comprehensive survey of the present state of research on the various aspects of language change, focusing on methodology and on various theoretical models.

The different types of language change – phonological, morphological, syntactic, and lexical – are examined, as well as the topics of language families, contact linguistics, creolization, bi- and multilingualism and similar contexts of changes.

This assessment of the different fields of study provides an introduction to the subject and the presentation is illustrated with numerous examples, mainly from Western languages. Not only are those areas of research which have been explored indicated, but those which need further investigation are also described.

mouton de gruyter Berlin · New York

Philip Baldi (Editor)
Linguistic Change and Reconstruction Methodology

1989. 15.5 x 23.0 cm. Approx. 650 pages. Cloth.
ISBN 3 11 011908 0 (Trends in Linguistics. Studies and Monographs)

   This collection of papers on historical linguistics addresses specific questions relating to the ways in which language changes in individual families or groups, and to which methodologies are best suited to describe and explain those changes. In addition, the issue of 'long distance' relationships and the plausibility of recovering distant linguistic affiliations is discussed in detail.

   Material is presented not only from the well-documented Indo-European family, but from Afroasiatic, Altaic, Amerindian, Australian, and Austronesian as well.

   Despite many claims to the contrary, the method of comparative reconstruction, based on the regularity of sound change, is the most consistently productive means of conducting historical linguistic enquiry.

   Equally important is the demonstration that the comparative method has its limitations, and that linguists must be cautious in their postulation of large super-families.

Dieter Stein
Natural Syntactic Change

1990. 15.5 x 23.0 cm. Approx. 400 pages. Cloth.
ISBN 3 11 011283 3 (Trends in Linguistics. Studies and Monographs)

   This research monograph presents a foundation for the examination of the mechanism of language change.

   As an example, a detailed analysis of the change in the semantics and syntax of English do is presented, showing that the Modern English syntactic pattern is the result of a complex interaction of language internal and external factors. The results of the study suggest a complex and heterogeneous methodology for the explanation of syntactic change, results applicable to other questions and languages.

mouton de gruyter Berlin · New York